A COMPLETE GUIDE TO

SCOUTING SKILLS

A COMPLETE GUIDE TO

SCOUTING SKILLS

Everything you need to know for your outdoor adventures

Written and compiled by Jacqui Bailey

DOUBLEDAY

A COMPLETE GUIDE TO SCOUTING SKILLS
A DOUBLEDAY BOOK 978 0 385 61698 0

Published in Great Britain by Doubleday,
an imprint of Random House Children's Books
A Random House Group Company

This edition published 2010

3 5 7 9 10 8 6 4 2

Copyright © The Scout Association, 2010

Written and compiled by Jacqui Bailey

The right of Jacqui Bailey to be identified as the author of this work has been
asserted in accordance with the Copyright, Designs and Patents Act 1988.

The Random House Group Limited supports the Forest Stewardship Council (FSC),
the leading international forest certification organization. All our titles that are printed on
Greenpeace-approved FSC-certified paper carry the FSC logo. Our paper procurement
policy can be found at www.randomhouse.co.uk/environment.

RANDOM HOUSE CHILDREN'S BOOKS
61–63 Uxbridge Road, London W5 5SA

www.kidsatrandomhouse.co.uk
www.totallyrandombooks.co.uk

Addresses for companies within The Random House Group Limited
can be found at: www.randomhouse.co.uk/offices.htm

THE RANDOM HOUSE GROUP Limited Reg. No. 954009

Designed by Dynamo Limited
www.dynamodesign.co.uk

A CIP catalogue record for this book is available from the British Library.

Printed and bound in China

This book is about Scouting skills. If you want to learn more, other guidance,
advice and publications are available from www.scouts.org.uk.
Scouting has rules as to where, when and who can take part in activities.
Scouts, from whatever section, should speak to their section leader to understand what these are.
UK Programme Advisory Team, The Scout Association

This book is a guide to outdoor activities and adventure but it is not a substitute for, not should it be relied on as,
professional instruction by qualified personnel. The author and publishers disclaim, as far as the law allows,
any liability arising directly or indirectly from the use or misuse of the information contained in this book.

CONTENTS

Already a Scout?
Remember, if you are taking part in any activity in this book in a Scouting capacity,
you need to follow The Scout Association's rules, as outlined in Policy, Organisation
and Rules, which can be found at www.scouts.org.uk

WHEN WAS THE LAST TIME YOU EXPLORED THE GREAT OUTDOORS?

I mean, *really* explored, when you've set out into the unknown with a map and compass, a rucksack, a tent and sleeping bag; the sort of exploring that makes your heart beat faster.

Can you remember the patter of rain on your tent, the sound of owls or the rustling of the wind in the leaves at night? It's a feeling of absolute freedom and belonging – re-establishing our relationship with both ourselves and Planet Earth. A night in the outdoors is also a reminder that not everything that's precious and valuable costs a lot of money.

One of the reasons I became a Scout was to spend more time with friends in the outdoors. It's among the greatest experiences in life and should be accessible to everyone, no matter where they live, what they look like or how they grew up. That is my mission as Chief Scout: to bring that opportunity of adventure to young people worldwide, wherever or whoever they are.

Into this book we've crammed the best and most useful skills you should have learned but never got around to, or once knew but have now forgotten. We'll show you how to identify plants and trees; how to light a fire, set a compass or rig up a waterproof shelter. This isn't a textbook. I hate textbooks! We won't bore you with the unnecessaries. When we show you knots, we'll only show you the most useful.

Nature and the outdoors are languages that can be learned. Once you can identify a beech tree, tie a clove hitch or cook a simple meal over a fire that you've built yourself, you'll never forget it.

This is the outdoor handbook brought to you by the people who wrote the rules.

See you out there!

Bear Grylls
Chief Scout

INTRODUCTION

The next generation is not only playing computer games and watching TV but also heading out for the adventure of the outdoors. Whether it's walking, climbing, canoeing, backwoods cooking or other accessible outdoor pursuits, the fun and challenge of getting outside and into a new activity is spreading fast. There's a T-shirt being worn at the moment that reads: *Nature is my X-Box*. It seems to just about sum it up.

Maybe that's one of the reasons why Scouting is making something of a comeback. People are rediscovering the outdoors and all those skills suddenly seem much more relevant. Camping has also seen a dramatic revival. Not only is it cheap (and what family doesn't need to make their money go further?) but it also reminds us that the simplest way of life is often the most rewarding. Sitting outside a tent on a warm summer's night after a long day spent on the hills – whether with your family, or with a group of friends – is one of life's most enjoyable pleasures.

But there's a challenge. To make the most of the outdoors it is essential to understand it – to be able to identify trees, plants and animals; to know which wood burns well and what food can be found and eaten in the wild. There are skills which have been passed from generation to generation which are being lost – how to predict the weather using signs in nature; how to navigate using the sun and the stars and yes – what knots to use and when.

Technology moves fast, and if we're smart, we'll use it to make our experiences in the wild even more enjoyable. This book looks at the most up-to-date tents, rucksacks and walking boots. The outdoors does not mean old-fashioned.

This book has all of these skills and more in one place. It draws on the experience and wisdom of Scout leaders, who have spent years accumulating an intimate knowledge of the outdoors. Whether it's knowing that hardwoods like apple, birch or hazel make great kindling for getting a fire going quickly, how to build a bivouac or the perfect way to make and cook campfire sausage rolls, then you've come to the right place.

By owning this book you are taking your place in a great tradition of the outdoors, helping to pass on these timeless skills, keeping them alive, and eventually even adding your own.

Be prepared . . . for adventure!

CHAPTER 1:

BEING PREPARED

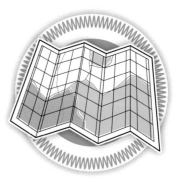

Whether you're a seasoned adventurer looking to brush up your skills or a complete beginner wanting to find a good starting point, this book is for you. It brings together for the first time Scouting knowledge, experience and expertise about all things outdoors.

You may not read it from cover to cover and there may be things here that are already second nature to you. But everyone should find something they didn't know – from how to set up a camp kitchen to cooking without a single kitchen utensil.

Using this book should be as much of an adventure as stepping outdoors. Of course, this book will not cover everything – it can take several lifetimes to learn every outdoor skill – but it will help you get a taste for adventure and, perhaps most importantly, be prepared for most, if not all, that nature has to throw at you.

MAKING PLANS

Whatever you want to do, whether it's exploring the countryside around your town, cycling through a national park, or a mountainside trek, it's best to have a plan. Even the simplest adventure can turn sour if you haven't put enough thought into how you will get there or what you will need.

WHAT WILL YOU NEED?

Begin by making a list. Every trip starts with a great idea, but writing those ideas down helps turn them into reality. If there is a group of you, get everyone else involved in the planning too.

Agree where you are going, how far away it is, and how you will get there. How long will your trip take – a few hours or a few days? Think about the time of year and what the weather will be like. Is it winter or summer? Are the days long or short? Is it likely to be cold, rainy, or hot?

Make sure you take the right kind of clothing. Begin with a list of any tools, tents, or other equipment you will need and work out how you will carry them. Will you be able to find food and water along the way or will you have to take them with you? If so, think about how you will carry the food and what you will cook it in. Do you have the right maps and a compass in case you get lost? What about a first-aid kit?

If you need places to stay, you will probably have to book them in advance. You may also need to get permission to travel across or camp on private land. If you are catching buses or trains, make sure you have their timetables, particularly if you have to make connections. If you are travelling by car, you will need to find out about parking. Alternatively, perhaps you could arrange for someone to drop you off and pick you up again?

TOP TIPS

+ Allow plenty of time in advance to plan and prepare for your trip.

+ Make a checklist of everything you plan to take with you.

+ Make sure any equipment you take is in working order before you leave.

+ Practise packing and carrying your gear.

+ If you are going somewhere new, find out what you can about it beforehand from guidebooks, websites, or by talking to people who have been there.

BE REALISTIC

Be realistic about what you can achieve. If none of you has ever hiked or camped before, it is probably not such a good idea to head off for a week-long trek in the wild. A weekend, or even a day hike might be a better way to start.

Think about the skills and abilities of everyone in the group. Are some of you stronger or more capable than others? Does your group include people of different ages? Adjust your plans to take into account the youngest, weakest, or less able members of the group rather than trying to push them into doing things they don't feel able to do.

BE FLEXIBLE

Do your best to think ahead, but don't insist on sticking too rigidly to a plan. Be willing to be flexible if the situation changes or things go wrong. Perhaps the weather has made a particular route more difficult and it would be better to go another way, for example. Or maybe you discover something new and want to make a detour.

TAKING TIME

Try to allow more time for your adventure than you think you need. It is easy to underestimate how long something can take and even small problems can cause lengthy delays. It is far better to be able to relax and enjoy yourselves than to rush and spend your time worrying about not keeping to your schedule.

If you are hiking or cycling, break down your planned route into stages based on your group's average speed of travel. If you are not sure what this is, do a few time trials. For example, time how long it takes each of you to walk or cycle one kilometre over fairly gentle terrain. Bear in mind that you will go more slowly if you are carrying heavy backpacks or cycling with panniers, and when travelling over hilly or rough ground.

Aim to reach a particular point at each stage so that when you are on your trip you have a rough guide to how close you are to your estimated timing. If it takes you two hours to reach your first rest stop when you estimated one hour, for example, you know you will have to speed up or else shorten your route.

In particular, remember to build in enough time for rest stops and meal breaks. Set aside a specific amount of time for these, say 10 minutes for a rest stop and 30 minutes for a meal break. Try to stage your meal breaks to coincide with interesting or useful sites, such as a spectacular view, or an ancient ruin, or at least a place where there may be somewhere dry to sit, or public amenities.

For more information on route planning and walking speeds see Chapter 3: Hiking and Hill Walking, pages 56–59.

IDEAS FOR ADVENTURES

1. Head for a beach. Check out the Marine Conservation Society's Good Beach Guide: **www.goodbeachguide.co.uk**

2. Take a walk in the woods. The Forestry Commission website: **www.forestry.gov.uk** is a good place to start, and if you don't want to walk, what about cycling or riding?

3. Go hunting for dinosaurs and other fossils, with Discovering Fossils: **www.discoveringfossils.co.uk**

4. Follow a National Trail, and explore some of the oldest pathways in Britain: **www.nationaltrail.co.uk**

TEAMWORK

It is not only safer to travel as a group, but it also allows us to share our knowledge, skills and experience and to build on each other's strengths. Those who are unsure of their abilities or who lack motivation may be encouraged to try new things and face new challenges – and gain self-confidence in the process. While those who have skills can discover the pleasure of sharing them and helping others.

LEADING THE WAY

To work well together, every group needs a leader. The leader may be elected by the rest of the group, or might naturally be the person best placed to lead in a particular situation, perhaps because of age or experience.

It is the leader's job to organize the others and help them to achieve their aim as successfully as possible. However, this does not mean that the leader has to take on all the different tasks that are required, or make all the decisions. It is best if everyone in the group is involved in each stage of the planning process.

At the planning stage, the leader should get everyone together to discuss what needs to be done and who should do it. People usually volunteer to carry out the tasks they feel most suited for, such as finding the right maps or guidebooks, booking campsites, checking timetables, or organizing food supplies.

If some members of the group are reluctant to volunteer, or there are jobs that no one wants to do, then the leader should share out the tasks evenly and offer help to anyone who may need it. The leader should make sure that everyone is clear about what needs to be done, when it has to be done by, and why.

INDIVIDUAL NEEDS

Everyone has different strengths and weaknesses, and a good leader will try to be aware of each person's needs and make sure that every member of the group feels wanted and involved. The leader must be willing to listen to other people's ideas and try to find a group consensus. If there is no workable consensus, then he or she must make the decision – and every member of the group should be willing to accept that decision.

The leader should also be aware of his or her own strengths and weaknesses, and keep in mind that his or her attitude and behaviour will affect everyone in the group.

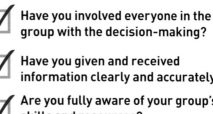

LEADERSHIP CHECKLIST:

✓ **Have you involved everyone in the group with the decision-making?**

✓ **Have you given and received information clearly and accurately?**

✓ **Are you fully aware of your group's skills and resources?**

✓ **Have you helped your group to work together effectively as a team?**

✓ **Have you helped individuals in your group to learn new skills?**

✓ **Have you considered each individual's needs?**

FIT FOR ADVENTURE

The third ingredient for any successful adventure, whether planned or unplanned, is each individual's ability to cope with whatever comes along – both mentally and physically. This does not mean that you have to be super-intelligent, or super-strong, but it does mean keeping yourself alert and fit and ready for action.

IT'S ALL IN THE MIND

Compared with other animals, the human body is not particularly well equipped to compete with nature. Yet we are excellent at survival, and this is largely because we use our brains.

Of course, the more you know about how your body works and what it needs to stay healthy, the better you will be at taking care of it. But how we feel about our bodies and the attitude we have to ourselves and the outside world also play an important part in our everyday lives. Being fit and healthy starts with a belief in ourselves and an open mind to everything the world has to offer.

People who survive against the odds in life-threatening situations often do so because of their determination and their ability to think positively. Humans are creatures of habit and it is easy for us to decide that we cannot do something, or to give up whenever a new or potentially difficult situation comes along.

But we are able to change the way we think.

TAKING CARE OF YOUR HEALTH

Our bodies are amazingly adaptable, and really quite efficient at maintaining and repairing themselves, but they do need looking after. This means eating the right kind of food, keeping ourselves clean, paying attention to any illness or infection, getting enough rest and sleep, and taking sufficient exercise.

To do anything at all our bodies need energy. This is where food comes in: our bodies convert food into energy. The potential amount of energy in food is measured in calories. When we use energy we burn up those calories, and the more energy we use the more calories we burn. The calories we do not use are stored in our body as fat. The aim, therefore, is to take in the right amount of calories for your body and lifestyle.

THINK POSITIVELY

Instead of always acting on your first impulse, try thinking about the situation in a different way. If your reaction is negative, ask yourself why. Is it based on a realistic assessment, or does it stem from lack of knowledge, or fear? What would be the benefits if you responded differently? Are there any alternatives you could explore? Is there someone you could ask for help or advice? What is the worst that could happen if you do or don't do something?

By thinking positively and creatively about the challenges you are faced with, you can learn to look at them in a different way – and achieve far more than you may have originally thought possible.

BRAIN GAMES

As with the rest of your body, your brain, and therefore your thinking, becomes lazy and inefficient unless it is exercised. Playing games such as word and number puzzles, trivia quizzes, IQ and memory tests, card and board games gives your brain a workout and keeps it alert.

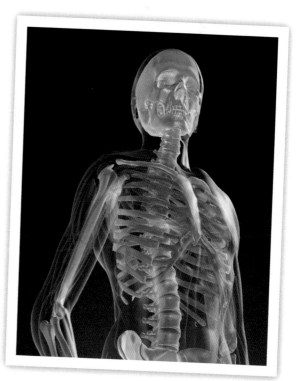

FOOD FOR LIFE

Our bodies do not only need calories. In order to work properly they also need the various chemicals that exist in food, and fibre to help us digest it. Broadly, these break down into the following groups:

Fats – such as oil and butter, and the fats found in milk, cheese, nuts and meat fat.

Carbohydrates – such as cereals, bread, rice, potatoes and other starchy vegetables, and sugary foods.

Proteins – found in meat, fish, beans, nuts, seeds, eggs and milk.

Vitamins – found in a great many foods, but mainly in fresh fruit and vegetables.

Minerals – also found in a variety of foods including meat, green vegetables, nuts and fruit.

Fibre – found in fruit, vegetables and whole grains.

To be healthy, we must eat foods from each of these groups every day, but unless we are incredibly active most of us need to balance our diet by eating less of some foods than others.

THE EATWELL PLATE

A well-balanced diet is made up of about one-third starchy foods, such as potatoes, bread, rice and other cereals, and one-third fruit and vegetables, along with smaller amounts of meat, fish and dairy foods, and even less fats and sugars.

Fruit and vegetables

Breads, cereals, potatoes and other starchy foods

Meat, fish, eggs, beans

Fatty and sugary foods and drinks

Milk, cheese and other dairy foods

BEING PREPARED

HOW FIT IS FIT?

Being fit means being able to enjoy your daily activities with energy and enthusiasm and, when necessary, being able to endure a certain amount of stress and physical hardship. Our bodies come in all shapes and sizes, and we all have different natural abilities. But no matter what type of body we have, if we do not regularly work and stretch our muscles, they become smaller and weaker and our heart works less efficiently.

TOP TIPS FOR A BALANCED DIET

+ Use less salt. Salt can be bad for your heart and young people over the age of 10 should eat no more than 6g of salt a day.

+ Drink more water. A good guideline is to aim to drink about 2.5 litres per day, and more if you are active or it's a warm, muggy day.

SAFETY CHECK : Your body needs to be kept in good working order. Minor wounds and infections can soon become major problems if not dealt with quickly. Prevent infections by keeping your skin, teeth and hair clean, and by washing your hands regularly, especially before handling or eating food.

A HEALTHY HEART

Your heart pumps oxygen around your body. Generally, a healthy and efficient heart pumps more slowly than an unhealthy one. One way of finding out your level of fitness is to check your pulse rate before you exercise, immediately after exercising, and again a minute or two later. This tells you what your normal, resting heart rate is, what your exercise rate is, and how quickly you recover your normal rate after exercising.

To keep your heart fit and strong, you need to exercise. Exercise makes your heart beat faster, and the harder you work the faster it beats. When your heart beats so fast that you are unable to carry on exercising, you have reached your maximum heart rate limit.

SAFETY CHECK : You can damage your heart if you regularly push it to its maximum heart rate limit.

Lots of things can affect your heart rate, including age (older adults have faster heart rates than younger), gender (women's hearts beat faster than men's), size (if you are overweight your heart has to work harder), and emotional state (anxiety or anger, for example, make your heart beat faster).

CHECK YOUR PULSE RATE

Pulse rate:

To find your pulse rate, place the index and middle fingers of one hand on the inside of your wrist, just below the base of the thumb. Press down lightly with these two fingers, until you feel your pulse beating. To find how many beats there are in 1 minute, count the number of beats in 15 seconds and multiply by 4. For example:

18 beats per 15 seconds x 4
= 72 beats per minute (bpm)

Resting rate:

In most adults, a resting heart rate of between 60 and 90 bpm is considered normal (although athletes can have a resting rate of between 40 and 60 bpm). To find your resting rate, sit quietly for a few minutes before counting your bpm. Make a note of the figure.

Exercise rate:

A formula that is often used to find the maximum limit of someone's heart rate is to subtract their age from the figure 220. The aim then is to achieve a heart rate during exercise of between 60% and 80% of that figure (starting with the lower target limit and gradually building up to the higher as your heart becomes stronger). For example:

At 16 years old:
220 – 16 = 204 bpm maximum heart rate
204 x 60% = 122 bpm lower target limit
204 x 80% = 163 bpm upper target limit

At 25 years old:
220 – 25 = 195 bpm maximum heart rate
195 x 60% = 117 bpm lower target limit
195 x 80% = 156 bpm upper target limit

Exercise for at least 3 to 5 minutes, then take your pulse immediately. Make a note of the figure. This is your current exercise rate.

Recovery rate:

To find your recovery rate, take your pulse again 1 minute later. Subtract this second pulse rate from your exercise rate. The difference between the two is your recovery rate, and the bigger the number the more quickly your pulse is returning to its resting rate and the fitter you are.

Pulse Points

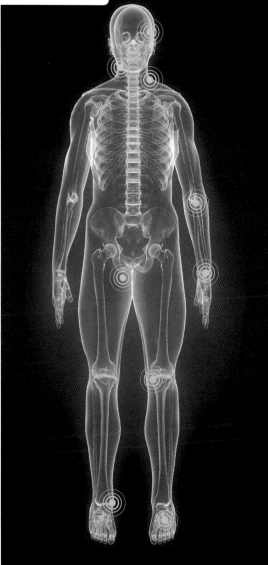

WARMING UP AND COOLING DOWN

Always start your exercise routine by warming your body up. Cold muscles and joints can strain rather than stretch. Spend 5 minutes on gentle aerobic exercise, such as walking or skipping, to get your heart and breathing rate up, then 5 to 10 minutes stretching (see pages 24–25).

At the end of your exercise routine it is important to spend another 5 to 10 minutes repeating the stretches and 5 minutes on gentle movement to allow your body to cool down slowly and for your heart rate to return to normal.

HOW MUCH EXERCISE?

This entirely depends on your age, level of fitness and how active you normally are. For adults, doctors recommend a minimum of 20 to 30 minutes a day of moderate to intense aerobic exercise, plus 10 to 20 minutes of stretching and strengthening exercises, five days a week. Younger people should aim to exercise for at least an hour a day.

TOP TIPS

+ Don't overdo it. It's better to start off slowly and gradually increase the amount and the intensity of the exercise you do.

+ You don't have to do all of your daily exercise in one go. You can break it up into three 10 or 20 minute sessions, for example.

+ Don't get dehydrated. When you exercise hard you sweat, which means your body is losing fluid. Drink plenty of water.

+ If you get tired, slow down and rest. As your body strengthens you will find that you will be able to work harder for longer.

+ Don't give up. It can take at least 4 to 6 weeks before you notice any real improvement in your fitness level. If you do not feel that you are improving, you may not be working hard enough.

GREAT WAYS TO STAY FIT

CYCLING

Cycling is great for exercising your heart and lungs so you get a good aerobic workout, and it exercises the muscles in your legs and buttocks. Because your body is supported by the bicycle, it's a low impact and low weight-bearing activity. This means there is little stress on your bones and joints, which is good for anyone with joint problems, but it will do little to maintain or improve your bone density or protect against osteoporosis.

RUNNING

Running or jogging is a very effective form of aerobic exercise. Because it is a high impact, weight-bearing sport, it is good for maintaining or increasing bone density and protecting against osteoporosis, and it builds up muscle mass. However, it can also put a lot of stress on joints and can cause injury if done incorrectly or to excess. If you are unsure of your level of health, begin with brisk walking. This will give you many of the same benefits as running but without the impact.

RELAX : Rest and relaxation are as important to your body as getting enough exercise. Try this: lie on your back with your legs and arms stretched out. Let the weight of your body sink into the ground. Now spread your toes and stretch your feet as much as you can. Hold the stretch for a second or two, then relax. Gradually work your way up your body, tensing and relaxing your legs, buttocks, abdomen, shoulders, arms, hands and face, until you feel totally relaxed. Stay lying down for at least 5 minutes.

SOME EVERYDAY STRETCHES

Stretching your body is great to do at any time, but particularly before being active. Take each position slowly and carefully. Do not jerk or bounce, and do not over-stretch. A stretch can feel difficult, but it should feel good – not painful! Each of these stretches can be repeated as many times as you wish.

2. Waist and sides

Stand with your feet apart and knees very slightly bent. Put one hand on your hip and raise the other arm straight up above your head. Slowly stretch the raised arm over to the opposite side, bending your waist towards the hand on your hip. Feel the stretch along the outside edge of your body from the shoulder to the hip.

HOLD FOR 10–15 SECS ON EACH SIDE.

1. Arms and shoulders

a) Stand with your feet slightly apart and your back straight. Interlace your fingers and turn your hands so the palms face out. Stretch your arms in front of you at shoulder height. Push your arms away to feel the stretch in your shoulders, upper back, arms and hands.

HOLD FOR 10–15 SECS.

b) Keep your fingers interlaced and lift your arms above your head, with your palms still facing outwards. Stretch your arms upwards and slightly backwards. Take a deep breath.

HOLD FOR 10–15 SECS.

c) Stretch one arm across the front of your chest and place your hand on the opposite shoulder. Gently use your other hand to pull the elbow towards the opposite shoulder. You should feel the stretch in your shoulder and upper back.

HOLD FOR 10–15 SECS ON EACH SIDE.

3. Back, hips and hamstrings

a) Stand upright with your feet apart and knees bent. Lower your chin and roll forward, slowly bending your chest, then your waist, then hips. Relax your head and neck and let your arms hang. Bend until you feel a stretch in your lower back and the backs of your legs.

HOLD FOR 15–30 SECS.

b) Keeping your knees bent, roll slowly upwards, bringing your head up last. The more you do this stretch, the more flexible you will become in your back and hamstrings.

c) Stand with your feet apart, knees bent, and toes pointing straight ahead. Keeping your body upright and your heels flat on the ground, bend your knees as if you were going to sit down. This stretch tightens the quadriceps muscles in the front of your thighs while releasing the hamstrings in the back of your thighs.

HOLD FOR 15–30 SECS.

BEING PREPARED

4. Achilles tendon & calf stretch

Stand with both feet on a low step. Move back slightly so that the ball of one foot is on the edge of the step and your heel is hanging over the edge. Carefully put your weight on the back foot pressing your heel below the level of the step. If needed hold onto a wall or handrail for balance. You should feel the stretch in your ankle, Achilles tendon and lower calf.

HOLD FOR 15–30 SECS
ON EACH SIDE.

5. Quadriceps stretch

Stand upright with your feet flat on the ground and bend one knee. Reach behind you to hold the top of your foot and gradually push the bent knee backwards, gently pulling the foot towards the lower back. If necessary, hold onto something to keep your balance. Try not to lean forward as you do this, or pull your foot outwards.

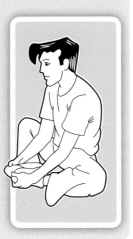

HOLD FOR 15–30 SECS
ON EACH SIDE.

6. Groin stretch

Sit on the floor and bring the soles of your feet together, letting your knees fall outwards. Hold your feet or ankles and gently pull yourself forward, bending from the hips. Try not to hunch your back and shoulders. If this is difficult, slide your feet further away until you find a comfortable stretch. You should feel this stretch in your groin and possibly in your lower back.

HOLD FOR 20–40 SECS.

6. Hamstring stretch

Lie on your back and bend your knees, keeping your feet on the ground. Now stretch one leg towards the ceiling, flexing your foot and pushing the heel uppermost. You should feel the stretch along the back of your hamstring. If you do not, keep your foot flexed and pull your raised leg gently towards you.

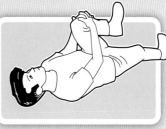

HOLD FOR 15–30 SECS ON EACH SIDE.

8. Lower back stretch

a) Lie on your back and stretch your legs out straight. Bend one leg towards your chest and interlace your fingers around your knee. Gently pull the knee towards your chest. Keep your head on the floor, tuck in your chin a little and relax your neck and shoulders. Keep the other leg as straight as possible. Breathe easily and do not strain.

HOLD FOR 15–30 SECS ON EACH SIDE.

b) Raise both knees. Clasp your hands around or behind your knees and gently pull them towards your chest. Keep your head on the floor and relax your shoulders as above. Hold as indicated, then gently circle your knees in one direction 5 to 7 times, and then in the other direction. This uses your own weight to massage your lower back and is excellent if your back aches.

HOLD FOR 10–15 SECS.

CHAPTER 2:

EXPLORING OUTDOORS

Most of us spend our time rushing from place to place – largely unaware of the natural world except perhaps when it crashes into our lives in the form of a storm, flood or some other natural disaster. But we are not as separate from nature as we may think.

We have a responsibility to support the natural world, just as it supports us by providing the food and materials we use, but in order to understand that responsibility we have to understand nature. And to do that, we must go outside and explore it.

OBSERVING NATURE

Of course, the most exciting way to experience nature is by getting out into the countryside – the wilder the better. But nature is all around you and you can start to explore it simply by standing outside your front door.

PAYING ATTENTION

Exploring and understanding something begins with paying attention to it. Instead of rushing around with all your awareness focused on your own thoughts, stand still and listen. Can you hear birds singing, or dogs barking? Can you feel the wind on your face? Can you smell flowers, mown grass, smoke? Look up at the sky. What do you see?

Observing the world and asking questions about your observations is the key to exploration, and the more you look the more you will see. As with any skill, being a good observer takes practice. For example, find a favourite spot and go back there at different times of day and in different seasons. Notice how the light changes, how the animals come and go, and how the plant life changes with the seasons.

TOP TIPS

+ Take a notebook and pencil whenever you go exploring, even if it's just to the local park. Get into the habit of jotting down the things you see and any questions you might have (so you can look up the answers later).

+ Look closely, then make sketches of what you see, whether it's a leaf or a landscape.

+ Take a camera with you. Even a mobile-phone camera can take useful photographs to help you identify things or remember them later.

LAND SHAPES

Wherever you go in the countryside, take time to look at the landscape around you. The shape of the land and its physical features have a story to tell if you know how to read it.

Geology teaches us that the Earth is continually shifting and changing, not just from season to season, but also from century to century as mountains crumble and rise, rivers widen and shrink, coastlines are built up or washed away, and woodlands and grasslands appear and disappear.

The shapes of mountains and valleys can tell you how they were formed – whether the Earth's crust fractured and shifted to make sharp jagged peaks and deep chasms, or was slowly squeezed into gentle curves and folds. Perhaps a valley was formed by the relentless pressure of a huge glacier that slowly scraped and scoured the land away thousands of years ago, or it may have been shaped by a river cutting through it.

ROCKS, TREES AND GRASS

Weather and climate change the landscape too. Wind and rain break down rocks into dust and soil, eventually washing them into the sea. Look carefully at the rocks and pebbles at your feet and you will see stripes and streaks, and flecks of different colours. In some you may see grains of sparkling crystals, or you may find the fossils of a long-dead creature or plant. Different types of rock have particular colours or patterns, depending on how they were formed. A rock identification guide can help you to discover which is which.

Britain has a temperate climate, and hundreds of years ago it was covered with woodland. However, another major force that changes the landscape is people, and over thousands of years people cleared away much of the woodland and forest to make space for farming, industry and settlement. As a result Britain now has large areas of grassland for grazing or is divided up into a patchwork of fields, with small scatterings of woodlands here and there.

EXPLORING OUTDOORS

WHAT TO TAKE?

What you take with you on your explorations will depend on the time of year and the weather conditions. But you might wish to consider the following:

▶ **A warm, waterproof jacket**

▶ **Comfortable footwear, waterproof if the ground is likely to be muddy or wet.**

▶ **Backpack – not too big but with enough room to take the following:**

   ▶ **Water bottle and food**

   ▶ **Notebook, pen and pencil**

   ▶ **Maps/guidebook**

   ▶ **Small plastic bag for collecting leaves, feathers, shells, seeds, etc.**

   ▶ **Larger plastic bag to sit on**

   ▶ **Mobile phone**

   ▶ **Camera**

   ▶ **Magnifying glass – useful for getting up close to rocks, plants and insects**

   ▶ **Binoculars**

SAFETY CHECK : If you go exploring the countryside alone, make sure someone else – family or friends – knows where you are going.

For more on travelling outdoors, see Chapter 3.

WATCHING WILDLIFE

To enjoy the countryside you do not have to be able to name all the plants and animals that live there. However, the more time you spend in the outside world, the more likely it is that you will want to know more about it – and it is very satisfying when you start to become familiar with some of the life forms you find there.

NATURAL HABITATS

'The countryside' is a very general term for what is, in fact, a number of different natural environments. Each environment has its own particular set of physical conditions and its own particular plants and animals that have adapted themselves to live there. These environments are known as habitats, and each is unique. If a habitat is destroyed its wildlife must either move or die, as each is dependent on the other.

WOODLANDS

MOORLANDS

MOUNTAINS

FIELDS

RIVERS

COASTS

HOW MANY HABITATS?

When you are out and about, make a note of the different habitats you find. Common habitats in Britain include woodlands, moorlands, mountains, fields, rivers, lakes and coasts. But not all habitats cover large areas. A city park has its own group of plants and animals, for example, as does a hedgerow, a pond and even a single tree.

CHAINS AND WEBS

Over hundreds of years, the plants and animals in a habitat adapt to their environment and also to each other. They form connections known as a food web. Each food web is made up of a number of food chains. Each chain contains a plant and a group of animals that feed either on the plant or on the animals that eat the plant.

The chain always begins with a plant and ends with a top predator – an animal that is not naturally hunted for food by any other animal.

SIMPLE FOOD CHAIN

For example, in a simple food chain grass is eaten by a rabbit, which is eaten by a fox. In this chain, the fox is the top predator because although it may be killed by people or dogs it is not killed by another animal for food.

The animals in a food web do not only feed on plants, they support them too. Animal droppings and dead bodies are broken down by bacteria and release nutrients into the soil. Plants absorb these nutrients through their roots and use them to make food and grow – and so provide more food for more animals.

A WOODLAND FOOD WEB

Another food chain in the same web might be: grass, rabbit, owl. The fox and the owl do not eat each other, but are linked because they both feed on rabbits – as does the sparrowhawk. Most predators eat a variety of prey, depending on what is available, but if any part of a food chain is lost it can affect the whole web.

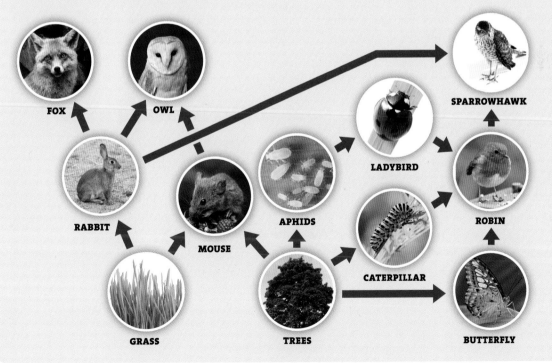

FOX OWL SPARROWHAWK

LADYBIRD

RABBIT MOUSE APHIDS ROBIN

CATERPILLAR

GRASS TREES BUTTERFLY

WOODLANDS

Woodlands are one of the most diverse habitats in the UK. Next time you are in a wood, see if you can identify some trees. Apart from developing your knowledge of the countryside it is a skill that will come in useful when collecting wood for a campfire.

Trees are either deciduous (shed all their leaves in autumn), or evergreen (have green leaves all year long). Evergreen trees are mostly cone-bearing with needle-like leaves, such as pines and spruce, although holly is also an evergreen. Evergreens usually grow in cooler climates. Deciduous trees include an enormous range of different types, from oaks and elms to apple trees. Most have flat, broad leaves that come in a great many shapes and sizes. Deciduous trees produce flowers, and seeds held inside a fruit. The fruit may be fleshy, as with cherries and apples, or hard, such as the spiky green casing around a chestnut, or the shell of a hazelnut.

IDENTIFYING TREES

One of the best ways to identify trees is by their leaf shape. Nuts, seeds, berries and other fruit and flowers are useful too, although only in the right season. In winter, the colour and pattern of the bark and even the tree's whole shape can help you to recognize different deciduous trees. Here are a few examples of the identifying features of some common British trees, but for a full range you will need an identification guidebook.

For more on the burning properties of wood, see Chapter 6, page 122.

EXPLORING OUTDOORS

SPOTTERS' GUIDE : IDENTIFYING TREES

OAK

HAWTHORN

SCOTS PINE

SYCAMORE

BEECH

HORSE CHESTNUT

BIRCH

YEW

IN THE UNDERGROWTH

Of course, trees are not the only plants to grow in woodlands. Depending on the density and types of trees, and the amount of light that finds its way through the leaves to the woodland floor, there will be thickets of lower-growing shrubs, such as blackthorn, dogwood and elder, as well as ferns, mosses and wild flowers.

The best time to see many of the most popular woodland wild flowers, such as violets, wood anemones and bluebells, is in spring when there are fewer leaves on the trees to block the light. But wherever there are spaces in woodland you can find summer flowers appearing such as white cow parsley and purple foxgloves.

SPOTTERS' GUIDE : WOODLAND WILD FLOWERS

Never pick wild flowers, however tempting. There are far fewer of them than there once were and they are best left where they can flourish and be enjoyed by everyone. Grow your own wild flowers instead. It is now possible to buy wildflower plants and seeds to grow in a pot, window box or garden.

BLUEBELL
Popular plant, found throughout the UK, flowers April to June.

DOG VIOLET
Another springtime flower, low-growing in large clumps.

FOXGLOVE
The plant is poisonous but is used to treat heart disease.

GREATER STITCHWORT
Found at woodland edges, has long straggly stems.

HERB ROBERT
Strong smelling plant, flowers from April to October.

PRIMROSE
One of the first signs of spring, flowers March to May.

RAMSONS
Also known as wild garlic, this plant smells of onions.

STINKING HELLEBORE
Pretty pale green flowers, February to March, strong smell.

IN THE LITTER

A woodland floor is often soft and spongy and covered with decaying leaves, fallen branches and sometimes entire tree trunks. It's the perfect place for fungi, such as mushrooms and toadstools, and also for a horde of tiny insects and other animals.

Grab a large handful of leaf litter and spread it out on a piece of cloth or paper (or a plastic bag or the inside of your jacket). Look at it through a magnifying glass and see how many different creatures you can find. You could also lay a groundsheet on the ground under a tree, then shake the tree to see what insects may fall out. Don't shake it too vigorously, make sure you check for loose branches or birds' nests first, and be careful not to damage the tree.

SPOTTERS' GUIDE : COMMON FUNGI

ARTIST'S FUNGUS
Inedible, brown-topped bracket fungus with white underside.

BEECHWOOD SICKENER
Very poisonous. Rich pink to white cap, with white gills.

BLUSHER
Not poisonous but not advisable to eat, especially if raw.

CHANTERELLE
Wavy-edged funnel-shaped yellow cap.

DEATH CAP
Common and deadly poisonous, varies from white to olive cap.

FLY AGARIC
Poisonous and fairly common, caps may be red or orange.

HONEY FUNGUS
Damaging to trees, these are not recommended eating.

STINKHORN
Strong smell but no taste. Cap may have sticky green coating.

 WARNING : Never eat wild fungi unless you are with an experienced gatherer. They can make you very ill and a few are deadly poisonous.

ANIMAL WATCHING

Woodlands are home to larger animals too, although you are more likely to see them at dawn or dusk than during the day as this is when many animals feed. Watching animals in the wild requires care and patience. Most will scatter as soon as they hear, or smell, you coming. You have to sit quietly and peacefully, and preferably at least partially hidden by a bush or tree, and wait to see what happens. Eventually any animals in the area will go back to business as normal and this is when you stand your best chance of seeing them.

The edge of a clearing is a good place to start as you will have a more unrestricted view than trying to peer through dense trees. Try to position yourself downwind from the area you are watching. This way an animal is less likely to catch your scent. Stay low, and keep to the shadows. Don't try to get too close, you do not want to disturb the animal or cause it stress, instead use binoculars to observe from a comfortable distance.

BADGER

Badgers are one of the shyest woodland animals. You may be able to spot the entrance to one of their holes or setts. Look for a largish hole in a bank or sloping ground, with a heap of soil around it and scratch marks on nearby trees. If you can, go back before dusk, and be prepared for a long wait.

FALLOW DEER

There are three main types of deer in Britain. Fallow and roe deer are the most widespread, while red deer are found mainly in Scotland. Muntjac deer, although not native to the UK, are also becoming increasingly common. Newly born roe deer can sometimes be seen lying among bracken or long grass. Do not disturb them, their mother will have left them to graze and will return regularly throughout the day.

EXPLORING OUTDOORS

FOX

There seem to be as many foxes in towns and urban gardens these days as in the countryside. Foxes can live pretty much anywhere but they are perfectly at home in woodland areas, which offer them plenty of opportunity to build their dens. Look out for chewed feathers and bird carcasses. Foxes also leave a very distinctive smell.

SQUIRREL

Squirrels are fairly widespread woodland creatures and are active throughout the day. Look out for split nutshells or the remains of cones. You are far more likely to see a grey squirrel than the native red squirrel, as these are now rare and are usually found only in parts of northern England, Scotland and Wales.

IN PARKS AND GARDENS

Many small animals are nocturnal – only active at night. This can make them difficult to watch, but if you have a garden or a nearby park or piece of wasteland try going there at dusk or early dawn.

HEDGEHOGS are favourite garden animals, as they eat many garden pests such as slugs and snails. However, their numbers are declining, so if you want to encourage them don't put slug pellets in your garden as these will poison them. It's also a bad idea to leave milk out for them, as it upsets their digestion.

WEASELS are likely to be found in parks or on wasteland or farmland. They look very similar to stoats, but are smaller and do not have a black tip on their tail. Weasels are hunters and feed on other small animals, especially mice and voles.

BIRDWATCHING

There are more than 500 species of birds in Britain (and around 10,000 species worldwide) and it is not always easy to tell them apart. However, it helps if you have a pair of binoculars and a good bird identification guide – and you remember a few basic guidelines:

What size is it?

Bird size in Britain varies from about 12 cm or less (blue tit) to more than 1 metre (swan). Compare the size of a new bird you see with one you know quite well. Is it bigger or smaller than a robin or a blackbird, for example?

What shape does it have?

Think about the bird's shape. Does it have a long, narrow body, or is it round and short? Does it have a long neck? What shape is its beak (bill): strong and stubby, long and curved, flat and wide, or hooked? A bird's bill can give you a lot of clues about how it lives. A sharply hooked beak is likely to belong to a bird of prey, for example, whereas a slender pointed beak is useful for digging insects out of tree bark.

How long are its legs? Short-legged birds spend most of their time perching, whereas those with long, slender legs are likely to be wading birds.

What colour are its feathers?

Some birds are dull greys and browns to help camouflage them from predators. Others have an amazing range of colours, often in patterns of patches and stripes (bars). The colour of a bird's feathers and the pattern its colours form are an important tool for identification. In particular, look at the colour of its upper body (back and wings), its lower body, and any strong markings on its head or tail.

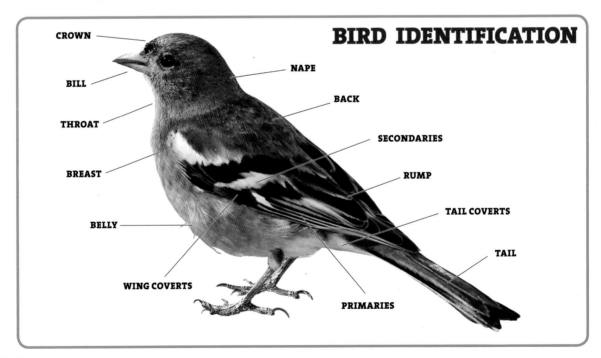

BIRD IDENTIFICATION

CROWN

NAPE

BILL

BACK

THROAT

SECONDARIES

BREAST

RUMP

BELLY

TAIL COVERTS

TAIL

WING COVERTS

PRIMARIES

SPOTTERS' GUIDE : TYPES OF BILL

WOODPECKER
Has a strong pointed bill to drill into tree bark for insects.

TREECREEPER
Uses its curved bill to probe into cracks in bark for insects.

HAWFINCH
Has a short powerful beak for cracking seeds and fruit kernels.

NIGHTJAR
Short but wide bill for catching insects while in flight.

COMMON BUZZARD
A sharp, hooked beak for killing and tearing at prey.

SPOONBILL
A wide, flat bill for scooping up fish and other water creatures.

Where did you see it?

The surroundings in which you saw the bird can also help. Many birds are happiest in a particular habitat. Woodpeckers and treecreepers are far more likely to be found in woodland than on an open moor, for example, whereas skylarks and kestrels like nothing better than wide open spaces. However, some birds, such as robins and blackbirds, occupy a variety of habitats.

What did you hear?

You cannot always see a bird from a clear angle, but you can usually hear it, and every species of bird has its own distinctive song. The only way to recognize bird songs is to listen to them and, as with most things, the more you do it the more familiar they will become. Try listening to recordings of bird songs as well.

TOP TIPS

+ You don't have to go far to watch birds, you can begin with the ones in your own back garden or local area.

+ Always carry a small notebook, so that when you see a bird you don't recognize you can jot down its main features and where you saw it, then look it up when you get home.

+ Learn from others. Go birdwatching with someone who is more experienced than yourself.

+ Visit the Royal Society for the Protection of Birds (RSPB) website on: www.rspb.org.uk It has lots of useful information and guidelines to watching birds safely and responsibly.

GRASSLANDS

Open grasslands, whether fields, parkland or rough common land, are good places to look for insects in summertime. Edges of fields, hillsides and grazing meadows often contain a wealth of plants, including flowering weeds and wild flowers which provide the nectar on which many butterflies feed. In return, the butterflies carry pollen grains from one flower to the next, like bees, ensuring that the plant will produce seeds that will grow into new plants the following year.

IN THE GRASS

Down on the ground among the grass stems, slugs, snails and scurrying beetles are all busily feeding and reproducing. If you look hard you might spot a few grasshoppers. Their green and brown bodies merge well with the undergrowth to protect them from

GRASSHOPPER
Male grasshoppers make their clicking whirring sounds by rubbing their hind legs against their abdomen.

the watchful eyes of hungry birds. But you can certainly hear the whirring, buzzing noise the males make as they 'sing' to the females.

Small mammals also live among the grasses. Colonies of rabbits usually build their burrows around the edges of fields or meadows, near to hedgerows or woodlands. They mainly come out to feed at dawn or dusk, but can be seen during

SPOTTERS' GUIDE : BUTTERFLIES

BLACK-VEINED WHITE

CHEQUERED SKIPPER

SIX SPOT MOTH
Moths far outnumber butterflies, although most are only seen at night. Brightly coloured daytime moths, like this one, are often mistaken for butterflies.

LARGE COPPER

PEACOCK

SWALLOWTAIL

SNAKES IN THE GRASS

There are three types of snake in Britain:

ADDERS can be found in various habitats, including hedgerows, open woodland, moorland and riverbanks. They are active during the day, but hibernate from early autumn through to spring. They prefer to live well away from people and will only attack if threatened, for example if they are picked up or trodden on. Their venom is not normally dangerous to a healthy adult human, but it is painful and requires medical attention as soon as possible.

GRASS SNAKES also like hedgerows, meadows and woodland edges, and particularly damp ditches, ponds or riverbanks. Like adders, they eat frogs, toads and newts as well as small mammals and birds. Their venom is poisonous, but only to small animals.

SMOOTH SNAKES enjoy dry, sunny places. They feed on lizards and other snakes, small mammals and earthworms. They have no venom but catch their prey by squeezing it in their coils and then swallowing it alive and whole. These snakes are now very rare in Britain.

ADDER

GRASS SNAKE

SMOOTH SNAKE

SLOW WORMS are not actually snakes – but are easily mistaken as such.

the day if there are few people about. Hares may be harder to see, as unlike rabbits they live alone and do not build burrows but hide in patches of long grass.

Field voles trample a network of pathways through long grass as they nibble on leaves and grasses, while their smaller, pointy-nosed counterparts, the shrews, chase insects, slugs, spiders and worms.

High above them all soar the birds of prey – owls, kestrels, harriers and hobbys. For these spectacular hunters the grasslands lay like a tablecloth, laden with tasty titbits.

KESTREL
Found in a wide variety of habitats, including urban areas. Eats small mammals and birds.

MOUNTAINS AND MOORLANDS

We do not have very high mountains in Britain, but even so they can seem wild, windswept and fairly empty at first sight. The higher a mountain is, and the further up you climb, the colder and windier it gets. At a certain point trees stop growing – this is the tree line, and beyond it is where the mountain habitat really begins.

In Britain, mountains are generally more than 600 metres above sea level. Many of Britain's high and mountainous regions are covered in moorlands. These are large areas of rough grassland scattered with low-growing shrubs of gorse and thorn. Great expanses of heather and bracken are also found there. In some parts the ground is wet and boggy and covered with mosses and other water plants.

A WEALTH OF WILDLIFE

In summer, when the heather blooms and many other low-growing plants come into flower, the moors are painted in swathes of pinks and purples, and humming with bees, butterflies and a variety of moths. Moorland bogs make an ideal habitat for frogs, toads and newts, and for the predators that feed on them, including adders, foxes, stoats and birds of prey.

The moors are important feeding and breeding grounds for many species of birds, including curlews, dunlins and wrens. A number of them are endangered, such as grouse, skylarks, golden plovers and the birds of prey – hen harriers, merlins, and the spectacular golden eagle which is now found only in the wildest parts of Scotland.

GOLDEN EAGLE

MERLIN

HEN HARRIER

GOLDEN PLOVER

MOORLAND MANAGEMENT

Few people live on the moorlands, but the terrain is not quite as wild as it seems. Hill farmers graze sheep and hardy breeds of cattle there, and ponies roam Dartmoor and Exmoor.

Because the moorlands are a unique habitat – Britain contains 75 per cent of the world's remaining heather moorlands – many areas are protected and managed. Moorlands are open to visitors, but there are guidelines which everyone should follow, both for their own protection and for that of wildlife.

Moorland can be a difficult environment to wander in. You may walk for hours without seeing anyone and there are many areas with no mobile phone signal. The weather can quickly turn cold and wet with poor visibility. There are many tracks but few roads or signposts, and it is easy to lose your way. Bogs, old mineshafts and hidden holes all provide potential dangers for the unwary. It is wise to add local maps, a compass and extra clothing to your backpack (see page 29), and always be prepared to turn back if in doubt.

MOORLAND VISITOR'S CODE

Visitors to moorlands should be careful to follow the Countryside Code (see pages 48–49), but because of the unique qualities of the habitat there are also some additional points to be aware of, known as the Moorland Visitor's Code. For details of the moorland code and for lots more information about Britain's moorlands, see: **www.moorlandassociation.org.uk**

For more on hiking and hill walking, see Chapter 3.

BRITISH MOUNTAINS

▶ **The highest mountain in Britain is Ben Nevis in Scotland – 1,344 metres above sea level.**

▶ **The highest mountain in Wales is Snowdon – 1,085 metres above sea level.**

▶ **The highest mountain in England is Scafell Pike – 978 metres above sea level.**

In comparison, Mount Everest is 8,848 metres above sea level.

COASTS

Coastlines are varied and exciting places to visit. There are stretches of fine, golden sands, often with sand dunes rising behind them, beaches of pebble and shingle, rocky shores, steep cliffs and muddy estuaries.

The tidal zone of any shore is a harsh environment. Alternately swamped with salty seawater or left literally high and dry, the wildlife that live here have found some remarkable ways to survive.

SEA PLANTS

Seaweeds are often referred to as plants, but in fact belong to a simpler life form known as algae. They do not have roots, but cling to rocks or the seabed using structures called holdfasts, or float in clumps on the surface of the sea. There are thousands of different types of seaweed and they grow in an amazing array of shapes, from feathery fronds and flat strips to large floppy 'leaves', but they can be broadly divided into three main groups according to their colour: green, brown or red.

SPOTTERS' GUIDE : SEAWEED

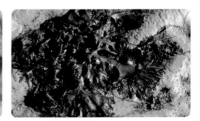

Green seaweeds can cope with the most exposure to the air and are often found growing high up on the shoreline. Leafy sea lettuce is a common green seaweed (above). It is edible and a good source of protein. In shallow waters, you might also find 'fields' of seagrass.

Brown seaweeds include the long ribbons of kelp that grow in forests on the floor of shallow seas. Branched bladder wrack (above), with its air-filled bubbles, is a common sight along the mid-tide area of rocky shores. It is a source of iodine and is often used in herbal medicines.

Red seaweeds form the oldest and largest group of seaweed species. Dulse (above) is a well-known variety that grows in the mid to lower tidal levels. It is an excellent source of vitamins and minerals and is widely used both as a food and as a health supplement.

PROTECTIVE SHELLS

Small creatures also live in the tidal zone, among the rocks and seaweeds. They too have to cope with the continually changing conditions and many of them do this by using a protective shell.

Limpets remain clinging to the rocks no matter how heavy the waves that crash over them. Once the tide water has covered them they release their grip and creep slowly over the rock face, scraping up algae. When the tide goes out the limpets return to their exact same spot and clamp their shells back in place.

Periwinkles are small sea snails that use seaweeds for shelter and for food. When the tide is out they hide beneath the damp weeds, or seal themselves inside their shells to avoid

drying out. They live high up on the tide zone among rocks and rock pools. Periwinkles are a good source of food for us and other animals.

Mussels are an even more popular food source. Their blue-black or brown shells are easily recognizable and large clusters of them may be seen fixed to rocks at the mid to low tide level.

Other shelled creatures, such as prawns, crabs (above), and starfish can be found at the edges of the low tide zone or hiding in the cracks and crevices of rock pools, while cockles and razor shells bury themselves in the sand to wait until the tide comes in.

SAFETY CHECK : Like other shellfish, mussels must be alive when they are cooked. An easy way to check is to make sure that their shells are pulled tightly shut. Before cooking, an open shell means that the mussel is dead and therefore likely to be poisonous. Fresh mussels open their shells naturally during cooking.

PROTECTING THE COUNTRYSIDE

The countryside is there for us all to explore and enjoy, but we should not assume that it will always be there. Without care and attention the countryside can become damaged or polluted, and habitats destroyed through overuse, overbuilding, or the introduction of invasive plants or animals that interfere with the natural balance.

WHAT THREATENS THE COUNTRYSIDE?

We are one of the biggest threats to the countryside. Our industries use up natural resources and create vast amounts of waste and pollution in the process. These waste products affect our air, soil and water and all of the life forms that depend on them, including us.

Farmers spray the land with chemicals, cut down trees and hedges and plough up natural habitats in order to produce the range and quantity of food we demand. We build more roads, towns and factories, thereby reducing even further the amount of land available to support our wildlife. We kill wildlife through collecting – plants, butterflies, moths and birds' eggs – through hunting, trapping, and overfishing, and by accident – on our roads, by starting forest fires, or by leaving behind litter which can injure or poison wildlife.

THE RED SQUIRREL: The introduction of grey squirrels from North America into Britain in the 1940s has resulted in the near extinction of the native red squirrel.

ENDANGERED!

The United Kingdom has about 65,000 different types of plants, and 37,000 different types of animals. But increasing numbers of these species are now under threat. In 2007, for example, the UK Biodiversity Action Plan listed 1,149 species and 65 habitats (such as hedgerows, marshes and dunes) as priorities for conservation action.

The species include hundreds of moths, beetles, butterflies, bees and wasps; 10 species of amphibians and reptiles including adders, grass snakes and common toads; 18 species of land mammals including bats, voles, dormice, hares and red squirrels; 59 species of bird; and far too many wild plants, fungi, fish and other marine wildlife to list here.

WHAT CAN WE DO?

We can group together to work towards protecting and conserving our planet and our wildlife for ourselves and for our children.

We can encourage our government to: a) create laws that will protect our habitats and species, b) take steps to limit pollution, and c) reduce our consumption of natural resources.

We can continue to learn as much as possible about the natural world and the dangers it faces. And adapt our own behaviour in order to lessen our impact on the natural world.

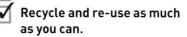

ACTION LIST

- ☑ Walk, cycle or use public transport as much as possible rather than travelling by car.
- ☑ Turn off lights and other electrical equipment when not in use. Avoid leaving items like computers on standby.
- ☑ Don't waste water.
- ☑ Recycle and re-use as much as you can.
- ☑ Don't buy products with lots of packaging.
- ☑ Don't drop litter.
- ☑ Do what you can to care for your local environment.
- ☑ Follow the Countryside Code (see pages 48–49).

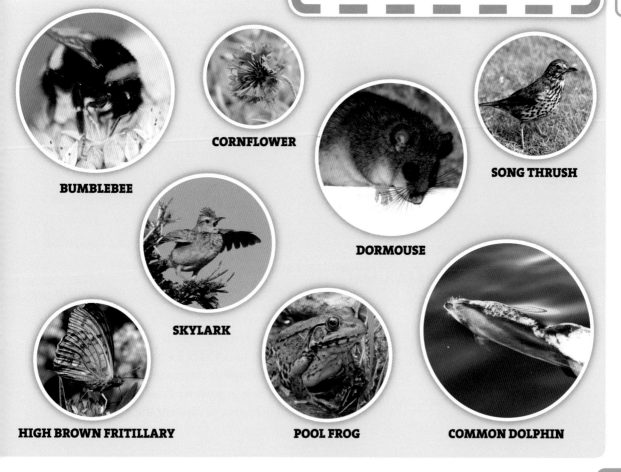

CORNFLOWER

SONG THRUSH

BUMBLEBEE

DORMOUSE

SKYLARK

HIGH BROWN FRITILLARY

POOL FROG

COMMON DOLPHIN

FOLLOW THE SIGNS

Whenever you go into the countryside it's advisable to get the right information about where you can go, and when. Public rights of way are shown on Ordnance Survey maps, but things can change so it is worth checking the OS website (see Useful Addresses, page 244) or the websites in the panel below.

Rights of way include footpaths, bridleways and byways and should be clearly signposted. Get to know the signs and symbols used for these paths. When crossing private land or farmland you must always stick to the path. Since the introduction of the Countryside & Rights of Way Act 2000, the public have the right to walk freely on mapped 'Open Access' areas without staying on the path. You cannot, however, camp, cycle, ride horses or drive vehicles on open access land. Occasionally, farmers and land managers may close access to their land while work is carried out, or for conservational or seasonal breeding reasons. See the access websites for specific guidelines to using rights of way and access land.

You and the other members in your group are responsible for your own safety, so be prepared for the type of terrain you will be crossing and check the weather forecast before you set out. Always make sure someone else knows where you are going and when you expect to get back.

For more information on maps and map reading, see Chapter 4.

THE COUNTRYSIDE CODE

In 2004, the old Countryside Code was updated and divided into 5 sections:

▶ **Be safe – plan ahead and follow any signs.**

▶ **Leave gates and property as you find them.**

▶ **Protect plants and animals, and take your litter home.**

▶ **Keep dogs under close control.**

▶ **Consider other people.**

A brief description of the key points is given on these pages, but for full details go to the Countryside Agency website: **www.countrysideaccess.gov.uk** for England; or **www.ccw.org.uk** for Wales, or visit **www.outdooraccess-scotland.com** for Scotland.

WAY MARKERS

Public rights of way are signposted with coloured arrows as shown below. The boundaries of access land should always display the Open Access symbol. National Trails have their own symbol. Some routes may also show local markings.

FOOTPATH WAYMARK

BRIDLEWAY WAYMARK

BYWAY WAYMARK

NATIONAL TRAILS

OPEN ACCESS

WILDFIRES : Accidental and uncontrolled fires can cause as much damage to wildlife and habitats as to people and property. Take particular care with matches at all times of year, not only during dry summers. Sometimes vegetation is deliberately fired in some fields, heaths and moors between October and early April so always check that a fire is not supervised before calling 999.

LEAVE IT AS YOU FIND IT

To protect their livestock, farmers usually keep their field gates closed, but there are occasions when they may deliberately leave them open so it is always best to leave gates as you find them. Always use the gaps, gates or stiles provided. Climbing over walls, hedges or fences damages them and increases the risk of farm animals escaping. When walking through crop fields, keep to the path as much as possible to avoid damaging the crops.

Remember that dropping litter and dumping rubbish are criminal offences, and it is also an offence to deliberately uproot wild plants, especially protected species.

RESPECT FOR OTHERS

Be aware of the needs of local people, other visitors and wildlife, particularly when travelling on small country roads. Do not block gateways or driveways. Give all wildlife, horses, livestock and walkers plenty of room on the roads.

WEATHER WATCHING

The sky is full of information and once you know what to look for, it will give you fair warning of the weather to come.

When you look up at the sky, you are really seeing the Earth's atmosphere. The atmosphere is like a safety blanket that encircles the Earth and protects it from the freezing airlessness of space and the searing, deadly radiation from the sun.

It's not a very thick blanket. As it extends up from the surface of the Earth it gets thinner and thinner, until it fades away.

Almost all of it lies within 100 kilometres of the Earth's surface (about the same distance as Portsmouth to London), but most of us are only aware of the first 16 kilometres or so, because this is where the weather happens.

WHAT MAKES THE WIND BLOW?

Weather happens largely because of the sun. The sun heats the Earth, which in turn heats the layer of air closest to the Earth's surface. Because the Earth is round, the equator is closer to the sun and receives more direct heat, while the North and South Poles are farthest away and receive less heat.

Areas of land heat up and cool down more rapidly than the oceans, and the height of the land and the type of vegetation it has affects this heating and cooling process even more, as do the seasons. Hot air rises and cool air sinks. As hot air rises, it pulls in cooler air below it. Then the rising hot air gradually cools and sinks down again, replacing air that has been warmed. This rising and falling of hot and cold air creates wind, and wind brings weather.

Different parts of the world heat up and cool down at different times, resulting in a wide variety of weather patterns. Meteorologists – who study the weather – do their best to try to predict what those patterns will be in any particular place at any particular time. But most of us can make very simple predictions of our local weather by keeping an eye on two things: wind speed and clouds.

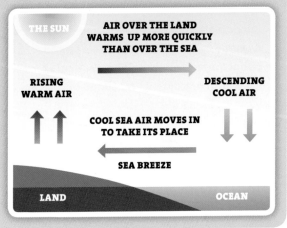

THE SUN

AIR OVER THE LAND WARMS UP MORE QUICKLY THAN OVER THE SEA

RISING WARM AIR

DESCENDING COOL AIR

COOL SEA AIR MOVES IN TO TAKE ITS PLACE

SEA BREEZE

LAND

OCEAN

BEAUFORT SCALE

The Beaufort scale was first devised by a British Admiral, Francis Beaufort, in 1805. It is widely used around the world as a way of estimating the force of the wind based on the visible effects it has on land and at sea. Originally the scale had 13 levels (0–12), but 5 more levels were added in 1946 to describe extreme typhoon and hurricane conditions, although these are rarely used. Changes in the wind signify a change in the weather, and the greater the force of the wind the more severe the change will be.

SCALE NO.		WIND SPEED IN KM/H	WIND SPEED IN MPH	DESCRIPTION	EFFECTS ON LAND
0		< 1	< 1	Calm	Smoke rises vertically
1		1–5	1–3	Light air	Smoke drifts in the wind
2		6–11	4–7	Light breeze	Wind felt on face, leaves rustle on trees
3		12–19	8–12	Gentle breeze	Leaves and twigs in constant motion, lightweight flags extended
4		20–28	13–17	Moderate wind	Dust and loose paper raised, small branches move
5		29–38	18–24	Fresh wind	Small trees sway
6		39–49	25–30	Strong wind	Large tree branches move, whistling in phone wires, umbrellas hard to hold
7		50–61	31–38	Very strong wind	Whole trees in motion, difficulty in walking against wind
8		62–74	39–46	Gale	Twigs and small branches break off trees, great difficulty in walking
9		75–88	47–54	Severe gale	Chimney pots, roof tiles and hanging signs damaged, larger branches break off
10		89–102	55–63	Storm	Trees uprooted, structural damage to buildings
11		103–117	64–72	Severe storm	Widespread damage to vegetation and structures
12		> 118	> 73	Hurricane force	Considerable widespread damage, rarely experienced on land

CLOUDS

Clouds are formed by moisture in the air. They are usually associated with rain and bad weather but this is not always the case. Clouds that are high up in the sky usually indicate good weather with stable conditions. Mid-level clouds can indicate changing weather conditions. Low-level clouds often bring drizzle, rain or fog.

Meteorologists use four basic words for clouds:

Cirrus – meaning a strand or filament

Cumulus – meaning a heap or pile

Stratus – meaning a layer

Nimbus – meaning rain-bearing

And they combine these four words to describe 10 different types of clouds.

WEATHER LORE

Many of the traditional sayings to do with the weather were based on long-term observation, such as:

▶ **Red sky at night, shepherd's delight. Red sky in the morning, shepherd's warning:** a red sky at night is often seen as a glowing red sunset and usually indicates dry weather the next day. On the other hand, a red sky at dawn often means there is moisture in the air, which could indicate that wet weather is on the way.

▶ **Rain before seven, fine before eleven:** most periods of rain last less than four hours, except when there is little wind and a weather front is slow-moving.

High clouds

Cirrus – are thin, white, wispy clouds, high up in the sky. Thread-like trails with curled ends are also known as 'mares' tails'. Cirrus clouds usually indicate fine weather, but can be an early sign of deterioration.

Cirrocumulus – patches or sheets of small clouds that form a pattern of ripples or can look like fish scales, which is why this pattern is known as a 'mackerel sky'. Usually indicates fair weather.

Cirrostratus – a thin sheet of cloud that usually covers the sky. Often the sun or moon can be seen through it, surrounded by a ring of reflected light called a halo. Often indicates a deterioration of weather conditions.

Mid-level clouds

Altocumulus – blobs of fluffy cloud in layers or patches, often form bands or rows across the sky. Can indicate the approach of rain or snow.

Altostratus – a flat, grey layer of cloud covering the sky, sometimes allows the sun to be seen as if through obscured glass. Often brings rain or snow.

Nimbostratus – a thick layer of dark, grey cloud that covers the sun. Usually brings moderate to heavy rain or snow.

Low-level clouds

Stratocumulus – sheets of rounded rolls or large, soft clumps with occasional gaps, often white with grey shading. May be dry but dull, or bring light rain or snow. Also often seen at the front or tail end of worse weather.

Stratus – low, flat, uniform grey. Can obscure the tops of hills or tall buildings, or even reach to the ground to cause fog. A 'cloudy day' usually features a sky filled with stratus clouds obscuring the sun. Sometimes produce light rain or snow.

Cumulus – separate, fluffy clumps of white clouds, sometimes with grey shading. May clump together to form billowing rolls or towers with a flat base. When scattered, usually indicate fair weather, but if accumulate can produce showers.

Cumulonimbus – these are the thunderclouds, large, dark, cauliflower-shaped towers, sometimes with flat 'anvil tops'. Often bring thunderstorms or heavy rain or snow. They are the tallest clouds and can stretch from low levels to the upper atmosphere.

STORMS AND FLOODS

Most of the time the weather in any part of the world follows a fairly predictable pattern for that region and time of year. But it is always a mistake to take nature for granted and warnings of severe weather should always be taken seriously.

Thunderstorms can seemingly appear out of nowhere, even on a sunny day. In the right conditions, fluffy cumulus clouds can soon build up into towering cumulonimbus clouds 20 kilometres high or more. The air below the clouds may be warm, but at the top the temperature is freezing. Inside the clouds, air currents rise and fall rapidly, carrying water vapour that quickly condenses into heavy rain.

If the downpour is very heavy or prolonged, or the ground is very dry, the water may not be able to soak away in its usual fashion. Instead it builds up on the surface, washing away soil, boulders, trees and other vegetation, causing rivers and reservoirs to overflow, damaging buildings and flooding into low-lying areas.

Flash floods can turn dry riverbeds, gullies and small streams into raging torrents in minutes, even though the storm that caused them is some distance away. Always be cautious when travelling in areas where flash floods are known to occur.

For more on water safety, see Chapter 8.

FLOOD SAFETY

▶ If you think there is danger of flooding, get to high ground or the upper floors of a building as quickly as possible.

▶ Do not try to walk or wade through flood waters. It is easy to underestimate the depth and power of the flow and impossible to know what objects may be under the water. If the water is above your ankles, it is too deep.

▶ Never attempt to travel by car along flooded roads. If the car stalls get out and climb onto higher ground. Most cars can be swept away in as little as 60 cm of water.

▶ If you have time, take supplies of drinking water, food, a flashlight, matches and warm clothing with you.

▶ Once you find a safe place, stay there until the flood waters drop or you are rescued.

LIGHTNING

Thunderstorms can also bring lightning. The jostling of air currents inside storm clouds creates static electricity. Eventually the build-up of electricity becomes so great it explodes in a massive electrical discharge – a bolt of lightning.

Lightning travels at enormous speeds, around 220,000 km/h, and is hotter than the surface of the sun. The air around it heats up so quickly and tries to expand so fast that it explodes, creating a shock wave that ripples outwards from the lightning. This is thunder. Sound travels more slowly than light so we see lightning first then hear the thunder.

Lightning is drawn towards objects on the ground, but not always the tallest ones. No one can tell where lightning will strike, although it does strike the Earth an average of 100,000 times each day. If lightning strikes an object, the combination of energy, heat and the vibrations from the shock wave can cause severe damage. Lightning can also strike people, although this is more rare than you might imagine.

LIGHTNING SAFETY

▶ Avoid exposed places, such as mountainsides, lakes or large meadows. Try to make for lower ground or dense woodland.

▶ If possible, take shelter in a building.

▶ Do not shelter beneath a single tree or overhanging rocks.

▶ If you are with a group, spread out until you are about 10 metres apart.

▶ Curl up and crouch down with your feet together so that only the soles of your shoes are on the ground.

▶ If you can, put something dry under your feet (your backpack, coat, sleeping bag) for more insulation.

▶ Do not lie down on the ground. If lightning strikes the ground nearby, the current will flow outward and could flow through you.

CHAPTER 3:

HIKING AND HILL WALKING

There are more than 220,000 kilometres of public footpaths and trails throughout England and Wales, and many public access tracks and trails in Scotland and Northern Ireland. You can walk along country lanes, through lush meadows, climb mountain peaks or follow winding river valleys. The choice is yours.

GETTING STARTED

Hiking is one of the simplest activities you can do. It's free, and it can be done pretty much anywhere at any time. If you do not walk much as a rule, start by building a walk into your daily routine. If you travel by bus, walk part of the way instead. Walk in your local park, to the shops, or to visit friends. Better still, get your friends to walk with you.

Walking exercises your heart and other muscles, reduces stress, and gives you more energy. But to get the most from it you need to walk briskly for at least 30 minutes a day. This means walking just fast enough to warm up and breathe a little more deeply than normal. If you get out of breath, you are probably going too fast. You do not have to walk 30 minutes in one go; you could do two 15-minute walks, for example. But if you want to improve, you should increase the length of your walk at least once or twice a week.

Once you can comfortably walk for a few hours at a time, try something more challenging. One way to sample a longer hike is to join an organized group walk. Look for walking groups in your area, or try the Ramblers Association (see panel for website). They have a regular schedule of walks in various parts of the country, graded for different abilities and often for different age groups.

PLANNING A HIKE

If you are keen to do it yourself, the first thing to decide is what sort of hike you want to do. Do you want to walk a particular footpath or trail, for example? How long do you want to walk for, and what route will you take? One way may be easier than another.

Who are you going with and what are their walking abilities? It is always sensible to tailor your plans to suit the least able member of your group. Think about the time of year too, and what sort of weather conditions are probable. Remember, the weather in Britain can change very rapidly.

Once you know where you are going and when, you can put together a route plan – see page 58. To do this you will need a map. Rights of way and national trails are often signposted, but it is never a good idea to set off anywhere without at least a guide map to the walk. And, because it is surprisingly easy to lose your way, an OS map and a compass are useful too, especially if walking in more remote or mountainous areas. Without them you have no way of working out where you are and how to get back onto your route. Some people also like to use a GPS unit.

COAST PATH

WHERE TO WALK

For specific information about trails, rights of way, national parks, nature reserves and links to other countryside organizations contact the following websites:

BRITAIN

Ramblers Association:
www.ramblers.org.uk

ramblers
at the heart of walking

ENGLAND

Countryside Access:
www.countrysideaccess.gov.uk

WALES

Countryside Council for Wales:
www.ccw.gov.uk

Cyngor Cefn Gwlad Cymru
Countryside Council for Wales

SCOTLAND

Scottish Natural Heritage:
www.snh.org.uk

Scottish Natural Heritage
All of nature for all of Scotland

NORTHERN IRELAND

The Countryside Access and Activities Network:
www.countrysiderecreation.com

OUTDOORNI.COM

For more general information on planning, see Chapter 1, pages 10–12.
For information on map reading, navigation and GPS, see Chapter 4.

A ROUTE PLAN

A route plan can be as simple or as complicated as you want to make it, depending on the length and difficulty of your proposed hike. It is basically a form on which you set out the key details of your route.

Start by breaking the hike down into stages, giving the start and finishing point for each stage, the distance you plan to cover in each stage, and how long you estimate it will take you to walk that distance – see the panel on Naismith's Rule. Include where, when and for how long you plan to take rest breaks and food stops. By adding all the stages, breaks and stops together you end up with your total travelling time. On average, it is best not to walk more than 6 hours in one day, excluding time taken for rest breaks and stops.

Your plan could also include descriptions of landmarks along the route, or notes about difficult terrain or uphill sections that will slow you down. It could include alternative routes if one is easier or shorter than another, or the quickest way to get help in case of an emergency. For greater accuracy, you could include map grid references or compass bearings for each stage of the hike.

FOR EMERGENCIES

If you are planning a long-distance hike and are camping or walking in wild or difficult terrain, leave a copy of your route plan with someone at home, along with the names of members of your group, their mobile numbers and contact numbers for any places you are likely to stop at along the way. (Remember to let your contact know that you have arrived safely at the end of each day.)

NAISMITH'S RULE

In 1892, a Scottish mountaineer called William Naismith set out a rule of thumb for working out how long, on average, it takes to walk a particular distance, including an allowance for slower walking up or downhill.

Naismith's basic rule for a fit person walking on flat terrain is:

> **Allow 1 hour for every 5 kilometres, plus 10 minutes for every 100 metres uphill.**

However, if you or any members of your group are carrying backpacks, are unfamiliar with long-distance walking, or are not so fit, it is better to begin more cautiously and:

> **Allow 1 hour for every 3 kilometres, plus 10 minutes for every 100 metres uphill.**

For example, if route A is 15 km in distance and climbs 600 metres it would take:

> $15 \div 3 = 5$ hours

> $600 \div 100 = 6 \times 10$ minutes $= 1$ hour

> 5 hours + 1 hour $=$ 6 hours
> **total walking time**

Downhill walking can also affect your timing, although this can vary depending on the steepness of the slope. In general, most people time it in the same way as level walking. However, a gentle decline can add to your speed, so you could subtract 10 minutes for every 100 metres downhill. On a steep descent, add 10 minutes per 100 metres. Use the contour lines on an OS map to estimate the height gained or lost for each stage – see page 80.

ROUTE PLAN: The Cotswold Way — Chipping Camden to Winchcomb

MAPS:	National Trail: Cotswold Way
	OS map: OL45 The Cotswolds
	OS map: OS179 Gloucester, Cheltenham and Stroud

START: Market Hall, Chipping Camden
STARTING HEIGHT: 150 metres

DATE: 19th August **DAY:** 1 of 2

WALKING TO	KM	HEIGHT GAINED	DESCRIPTION	EST. TIME (HRS:MIN)
The Inn, Broadway	9.6	163 m	Take 10 min. break at Broadway Tower on Broadway Hill. The hill is 313 m – one of highest points on Way	3:38
TOTAL FOR DAY 1	**9.6**			**3:38**

START: The Inn, Broadway
STARTING HEIGHT: 100 metres

DATE: 20th August **DAY:** 2 of 2

WALKING TO	KM	HEIGHT GAINED	DESCRIPTION	EST. TIME (HRS:MIN)
Wood Stanway	10.5	200 m	High point: Shenberrow Hill 300 m 10 min. break at Shenberrow Hill 30 min. lunch break at Stanway House	4:30
Winchcomb	8.8	140 m	High point: Stumps Cross 250 m 10 min. break at Stumps Cross	3:20
TOTAL FOR DAY 2	**19.3**			**7:50**

TOTAL DISTANCE WALKED: 28.9 km

This example of a simple route plan is based on allowing one hour for every 3 kilometres distance. As you become more familiar with hiking you can adjust your timing to suit your own walking speed.

WHAT TO WEAR

You don't need a vast array of expensive specialist clothing to go walking; the main considerations are to keep warm, dry and comfortable. Badly fitting or uncomfortable clothes can become excruciating after an hour or so, and being cold and wet is not only miserable but can also be dangerous (see page 62 and Chapter 9).

BOOTS MADE FOR WALKING

The one thing you really do need if you are planning on hiking any distance at all is a good pair of walking boots or shoes. The wrong kind of footwear can leave you with aching feet, blisters, or even a twisted ankle. Fashion trainers or boots are useless on any kind of rough or wet terrain, and although wellingtons are waterproof they do not give your feet or ankles the support they need.

Walking boots or shoes are designed to protect and support your feet and ankles and to keep your feet comfortable. They come in a vast range of styles, materials and sizes and it is important to find the right ones for your feet and your needs.

When buying new boots it is best to go to a specialist shop. Think about the sort of walking you want to do. Low-cut, lightweight boots and shoes without ankle support are meant for easy terrain without too much hill climbing, or for summer walking. If you want to walk all year round on varied terrains or with a full rucksack, you will want high-cut, hill walking or trekking boots made from leather or waterproof fabric. These will support your ankles and the tough tread soles will grip well on steep or slippery tracks.

SANDALS

+ **Lightweight for carrying**
- **No support**
- **Limited foot protection**

TRAINERS

+ **Comfortable to wear**
- **No foot protection**
- **Limited warmth**
- **No waterproofing**

WELLINGTONS

+ **Waterproof**
- **No ankle support**
- **Not recommended for long-term wear**

WALKING BOOTS

+ **Excellent ankle support**
+ **Sturdy grip**
- **Limited waterproofing**

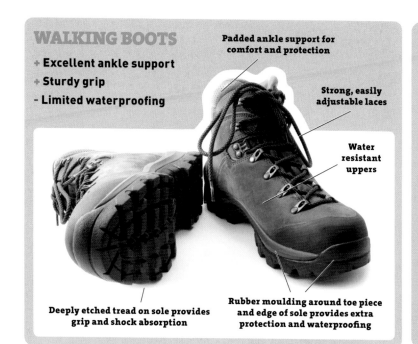

Padded ankle support for comfort and protection

Strong, easily adjustable laces

Water resistant uppers

Rubber moulding around toe piece and edge of sole provides extra protection and waterproofing

Deeply etched tread on sole provides grip and shock absorption

SOCKS

It is worth investing in a couple of pairs of walking socks. These are usually made from special materials to help absorb sweat. They should be soft with minimal seams so as not to add pressure or rub. Many walking socks also have a bit of extra padding around the heel and toe. In cold weather or for extra comfort, wear two pairs – a thin pair on the inside and a thicker pair on top.

TRY BEFORE YOU BUY

Always try boots on before buying them. Take your time and wear them in the shop. Most specialist stores will have an incline board so you can find out what the boots feel like when your foot is at an angle.

Remember that walking boots are usually worn with thick socks for added comfort and protection, so take some walking socks with you or ask the shop to lend you some. You may decide you need to buy a size bigger than your normal shoe size, especially as your feet could swell a little during a long walk.

The boots should feel comfortable when laced up. You should be able to flex your toes, but your feet should not slide around. The boots should not press on any part of your foot, such as your big toe or heel, and should not feel tight across the top of your foot as you walk. If one of your feet is bigger than the other, try going for a larger size with combinations of insoles.

Once you have your boots, take care of them. Keep them clean and waterproofed. It is also a good idea to wear them in a little before going on a long-distance hike.

TOP TIP

+ To remove sweat and odour from your boots, cut the legs off an old pair of tights – up to about knee level – then fill each leg with a few handfuls of bicarbonate of soda (or baking soda). Push it down to the bottom to make a ball about 4–6 cm diameter in the foot. Make a knot in the top of the ball. Wrap the remaining leg material around the ball one more time and knot it again to create a double layer of material. Cut away any excess. When you take your boots or shoes off, put a ball in each boot. The bicarb will absorb the moisture and any odours.

LAYERING UP

As you walk through the day your body temperature will vary depending on the weather and the amount of energy you are using. For this reason it is far better to wear three or four layers of thin but warm clothing that you can easily take off or put on, than to rely on a heavy coat or jacket for warmth.

Layers of thin clothing trap air between them, providing good insulation without too much weight or bulk. Damp clothing soaks up the heat from your body and wind can lower your body temperature even more, creating the danger of hypothermia. Similarly if your body overheats, you can suffer from hyperthermia.

FROM THE INSIDE OUT

LAYER 1

The first layer, nearest your skin, should be light and well fitting, but not too tight. In winter a long-sleeved thermal vest is a good choice, or in summer a sleeveless or short-sleeved top. Cotton is soft and hardwearing, but can get clammy when you sweat. A synthetic 'breathable' material will dry more quickly.

LAYER 2

The second layer should be looser with long sleeves that button or are fitted at the wrists so they can be rolled up or folded down, and a high neck – such as a polo neck or warm shirt in winter, or a lighter cotton shirt in summer. In warm weather, these two layers plus a lightweight wind- and waterproof jacket would be plenty.

LAYER 3

The third layer for extra warmth should be a loose fleece or woollen pullover, preferably with a zip front that you can open or close as needed. In mild, dry weather this can also act as the final layer (although a waterproof shell that folds up small is always useful).

LAYER 4

The final layer should be a windproof and waterproof jacket, preferably with a raised collar and a hood. Overlapping fastenings and pocket flaps help keep the wind out and shed water. Adjustable cuff fastenings and vents under the arms help to avoid overheating, and 'breathable' material will help prevent sweat building up on the inside.

For information on how to recognize and treat extreme loss of body temperature (hypothermia), or excessively high body temperature (hyperthermia), see Chapter 9, pages 218–219.

TROUSERS

On a short or easy walk any pair of comfortable, loose-fitting trousers will do, but for longer or more arduous walking it is worth getting a pair of walking trousers. These are made of lightweight synthetic materials that dry quickly. Denim jeans are the worst things to wear as they hold onto water and become heavy. This can cause chafing and make you very cold.

In cold weather wear a pair of thermal leggings under your trousers, or if it is very cold or snowy you may need a pair of quilted trousers. In very wet conditions you could get a pair of waterproof trousers to wear on top of your walking trousers. You should put these on as soon as it starts to rain, but take them off again when the rain stops as they can make you very sweaty on the inside. In summer people often walk in shorts. However these do not offer much protection from thorns or nettles, or from the possibility of ticks – see panel.

TICKS

Ticks are small blood-sucking mites. They are parasites and feed on birds or mammals, including humans. Some carry diseases, such as Lyme disease, which an infected tick can pass on to its host through its bite. Ticks are found in most parts of the world, especially in slightly damp, shady areas such as long grass, bracken or woods. For more information, go to **www.lymediseaseaction.org.uk** or the Ramblers Association website – see Useful Addresses, pages 244–247.

HATS AND GLOVES

In summer a hat will protect your face, ears and the back of your neck from sunburn, and you will need a good sun cream on every part of your body that is exposed to the sun. A lightweight hat with a brim or a peaked cap will also keep the sun out of your eyes. In bright sunlight you might find a pair of sunglasses useful.

In cold weather it is essential to keep your head and ears covered. A fitted fleece or knitted hat is ideal. If it's very cold you might want to wear a balaclava to keep the sides of your face and neck warm (as shown left).

To keep your hands warm, fleece or thermal gloves are both warm and light. In very cold weather you could wear a pair of thin gloves underneath heavier mittens.

OTHER EQUIPMENT

How much personal kit or equipment you need to carry with you when you walk depends on the length of walk you are doing, the terrain and, of course, the weather.

HALF DAY HIKING

Obviously, a short walk – less than three or four hours, say – over gentle terrain will have fewer demands than a two or three day hike. But even so, there are some basics that you should always consider carrying:

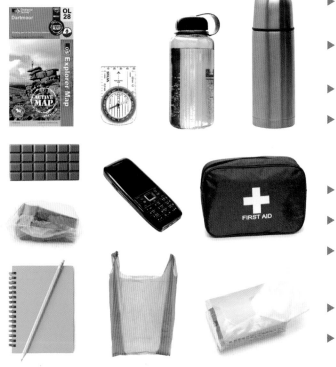

- ▶ Maps and, possibly, a compass depending on how well populated or well marked the route will be.
- ▶ Full water bottle – recyclable plastic bottles are lighter to carry than metal ones.
- ▶ Thermos of hot drink (tea, coffee, hot blackcurrant, etc.) if the weather is cold.
- ▶ Snacks – hiking can really burn up calories so it is always useful to carry something that will give you a quick energy boost, such as cereal bars, dried fruit, nuts, chocolate, or a sandwich.
- ▶ Mobile phone – bear in mind that you will not always get a clear signal.
- ▶ Personal first-aid kit – see page 66. See also Chapter 9, page 212.
- ▶ Notepad and pencil – useful for jotting down notes about the route, directions if you get lost, or for working out your bearing – see Chapter 4.
- ▶ Plastic bags – to sit on, put rubbish in, etc.
- ▶ Packet of wet wipes, or tissues and a small bottle of antiseptic handwash gel.

TOP TIPS

+ Keep your maps and route plan inside some kind of protective waterproof carriers, such as transparent plastic folders or bags.

+ Carry your mobile phone in an easy-seal plastic bag to make sure it is protected from cold and damp. Make a few small air holes in the bottom of the bag to prevent condensation.

+ Buy a spare phone battery and carry it in a separate sealed bag. Make sure both batteries are fully charged before setting out.

+ If you take a torch, also take a spare bulb and spare torch batteries.

DAY HIKING AND HILL WALKING

When you are planning a longer walk and/or walking in remote or more difficult terrain it's best to be prepared for possible emergencies. You will need sufficient clothing of the right kind, the correct navigational aids and a spare copy of your route plan to leave with a responsible person. You might also want to add the following equipment:

▶ **Whistle** – to attract attention in case of emergency.

▶ **Torch** – for map reading, etc., in case it gets dark, and for attracting attention.

▶ **Wristwatch** – as a backup to the clock on your phone.

▶ **Lots of high calorie, nutritious food** in case you are out for longer than expected.

▶ **Extra supplies of water.**

▶ **Emergency water purification tablets.**

▶ **In remote areas you should not assume that you will be able to find emergency shelter,** especially if someone is injured. Take a survival bag – a strong plastic or foil bag that is big enough to fit over one or two people yet folds into a compact pouch. It is designed to be wind- and waterproof and will prevent heat loss. Alternatively, for a group you may prefer a nylon bothy bag which can accommodate several people.

Don't forget you'll need these items from the Half Day Hiking list as well:

▶ **Personal survival kit** – may include some of the items above, see Chapter 9, page 233.

LONG-DISTANCE WALKING

If you are planning a longer hike and intend to camp along the way, you will need sleeping bags, tents and other camping gear. For information on camping equipment, see Chapter 5.

The internationally recognized emergency signal is six short blasts on a whistle, or six flashes with a torch, repeated every minute.

For more information on survival skills, see Chapter 9, pages 232–243.

A PERSONAL FIRST AID KIT

For long trips it is advisable for one member of the group to take a fully equipped first aid kit – see Chapter 9, page 212 – but for day hikes it is useful if everyone carries a small personal kit. Pocket-sized first aid kits are widely available from chemists, and kits for walkers are supplied by outdoor clothing and equipment shops and online from the British Red Cross and St John Ambulance – see Useful Addresses, pages 244–247.

DO IT YOURSELF

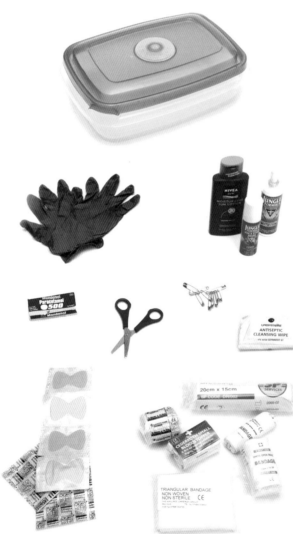

However, you could also put one together yourself. It should include:

▷ **Individually sealed antiseptic cleansing wipes.**

▷ **Small tube of antiseptic cream.**

▷ **Small pair of blunt-nosed scissors (you can buy folding scissors).**

▷ **Pair of tweezers.**

▷ **Safety pins, for securing bandages.**

▷ **Surgical tape.**

▷ **Small phial of eyewash.**

▷ **Steri-strips for closing wounds.**

▷ **Sterile gauze swabs.**

▷ **1 large and 2 medium sterile dressing pads.**

▷ **Crepe bandage.**

▷ **Triangular bandage to support broken bones or sprains.**

▷ **Selection of plasters.**

▷ **Corn cushions, foot felt or a blister kit in case of blisters.**

▷ **Insect bite or sting pads.**

▷ **Disposable gloves.**

▷ **Paracetamol tablets.**

▷ **Also, be sure you take any regular medication you require, such as inhalers.**

▷ **Washbag or other waterproof pouch or tin to put everything in.**

BLISTER CARE

The most common ailment suffered by walkers is blisters, and they can turn a pleasurable walk into a nightmare. Blisters are usually caused by friction.

1. To avoid blisters:

▶ Wear comfortable, well-fitting walking boots that allow your feet to 'breathe'.

▶ Make sure the boots have gusseted tongues to prevent small stones or other irritating objects from getting inside. If something does get inside your boots or socks, remove it immediately.

▶ Wear a fresh pair of walking socks every day.

▶ Keep your feet dry. If they get tired and sweaty, rest and remove your boots and socks for a while. Take a spare pair of socks so you can change them along the way.

▶ Take action the minute you feel any soreness or pressure on your feet.

2. To treat blisters:

▶ If you feel a blister forming, take your boots and socks off and let your feet cool down and dry.

▶ Apply some kind of protective cushioning or padding to the area, such as a corn or blister plaster, an ordinary plaster, or a piece of folded material held in place with surgical tape.

▶ Remove the covering overnight to let the area heal.

▶ Keep the blister area clean and dry, and put on a fresh dressing each day for as long as you need to.

CARING FOR YOUR FEET

It pays to keep your feet in good condition. Don't let the skin on your heels or soles get too thick and hard – it will not prevent blisters but can lead to cracked and sore feet. File hard skin away with an emery board or pumice stone and rub in moisturizing cream. Cut toenails straight across, never rounded at the sides. Don't cut them to the quick, but do not let them get too long as they may press against your boots.

COUNTRYSIDE HYGIENE

If you are walking in a remote area and are unable to find a proper toilet, please be aware of environmental health. Human waste, or faeces, should be buried about 20 cm (a hand and a half) deep and well away from any watercourse. You might want to carry a small plastic hand shovel or scoop for this purpose. If the soil is too thin or hard to dig, the waste should be carried away in plastic bags. Always carry away or burn used toilet paper, and take used sanitary products away with you.

For more information on dealing with personal waste, see Chapter 5, pages 116–117.

RUCKSACKS AND BACKPACKS

Once you have decided what equipment and supplies to take, you will need something to carry them in. Even for a short walk it is best to have a proper backpack. These are designed to place the weight of your load evenly on your back so it does not interfere with your balance.

Rucksacks or backpacks come in a variety of types and sizes. They should all have wide, adjustable, padded shoulder straps to prevent the loaded bag biting into your shoulders and neck. Many also have a hip pad that belts below your waist and a chest strap that pulls the shoulder straps together to prevent them cutting into your armpits. These additional straps help spread the weight of the pack and hold it firmly to your body.

Small backpacks, or daypacks, are the simplest and do not usually have a frame. Larger packs will have an internal or external supporting frame to transfer some of the weight of the pack to your hips.

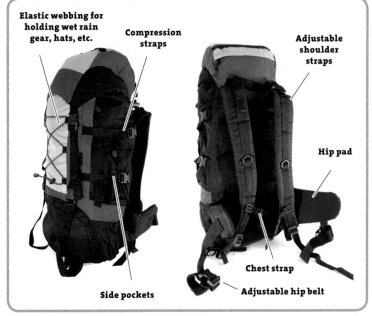

Elastic webbing for holding wet rain gear, hats, etc.

Compression straps

Adjustable shoulder straps

Hip pad

Side pockets

Chest strap

Adjustable hip belt

Compression straps allow room for expansion when you need it or make the backpack smaller when it is not full. Most backpacks also have a variety of compartments and side pockets to hold different items separately. Rucksacks are water resistant, but will let in water in heavy rain. You can buy rucksack liners and dry sacks to pack your gear in, or just use plastic bags. This keeps your belongings dry, keeps your pack neater and makes things easier to find.

SIZE MATTERS

It is best to choose the right size of pack for your purpose. Think carefully about what you need. It is uncomfortable to carry a small pack that is stuffed full, but pointless to carry a large backpack that is half empty. Rucksacks are usually measured in terms of their capacity in litres.

| 15 TO 30 LITRES | 35 TO 50 LITRES | 55 TO 75 LITRES | 75 TO 100 LITRES |

▶ 15 TO 30 LITRES

These are usually known as daypacks. The smaller sizes are often bought for general use and for school/college backpacks but also work well for short hikes. The larger sizes are good for day hiking in winter, or even an overnight stay if you are packing light and staying in a hostel or B&B.

▶ 35 TO 50 LITRES

Good for winter walking and two- to three-day hikes if you are not camping.

▶ 55 TO 75 LITRES

Generally good sizes for hiking and camping. Most people carry the 55–75 litre size.

▶ 75 TO 100 LITRES

The largest sizes of rucksack are used for major expeditions.

For more information on the best way to pack a rucksack when you go camping, see Chapter 5, pages 108–111.

SAFETY CHECK : Generally a loaded pack should not weigh more than a quarter of your body weight. However, it is not advisable to regularly carry more than 13.5 kg (about 30 lbs) as it can affect your posture, and young people in particular should not carry more than about 9 kg (20 lbs).

CHOOSING A BACKPACK

It is advisable to go to a specialist outdoor equipment shop where you can try on different packs and get the feel of them. If you can put something in them to see what they feel like with weight in them, so much the better. The staff in specialist stores should be able to give you advice on the best size and style of pack for your needs. When you find a pack you are happy with you can also ask them to help adjust the straps to fit you.

You will want to be able to get at your water bottle without taking the pack off, so make sure the side pockets will take a drinks bottle and that you can reach it easily. Alternatively, some packs have a built-in 'hydration system' – an internal water bladder with a pipe that you can suck on. However, these require special equipment to keep them clean and unless you particularly need to keep your hands free, for rock climbing or cycling for example, can seem more trouble than they are worth.

TOP TIPS

+ Put the things you use all the time, such as maps, sunglasses and snacks, in the front or side pockets so they are easily accessible.

+ Get into the habit of putting the same bits of your equipment into the same part of the rucksack. That way you will always know where to find them.

+ Carry a small roll of Duct or Gaffer tape with you. This reinforced fabric sticky tape is excellent for carrying out instant repairs on rucksacks, boots, anything.

+ Practise packing and carrying your pack before you set off on a long walk; you may want to lighten your load.

HOW TO PUT ON A RUCKSACK

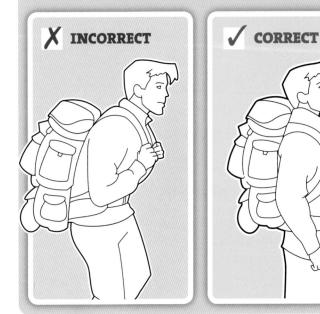

✗ INCORRECT

✓ CORRECT

A rucksack should sit comfortably and evenly on your shoulders. When full, the rucksack should be packed so that heavier items are in the upper part; this balances the load so that the weight sits mainly on your shoulders and does not drag on the small of your back. When the hip belt is done up it should rest on top of your hips, not around the waist, and should fit snugly. The hip belt will help to transfer some of the weight from your shoulders to your hips.

WALKING SAFETY CHECK

✓ Do not overestimate your own or your group's abilities.

✓ Be sure to check the weather before you set out.

✓ Be prepared to shorten or change your route, or to turn back if the weather worsens, you become tired or cold, or face some other difficulty.

✓ At least one member of your group should be familiar with basic first aid skills. See Chapter 9, pages 214–225.

✓ When walking in remote or challenging terrain, ensure that at least one member of your party is an experienced hill walker.

✓ Be sure to carry plenty of water and drink regularly. Avoid drinking unpurified water from streams.

✓ When walking on roads where there is no pavement, always walk on the side facing oncoming traffic. But cross to the other side before sharp right-hand bends.

✓ Use level crossings to cross railway lines, and pay attention to warning signals and lights.

✓ Keep to public footpaths and rights of way, and do not walk on private land without permission.

✓ Be cautious near untethered bulls or dogs. If cattle or other curious livestock come too close, the Ramblers Association recommends turning to face them with both arms raised and speaking in a firm, ordinary voice rather than shouting. Do not brandish sticks at them.

CHAPTER 4:

FINDING THE WAY

Even on well-marked trails, it can be annoyingly easy to lose your way, especially if trail markers have become worn or obscured by vegetation. In more remote areas, good map-reading and compass skills are essential. But there is more to navigation than reading a map – you also need to remain constantly alert and be a keen observer of your surroundings.

A SENSE OF DIRECTION

A map is simply a diagrammatic representation of the landscape. Because it is two-dimensional it relies on using lines and symbols to indicate the physical features of an area (see pages 80–81). To find your position on a map you have to be able to relate it to your surroundings, and to do this it is helpful if you can visualize the area the map is representing. This is a skill that comes with practice, and a good way to start is by paying attention to the landscape.

LOOKING AT THE LAND

As you walk a route, develop the habit of noticing particular features or landmarks as you pass them, and their relationship to you. Begin with the start of the walk. Notice the direction it takes – heading towards woodland, a hill on the left, for example. At regular intervals, compare the landscape you see with the lines and symbols on your map.

Bear in mind that artificial structures, such as buildings and roads, can change from one year to the next, whereas natural features like hills, valleys and rivers rarely do. The more familiar you become with the shapes of these natural features, the more easily you will be able to relate them to what you can see on a map.

If you are returning by the same route, turn round every now and then and look back at the path you have just walked. Things can look different when approached from the opposite direction and it is useful to familiarize yourself with this.

FOLLOW THE SUN

Practise learning how to find north, east, south and west. Of course, you can always check your direction with a compass (see pages 82–89), but it is useful to develop some sense of where these direction points are in case of an emergency or a lost or damaged compass. Before compasses were invented, people relied on celestial navigation – using the sun, moon and stars. The sun always rises in the east and sets in the west. In the northern hemisphere when the sun reaches its highest point in the sky, at around midday, its direction is in the south. (In the southern hemisphere it will be in the north.)

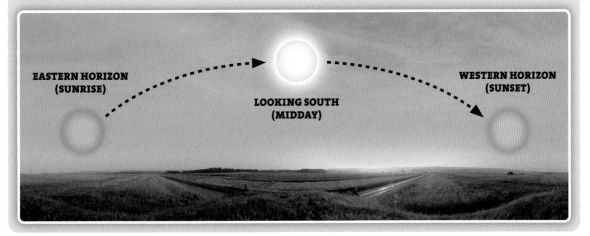

EASTERN HORIZON
(SUNRISE)

LOOKING SOUTH
(MIDDAY)

WESTERN HORIZON
(SUNSET)

FINDING NORTH

If you want to find out where north is more accurately without a compass, you will need a sunny day, a straight stick about 1 metre long, a bare piece of flat ground, and a couple of markers (stones or twigs).

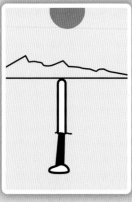 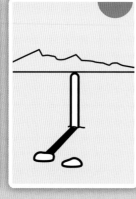 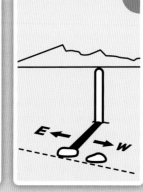 

1 Push the stick into the ground so that it casts a clear straight shadow. Place one marker at the tip of the shadow.

2 Wait half an hour, until the shadow has moved some distance from the first marker. Place a second marker at the tip of this second shadow.

3 Draw a line between your two markers. This is the east–west line. The first marker is pointing west, the second is pointing east.

4 Stand facing the line, with the first marker on your left and the second marker on your right. You are now facing north.

BY MOONLIGHT

When the moon is very bright it will also cast a shadow and sometimes this is strong enough to use the stick method described above. Of course, the moon does not produce any light of its own; it only reflects the light from the sun, and the shape of this reflected light varies as the moon moves around the Earth.

When the moon is on the opposite side of the Earth from the sun, the Earth blocks the sun's light and we cannot see the moon at all. This is called a new moon. As the moon moves out of the Earth's shadow, it begins to reflect a thin crescent of light on its right side. As the nights pass, this crescent gradually becomes fuller and spreads across the face of the moon until we see a full moon. After this, the light begins to slowly shift back to a crescent but this time on the left side.

If you see the moon rise before the sun has set, the lit side of the moon will be on the west. If the moon does not rise until after midnight, the lit side will be on the east.

STAR GAZING

The patterns that certain groups of stars make in the sky are called constellations. There are 88 officially recognized constellations and it can take a lifetime to learn them all. However, for direction-finding in the northern hemisphere you only really need to know one or two constellations – the ones that will help you find Polaris, the North Star.

The North Star or Pole Star has this name because it appears to sit almost directly above the North Pole and it is the only star that does not seem to move. So when you find the North Star you know you are facing north.

The constellation that is commonly used to help find the North Star is called the Plough, Ursa Major (the Great Bear) or the Big Dipper.

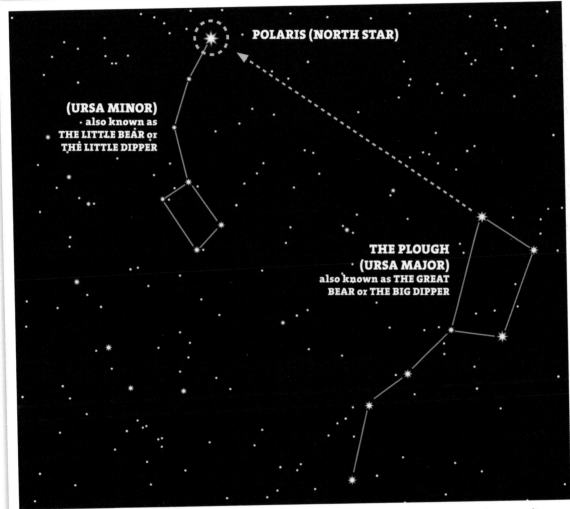

POLARIS (NORTH STAR)

(URSA MINOR)
also known as
THE LITTLE BEAR or
THE LITTLE DIPPER

THE PLOUGH
(URSA MAJOR)
also known as THE GREAT
BEAR or THE BIG DIPPER

The Plough takes its name from the shape of an old-fashioned horse plough, although to modern eyes it looks more like a saucepan with a 'bowl' and a long 'handle'. Find the two stars that form the right-hand side of the bowl. Now imagine a line extending straight up from the side of the bowl and about five times longer. The brightest star you will see there is the North Star, which also forms the northernmost point of the constellation Ursa Minor (the Little Bear).

MAP READING

The most useful maps for finding your way across country are topographical maps. Unlike standard road maps, topographical maps are highly detailed and contain all the natural and artificial features of an area, including the shape of the land – its hills, valleys, ridges and so on. In Britain these maps are produced by the national mapping agency, Ordnance Survey.

DRAWN TO SCALE

Maps are usually drawn to a particular scale. This tells you how the area shown on the map compares in size to the actual area of the land it covers.

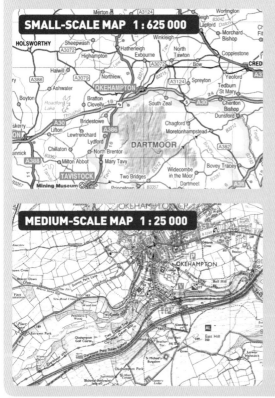

For example, a 1 in 625,000, or **1 : 625 000** scale map means that 1 centimetre on the map is equal to 625,000 centimetres (6,250 metres or 6.25 kilometres) on the ground. So if 1 centimetre equals 6.25 kilometres, 4 centimetres on the map will equal 25 kilometres on the ground, and so on. This is a very small-scale map, designed to show a large area but without a lot of detail. It will show all the major road and rail networks, cities and rivers, for example, but not much else.

On the other hand, a **1 : 25 000** scale map means that 1 centimetre on the map equals 25,000 centimetres (250 metres or 0.25 kilometres) on the ground. So 4 centimetres on the map equals 1 kilometre on the ground, 8 centimetres equals 2 kilometres, and so on. This is known as a medium-scale map, and it will show individual buildings and farms as well as villages and roads.

MEASURING THE DISTANCE

The scale of a map is clearly shown on its cover, and a scale bar like the example below will be printed on the margins of the map or inside a panel with other information about the map. You can use the scale bar to work out how far apart any two points on the map are.

	1000		Metres 0 Kilometres		1

1 kilometre = 0.6214 mile
1 metre = 3.2808 feet

3000		1000	Feet 0 Miles	1

MEASURING DISTANCE WITH A PIECE OF STRING OR PAPER

1 Lay a piece of string along the twists and turns of your route.

2 Or mark each section of the route along the edge of a piece of paper.

3 Measure the length of string or the combined paper marks against the scale bar to get an estimate of the distance.

IN THE GRID

Whenever you look at a map you will see a series of light-coloured vertical and horizontal lines dividing the entire map into a grid of squares. Each line is numbered on the edges of the map, so that each square can be identified by its vertical and horizontal numbers. The vertical lines are called 'eastings', because their numbers always increase from east to west (left to right). The horizontal lines are called 'northings' as their numbers always increase from south to north (bottom to top).

To identify a particular place on a map you give it a grid reference by quoting the numbers of its grid square. This usually consists of two sets of figures giving the number of the easting on the left side of the square, plus the number of the northing at the bottom of the square. For example, the coloured square in the diagram below would have the grid reference 6594. This is known as a four-figure grid reference. (Note that the easting is always given before the northing. One way of remembering this is: 'along the corridor and up the stairs'.)

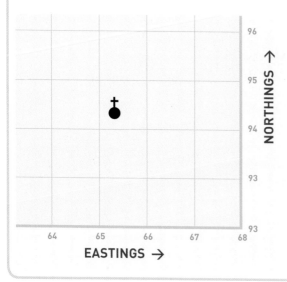

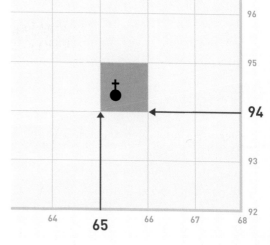

THE UK GRID

For mapping purposes, Ordnance Survey have divided the whole of Britain into 100 x 100 kilometre squares, known as the National Grid. Each square is identified by a two-letter code, such as NY or SX. **See diagram 1.**

Each of these 100-kilometre squares is then divided into a grid of smaller squares with eastings and northings numbered from 0 to 9. On small-scale Ordnance Survey (OS) maps, each smaller square is equal to 10 kilometres in real distance. **See diagram 2**.

On medium-scale OS maps, each 10-kilometre square is broken down even further into grid squares representing 1 kilometre and the eastings and northings are numbered in double digits from 00 to 99. **See diagram 3.** (Note that you can get a rough estimation of distance from one place to another simply by counting the number of squares between them.)

SIX-FIGURE GRID REFERENCE

A two-letter code and a four-figure grid reference, such as SX 7734, for example, allows you to pinpoint any place on a map within a 1-kilometre-square area. However, if you want to give a very precise location, you need a six-figure grid reference. To do this you mentally divide the grid square into tenths. Work out how many tenths your location is from the grid easting – let's say 6 – and then how many tenths it is from the northing – let's say 3. This would make your grid reference SX 776343 and it will be accurate to within 100 metres.

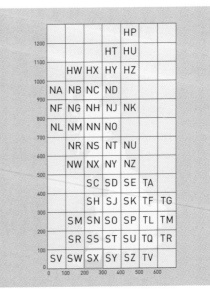

100-KM-SQUARE NATIONAL GRID REFERENCE = SX

10-KM-SQUARE GRID REFERENCE = SX 73

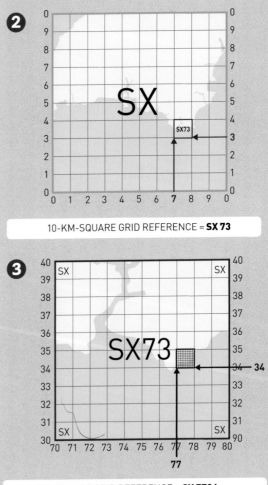

1-KM-SQUARE GRID REFERENCE = SX 7734

MAP SYMBOLS

Maps use lots of small diagrams or symbols to indicate the position of a variety of features common to most places. This saves labelling each one individually, which would make the map almost impossible to read. The symbols used may vary depending on the map, but on OS maps the symbols for each feature are shown in the same way.

A key to what the symbols mean will be shown somewhere on the map itself – this is called the map legend. However, it is useful to familiarize yourself with some of the most common ones.

ROADS AND PATHS

M1 or A6 (M)	Motorway
A 35	Dual carriageway
A 31 (T) or A35	Trunk or Main road
B 3074	Secondary road
	Narrow road with passing places
	Road under construction
	Road generally more than 4 m wide
	Road generally less than 4 m wide
	Other road, drive or track, fenced and unfenced

RAILWAYS

Multiple track / Single track — Standard gauge
Narrow gauge / Light Rapid Transit System with station
Road over; road under; level crossing
Cutting; tunnel; embankment
Station, open to passengers; siding

PUBLIC RIGHTS OF WAY

Footpath
Bridleway
Byway open to all traffic
Road used as a public path

OTHER PUBLIC ACCESS

Other routes with public access
National Trail / Long Distance Route; Recreational route
Permitted footpath
Permitted bridleway
Off road cycle routes

BOUNDARIES

National
County
Constituency (Const), Electoral Region (ER) or Burgh Const
Civil Parish (CP) or Community (C)
Unitary Authority (UA), Metropolitan District (Met Dist), London Borough (LB) or District
National Park

ARCHAEOLOGICAL AND HISTORICAL

Site of antiquity
✕ 1066 — Site of battle (with date)
VILLA — Roman
Castle — Non-Roman
Visible earthwork

GENERAL FEATURES

Current or former place of worship — with tower / with spire, minaret, or dome
+ Place of worship
Building; important building
Glasshouse
Youth hostel
Bunkhouse/camping barn/ other hostel (selected areas only)
Bus or coach station

HEIGHTS AND NATURAL FEATURES

52 · Ground survey height
284 · Air survey height
Vertical face/cliff
Loose rock, Boulders, Outcrop, Scree
Water, Mud
Sand; sand and shingle

VEGETATION

Coniferous trees
Non-coniferous trees
Coppice
Orchard
Scrub
Bracken, heath or rough grassland
Marsh, reeds or saltings

ACCESS LAND

Access land boundary and tint
Access land in wooded area
Access information point
DANGER AREA — Firing and test ranges in the area. Danger! Observe warning notices
MANAGED ACCESS — Access permitted within managed controls, for example, local byelaws

TOURIST AND LEISURE INFORMATION

Building of historic interest
Camp site
Caravan site
Camping and caravan site
Castle / fort
Cathedral / Abbey
Cycle trail
Fishing
Golf course or links
Information centre
Museum
Nature reserve
Parking
Picnic site
Preserved railway
PC Public Convenience
Public house/s
Viewpoint
V Visitor centre
National Park Information Point
Walks / trails
Water activites

Symbols taken from OS EXPLORER series (1 : 25 000 scale)

HIGHS AND LOWS

The other key piece of information you will find on a topographical map is the physical shape of the landscape and its height above sea level. This is shown by a series of lines (usually printed in brown) called contour lines.

Each contour line represents a particular height above sea level and it follows the shape of the land at that level. So a single hill, for example, might be shown as a series of ever-decreasing roughly shaped circles, whereas a range of hills might appear as a series of wavy lines.

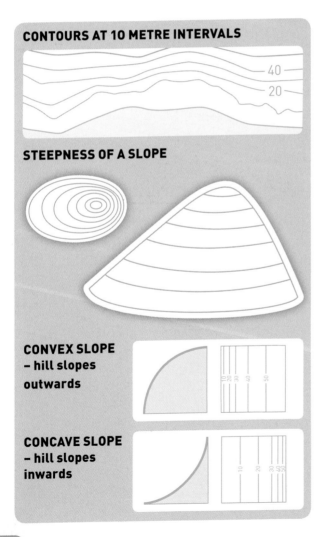

CONTOURS AT 10 METRE INTERVALS

40
20

STEEPNESS OF A SLOPE

CONVEX SLOPE – hill slopes outwards

CONCAVE SLOPE – hill slopes inwards

The height of a particular level is indicated by small numbers written at intervals on the lines themselves. On a medium-scale map, the contour lines are usually 5 metres apart (on small-scale maps or in very mountainous areas they may be 10 metres apart). The lowest number is closest to sea level, so a contour line marked 5 would be only 5 metres above sea level. The highest number marks the highest point, so a line marked 30 would be 30 metres above sea level.

When there are few contour lines on a map, you know the land is very flat. When there are lots of contour lines, you know the land is very variable. When the lines are drawn close together, this indicates that the rise, or elevation, of the land is steep. When they are far apart, the elevation is more gentle.

When the lines are close together at the lower levels, but open out at the higher levels, the hill will slope outwards. When they are further apart at the lower levels but close together at the higher levels, the slope will curve inwards.

CONTOUR FEATURES

RIDGE – a series of pointed or finger-like contour lines usually indicates a high ridge.

VALLEY – low-level contour lines spaced quite widely apart, often with a river following the same direction as the lines.

PASS – two sets of circles joined by lower contour lines, a little like the eyes in a face mask, indicate a saddle or pass between two high points.

FOLLOWING A MAP

When following a route on a map, turn it round until it faces the way you are walking. Make sure the map is correctly aligned by choosing two or three landmarks or features you can easily see ahead of you. Find these same landmarks on your map and position the map so that you could draw imaginary lines from the landmarks in the landscape to those on the map.

TOP TIPS

+ Keep checking for identifiable features on your map and mentally tick them off as you pass them along your route. (Remember that artificial structures can change.)

+ If you get lost, always go back to the last point you clearly recognized on the map. If you try to take short cuts you are likely to make matters worse.

+ When deciding on a trail, remember that when a path runs alongside a contour line it will be fairly level at that height. If it crosses contour lines, it will climb, and it will be steep if the contours are close together.

USING A COMPASS
THE POINTS OF A COMPASS

Geographical directions are usually described in terms of the points of a compass.

The four main or cardinal points of a compass are: North, East, South and West – and they are always described in a clockwise direction. An easy way to remember which order they are in is to use a simple memory device such as '**N**ever **E**at **S**hredded **W**heat'.

The four cardinal points divide the compass into quarters. For greater accuracy, these four quarters are then divided again to show the halfway mark between each quarter. So if you

PARTS OF A COMPASS

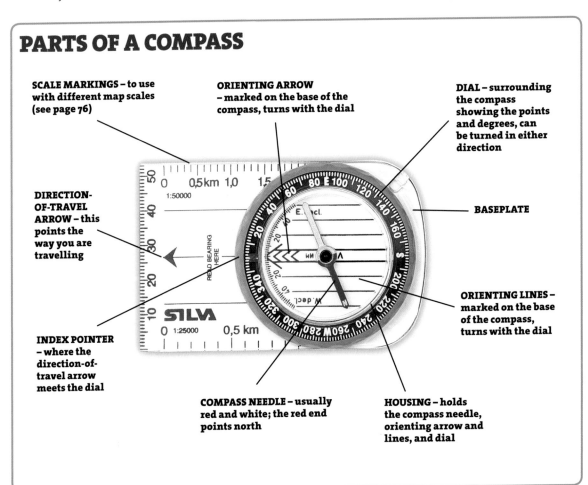

SCALE MARKINGS – to use with different map scales (see page 76)

ORIENTING ARROW – marked on the base of the compass, turns with the dial

DIAL – surrounding the compass showing the points and degrees, can be turned in either direction

DIRECTION-OF-TRAVEL ARROW – this points the way you are travelling

BASEPLATE

INDEX POINTER – where the direction-of-travel arrow meets the dial

ORIENTING LINES – marked on the base of the compass, turns with the dial

COMPASS NEEDLE – usually red and white; the red end points north

HOUSING – holds the compass needle, orienting arrow and lines, and dial

are heading in a direction halfway between north and east, for example, you can say you are heading north-east. These are called the intercardinal points. The others are south-east, south-west and north-west.

To make it possible to pinpoint directions even more precisely, the circle of a compass face is also divided into 360 degrees (360º). North is always 0º and each quarter adds 90º, so east is 90º, south is 180º, and so on. (Take care to notice how the degree numbers are marked on the dial. Most compasses show degree numbers in units of 20, with each small line between the numbers worth 2 degrees; however, compasses do vary. The one shown top left, for example, has units of 5 degrees.)

TYPES OF COMPASS

A simple, or nautical, compass is just a round dial showing the compass points and a lightly balanced needle in the centre that turns as you turn the compass. One half of the needle is usually coloured red, and this is the side that points north. When you turn the compass so that you line up the red pointer with the 'N' mark on the dial you know which direction is north, south, east and west.

For map-reading purposes, however, you need a compass that can give you more information than this. The best type of compass to use is an orienteering compass.

READING A COMPASS

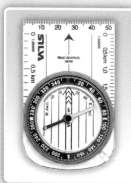 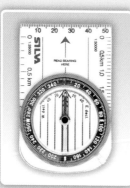 

1 Hold the compass level, with the direction-of-travel arrow on the baseplate pointing away from you. Turn the dial until the letter 'N' and the orienting arrow line up with the direction-of-travel arrow.

2 Keeping the compass steady in front of you, turn your body slowly around. As you move your body, the needle also turns. Keep turning until the needle points to the letter 'N'. You are now facing north.

3 Now turn a quarter circle to the right. The dial, orienting arrow and direction-of-travel arrow are pointing north, but the needle is now pointing west, right? Wrong! The needle is pointing north; it is your position that has changed.

4 Turn the dial so that the letter 'N' and the orienting arrow line up with the needle again. Now the dial shows that the direction-of-travel arrow is pointing east, so you know that you are facing east.

Remember, regardless of what the dial is telling you, the needle always points north. To find the direction in which you are heading you turn the dial until the 'N' mark and the orientation arrow line up with the needle. Then you read your direction-of-travel arrow to find out which direction you are facing. **FOLLOW THE DIRECTION-OF-TRAVEL ARROW, NOT THE COMPASS NEEDLE.**

WHICH NORTH IS NORTH?

Having said that all compasses point north, there is one other point to remember – not all norths are the same! For navigational purposes, there are three different norths:

TRUE NORTH – is the geographical point at the northern end of the Earth's axis – the North Pole.

GRID NORTH – is represented by the vertical north–south grid lines on a map. The difference between grid north and true north in the UK is very little, about 1.5°, and can usually be ignored.

MAGNETIC NORTH – is the direction shown by a compass.

NORTH

SOUTH

TRUE NORTH

MAGNETIC NORTH

MAGNETIC NORTH

Imagine a gigantic bar magnet sitting in the centre of the Earth. One end of the 'magnet' points north, and the other end points south. This 'magnet' gives off a weak magnetic field that surrounds the Earth.

A compass needle is magnetized so that one end is always pulled in the direction of north. However, the Earth's 'magnet' does not go exactly through the centre of the planet, but is angled slightly to one side. This means that the 'north' a compass points to is not true north, at the North Pole, but is some distance away at a point called magnetic north. Added to which, magnetic north does not stay in the same place but is always gradually shifting its position. In the past fifty years in the UK, for example, it has moved from roughly 9°W of the Greenwich Meridian to approximately 2°W.

MAGNETIC VARIATION

The vertical grid lines on a topographical map always point north. (This may be true north or grid north depending on the country.) In most parts of the world, this means that the magnetic north shown on your compass will be some degrees either east or west (right or left) of the grid north on your map.

Because the difference between true north and magnetic north varies from place to place and year to year, each map has a small diagram somewhere in the margin showing the degree of magnetic variation for that map. On OS maps the diagram shows all three

The map will also tell you what the actual difference is between the various norths for that part of the country, the date at which the

value of that difference was set, and the rate at which it is changing. With this information it is possible to calculate the magnetic variation for any particular place at any particular point in time. There are also online calculators that will work out the Magnetic Declination or Grid Magnetic Angle for you. For example, see the British Geological Survey website at:
www.geomag.bgs.ac.uk

Magnetic variation becomes important when you are using your compass and a map to take route bearings (see pages 86–87). If you do not adjust your compass bearing or your grid bearing by adding or subtracting the number of degrees of a given variation, for example, it is possible to end up some kilometres off course from your intended destination.

On an OS map, you will find a small diagram looking something like this:

GRID NORTH

– is always vertical, as it aligns with the vertical grid lines on the map.

TRUE NORTH

– indicates the difference between grid north and true north.

MAGNETIC NORTH

– indicates the degree of magnetic variation east or west of true and grid north.

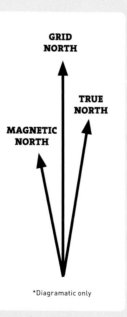

In the UK at the moment, magnetic north is roughly 2° west of grid north.

GETTING YOUR BEARINGS

Reading compass points is fine for giving you a general idea of your direction, but to find your way from one specific point to another you need to set a bearing. A bearing is the angle of a direction away from north and it is expressed in terms of the 360° circle on your compass.

The best way to follow these instructions is to read them with an orienteering compass in your hand.

TOP TIPS

+ Familiarize yourself with different map symbols and contour lines.

+ Practise using a compass by taking bearings around your house or garden.

+ Use your local street map to find bearings in your area and walk to them using the map and compass.

+ Keep your compass away from metal objects, including watches, steel pipes or fences, cars, even keys. The metal will interfere with the magnetic reading.

+ Take your time and try to be as careful and as accurate as you can in setting your bearings.

FINDING A BEARING

To find a bearing from where you are (Point A) to a visible landmark (Point B):

BEARING = 150°

1 Hold the compass so that the direction-of-travel arrow on the baseplate is pointing directly away from you towards Point B (a hill, for example).

2 Turn the dial and line up the orienting arrow on the bottom of the housing with the red end of the compass needle (which will be pointing north).

3 Read the number on the dial that lines up with the direction-of-travel arrow – the index pointer will help you. The degree number indicated on the dial is your bearing to Point B.

TO FIND A BEARING BETWEEN TWO POSITIONS ON A MAP

If you cannot see your destination, or do not know which direction to walk in, you will need to find your bearing on a map.

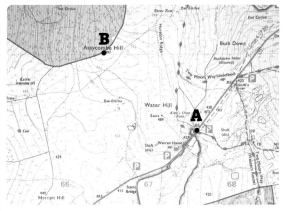

1 First locate your position on the map (Point A), and the position of the place you want to go to (Point B).

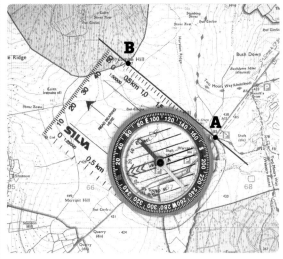

2 Imagine a straight line running directly between these two points and place your compass on the map so that one side of the baseplate lines up with your imaginary line. Make sure the direction-of-travel arrow is pointing towards the place you want to go to. (If your two points are very far apart you might want to draw a pencil line between the two points on the map first, or use a ruler or piece of paper to give you a straight line.)

3 Without moving the compass, rotate the dial until the orienting lines on the bottom of the housing line up with the north–south (vertical) grid lines on the map, and the orienting arrow is pointing to the top of the map.

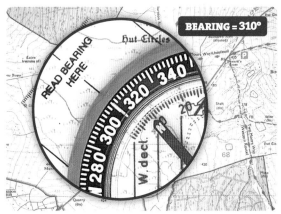

4 The bearing is indicated by the index pointer on the dial. If you know the magnetic variation between your map grid and your compass, you now add it to the bearing shown on the dial. (For example, if the bearing taken from the map is 75° and the magnetic variation is 5°, you turn the compass dial 5° to the left to give you a bearing of 80°.)

WALKING A BEARING

Once your direction-of-travel arrow is set to a bearing (310°, for example), pick up your compass and turn yourself around until the compass needle is pointing north ('N' on the dial) and is inside the orientation arrow. Do not turn the dial. The direction-of-travel arrow is now showing you the direction in which you must walk to follow your bearing.

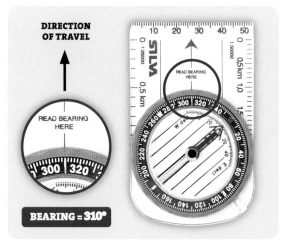

To stay on this bearing, you must keep the compass needle pointing north. However, any trail you are using is bound to meander all over the place, which means that your compass needle will be continually moving on the dial. It's hard to walk with your eyes always on the compass, and even if you try to keep the needle pointing north, you are bound to come across obstacles that you have to walk round.

An easier way to follow a bearing is to take a sighting along the direction-of-travel arrow and look for a nearby landmark to walk to – a hilltop, building or church spire, for example. When you reach this landmark, check your dial has not moved. Position yourself so that the needle is pointing north, look along your direction-of-travel arrow and find another landmark to walk towards. Carry on until you arrive at your destination.

TO FIND WHERE YOU ARE ON A MAP

You can also use compass bearings to find your position on a map – as long as you are able to identify two or three specific landmarks from your surroundings on the map. This is known as triangulation, or taking back bearings. Ideally your three landmarks should be about 90° apart.

First, you must orient, or set, your map so that grid north is facing true north.

FINDING THE WAY

TO ORIENT YOUR MAP

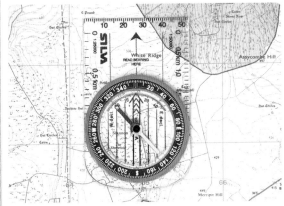

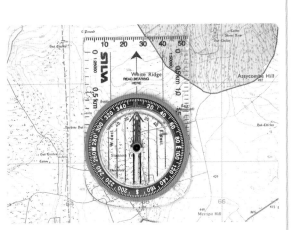

1 Place the compass on the map so the direction-of-travel arrow lines up with a vertical grid line on the map and is pointing to the top of the map.

2 Holding the compass in place, turn the map until the red compass needle lines up with the orienting arrow on the housing. Your map is now facing north.

(Note: if you know the magnetic variation for the area, you should first turn the dial to line up the index pointer with that degree number. For example, if the magnetic variation is 5°, the index pointer should be set to 5° on the dial.)

TRIANGULATION

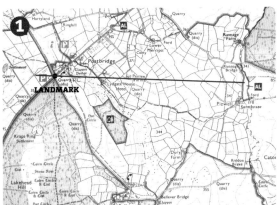

1 Without moving the map, pick up the compass and take a bearing to one of the identifiable landmarks – as described on page 86 .

2 When you have your bearing, place the compass back on the map so the top corner of one side of the baseplate is pointing at the landmark on the map.

3 Without moving the map or the dial, slide the whole compass round until the orienting lines are parallel with the map's vertical grid lines. Make sure the end of the baseplate is still on the landmark.

4 Draw a straight line along the side of the baseplate. *Picture 1.*

5 Next do the same thing with the second landmark. This line should cross the first. Your position on the map will be close to where the two lines cross.

6 For greater accuracy, repeat the process with the third landmark. Where the three lines cross there should be a small triangle. This is your location on the map. *Picture 2.*

(Note: if you added magnetic variation to orient your map, you should subtract the variation on your compass dial before taking your landmark bearings.)

ORIENTEERING

Orienteering is a great way to practise navigation skills. It involves finding your way round a series of control points marked on a specially prepared map. The challenge is in choosing the best route so as to complete the course in the shortest time.

Each course is set up with a series of control markers. These markers are highlighted on the map with a red circle. Competitors carry a control card which is punched or marked at each control marker to show that they have visited every marker to complete the course.

Orienteering is a recognized world sport and can be done at many different levels and in different ways. The most common form is by foot, although there are also courses using mountain bikes, canoes, skis or horses. Foot orienteering might take place around a local park or over a long-distance cross-country trail, and competitors might walk, jog or run.

An example of a control marker

The only equipment required is a compass and appropriate clothing. GPS devices are not usually allowed.

UK orienteering events are mostly organized by local clubs, and there are also some permanently fixed courses in the UK. These are mainly designed for beginners but can also be used by those wanting to improve their skills. To find a course or event, go to the British Orienteering website at:
www.britishorienteering.org.uk

GPS NAVIGATION SYSTEMS

receiver must have a clear line of sight to the sky and a full GPS signal, which is not always available, especially if you are walking in a forest. It relies on batteries to power it, and batteries can run out. Many do not display maps, although advanced models can be loaded up with map software. However, if you want anything other than the base map of the country you bought it in, you have to buy the software separately, which can be expensive.

All in all, if you do use a GPS receiver, it is advisable to carry a magnetic compass and paper maps as a backup, and know how to use them.

> **A GPS receiver will affect the reading on a magnetic compass if the two devices are too close together.**

A handheld GPS (Global Positioning System) receiver is a navigation system that can pinpoint its location just about anywhere on the planet by picking up information from a network of satellites orbiting Earth. About the size of a large mobile phone, a GPS receiver can give you the grid reference for your location, your height above sea level and plot your position on an electronic compass – as long as you are moving. If you load it up with a series of coordinates, it will calculate the bearings and distances for each one.

Some walkers never go anywhere without one, while others think they are just expensive toys. The truth is probably somewhere in between. They are undoubtedly useful and can save a lot of time and effort, but they do have their limitations. You still need reasonable navigation skills in order to use them. Your

GPS software is now increasingly available on mobile phone handsets, which means fewer devices to carry. But it is still early days, and unless your phone has GPS built in, you need a Bluetooth GPS receiver as well as buying or licensing the GPS software. You are also still reliant on your phone battery and a clear signal.

CHAPTER 5:

SLEEPING OUTDOORS

If you are planning on spending a few days or longer in the outdoors, you will need somewhere to stay. Of course, you might prefer to stay in a B&B or a Youth Hostel, but if not you will need to take your own shelter with you.

CHOOSING A TENT

Tents can be expensive and there are a great many different styles to choose from, so spend a bit of time thinking about the type of tent that's best for you.

THE PARTS OF A TENT

All tents have certain features. They should be waterproof and windproof. Many tents have two layers, with a built-in waterproof groundsheet to keep the tent floor dry. The outer layer, or flysheet, does most of the work of keeping out the wind and rain. The inner layer keeps the warmth in, but allows moisture out to prevent condensation. The two layers should not touch each other. If a tent has just one layer, the material must be both waterproof and breathable.

A flysheet that extends beyond the inner tent to provide a covered overhang or porch area at one end is useful for storing your gear, especially in wet weather. The tent should also have panels that can be opened and closed for ventilation, preferably with mosquito netting so they can be kept open on summer nights.

PARTS OF A TENT

VENTILATION FLAP

ENTRY FLAP

CURVED RIDGE POLES

GUYLINES stretch and support the sides of tent

LOOPS hook over tent pegs to hold the edges in place

FLYSHEET should be taut so it does not sag onto the sides of the inner tent

MOSQUITO FLAP zips separately from the entry flap

GROUNDSHEET

WHAT'S RIGHT FOR YOU?

The main points to consider are: size, season, weight and shape.

SIZE – Tents are sized according to the number of people that will fit in them when sleeping, from a one-person tent to a family or group tent that will sleep six people or more.

SEASON – When are you most likely to use your tent and where? If you are mainly using it in spring, summer and autumn in general terrain, a three-season tent should be fine. If you will be camping in winter, in the snow, or mountaineering, you will need a four-season or mountain tent. These are designed to withstand extremes of temperature and are more durable and stable, but are often heavier and more expensive.

WEIGHT – If you are hiking and carrying your tent in your pack, weight will be a key consideration. Some tents are designed specifically for backpacking. They are lightweight and pack down to fit into a rucksack, yet are durable and stable. However, they tend to be less roomy than other styles.

SHAPE – There are many variations, but the basic shapes are: ridge or A-frame, dome, and tunnel or hoop.

TOP TIPS

+ Bear in mind that most tents are sized to minimum space requirements and do not usually allow much room for kit. If you intend to spend more than a night or two in your tent, you may want to size-up, to a two-person tent for one with kit, or a three-person tent for two with kit, and so on. If you are carrying the tent, however, you may decide to sacrifice space for weight. If possible, try the tent out in the shop before you buy it.

TYPES OF TENT

RIDGE OR A-FRAME – the traditional tent shape with two rigid vertical poles supporting a straight or sloping horizontal pole. They usually have two layers and come in virtually any size, although can be heavier than other types. Modern ridge tents often use a curved hoop pole to support the front of the tent while the ridge pole slopes to the ground at the back. Ridge tents allow for a reasonable amount of headroom in the middle, but the sloping sides can be restrictive.

DOME — these tents are supported by two or more lightweight curved poles that cross in the centre, giving a square or hexagonal floor space. They are simple to put up, pack well and provide good headroom. A favourite for general use, their round shape sheds water well, but a high dome can make them less wind resistant. They are more stable than hoop or tunnel tents but in very windy conditions it may be best to pitch them behind trees or a wall or earth bank to shelter them from the wind.

HOOP OR TUNNEL – these may have a single hoop, or two or three hoops forming a tunnel. Single hoop tents are effectively small, lighter-weight versions of a ridge tent and have the same space restrictions. Tunnel tents are roomy and may have entrances at both ends.

A BIVI BAG

If you want to travel seriously light, you could consider a bivi bag. These lightweight waterproof sacks are designed to hold your sleeping bag, your gear and you, and keep you dry and warm without the benefit of a tent. Some have a small hooped pole to raise the head of the bag, giving you a little more room and allowing the bag entrance to be completely closed in the rain. Others have a drawstring which does not entirely close. Bivi bags are fine for one or two nights in the open, but get very cramped after a while. Some people use them as extra protection within a tent.

TOP TIPS BEFORE YOU BUY

+ **Check the tent seams. They should be double sewn or taped for added strength as they can tear if put under too much strain.**

+ **Make sure tent fastenings are well secured, and that the zips work smoothly and have protective flaps to keep the rain out.**

+ **A groundsheet that is raised at the sides to form a rim around the floor of your tent will protect against ground water.**

+ **If you intend to camp in hot, sunny places, check the tent's resistance to UV rays – it is possible to get sunburnt inside a tent.**

+ **Check that full pitching instructions come with the tent.**

TENT CARE

Your tent needs to stay in good condition to remain properly waterproof and windproof. Before your trip, check all the seams and fastenings and repair them as soon as you see any signs of wear. You can buy repair patches, tapes and sealant for tents and there are companies that will repair tents for you.

Avoid walking on your tent when putting it up or taking it down as this can damage the material. Always leave your shoes or boots at the entrance. Bringing mud, dirt or dust into your sleeping area can damage the groundsheet as well as making your surroundings uncomfortable and potentially unhealthy.

Do not touch the walls of your tent when it is raining as it can affect the waterproofing. Regularly open up the flaps to air your tent and prevent condensation.

PITCHING YOUR TENT

How you go about pitching your tent will depend on the style of tent you have. It is advisable to read the instructions that come with the tent and practise putting it up and taking it down a few times before setting out on your trip. You may find yourself having to pitch the tent in less than ideal conditions – in the rain, wind or dark, for example – and familiarity with the process will make all the difference.

That said, there are some basic principles that apply to any tent.

BEFORE YOU START

▶ When you arrive at a campsite check in with the site owner. If you haven't been designated a space, find a suitable location. Put up your tent straight away.

▶ Make sure the ground where you place your tent is flat and level, with no lumps, roots, or insect nests, and clear away any twigs or stones.

▶ Check there is nothing immediately overhead – you do not want dead tree branches crashing into your tent.

▶ If the tent has guylines, check that there will be enough space around the tent to stretch them out.

SETTING UP

Unpack all your tent equipment and lay it out neatly near your chosen area. It is important to keep your tent dry, so if the ground is wet lay all the parts on top of a waterproof sheet. An extra groundsheet or a tarpaulin is ideal. If the weather is particularly bad, you can use one to erect a temporary shelter and set up your tent underneath it.

Be careful with small items. It is best to place these together – on top of the empty tent bag, for example. Sort out the tent poles and fit them together. If the poles are separate, make sure you put them together in the right order.

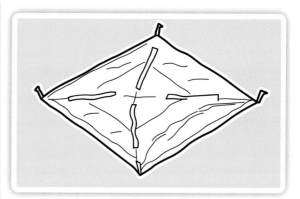

With some tents you begin by pitching the flysheet. Otherwise, unfold the tent and spread out the groundsheet, pegging the corners firmly in place so the wind cannot blow it away. Make sure the groundsheet is flat and taut with no wrinkles.

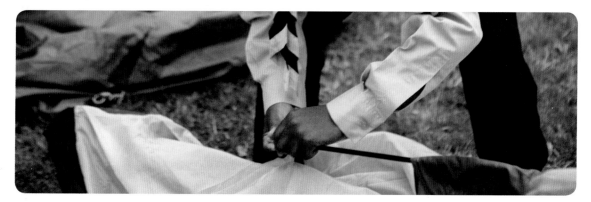

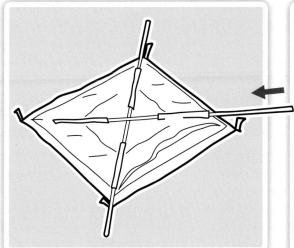

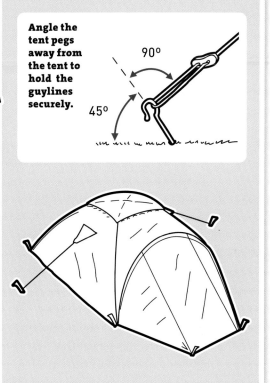

Angle the tent pegs away from the tent to hold the guylines securely.

90°

45°

Insert the tent poles with great care. It is all too easy to tear the tent by using too much force or dragging on the tent material. If you have to climb inside or onto the tent, take off your shoes and go on your hands and knees to avoid damaging the sides or groundsheet.

Fix any remaining pegs and guylines in place, making sure the sides are taut and the inner and outer walls do not touch. If the sides sag together, moisture can form on the inside of the tent and run down the walls.

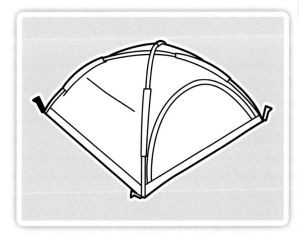

Once the poles are in place make sure the doors and vents are zipped up and lift the tent into position. If you have a separate flysheet, place it on top of the inner tent, making sure the doors align, then insert any poles or pegs that hold it in place. Alternatively, if the inner tent hangs from the flysheet, you will need to put the flysheet up first.

TOP TIPS

+ If the ground is too soft or hard to hold your pegs securely, tie the guylines to trees or heavy rocks or logs to secure them.

+ If you need to reposition any tent pegs, do not pull them up by the loops as this can weaken or tear the loops. Lever them out with a skewer, another tent peg or a proper peg puller.

For more information on choosing and laying out a campsite, see pages 112–115 in this chapter.

TAKING IT DOWN

When you are ready to move on, clear away and pack the rest of your campsite before dismantling your tent. That way you have somewhere safe to store your gear while you are clearing up, and somewhere to go if the weather is bad. When you are ready to start, make sure you take everything out of the tent before collapsing it.

Your tent must be dry when it is packed – or completely dried out as soon as possible when you get home. Otherwise it will rot. Be careful to clean and pack all the tent pegs, poles and any other equipment. Check that you have everything before packing the tent away. Fold the tent and guylines as neatly as possible. Put the pegs and poles in separate bags before putting them in the tent bag so they cannot damage the tent.

BUILDING A SHELTER

If you need an additional shelter, or are caught outside without a tent, it's useful to know how to build a lean-to or bivouac shelter. The shape and style of your lean-to will depend on the materials you have to build it.

Using a sheet

If you have a plastic sheet or a tarpaulin and some strong cord, there are a number of fairly quick options you can choose from. The illustrations shown here will give you some ideas. Make the best use you can of nearby trees. Hold down the edges of your tarpaulin with heavy stones, or carve wooden stakes to use as pegs.

Using sticks

If you need to build a frame, look for long, straight sticks to use as a ridge pole and two supports. If you can find forked sticks for the supports, so much the better.

Trim any protruding twigs or leaves from the sticks and sharpen the bottom end of the two supports. Hammer them firmly into the ground with a heavy rock. Balance the ridge pole between the two support poles, lashing them in place (see pages 164–167 for information on lashing). The ridge pole should be strong enough to support the shelter roof. Let it extend beyond the support poles at both ends.

Cut more long sticks to form a 45-degree angle from the ridge pole to the ground and lash them in place to make a roof frame. If you do not have a tarpaulin, build a roof by weaving thinner sticks across the frame. Then push leafy branches in and out of the sticks. If the structure can support them, you could line the roof with strips of turf, but be sure to replace the turf when you leave.

For more information on clearing a campsite, see pages 118–119 in this chapter.

Using a sheet

Using sticks

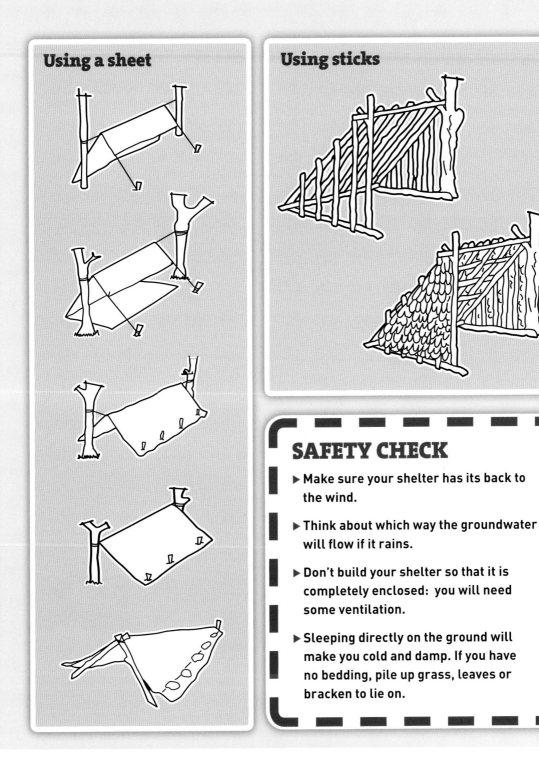

For more information on building shelters, see Chapter 9, pages 234–237.

SLEEPING BAGS

As with a tent, a good sleeping bag makes a big difference to whether or not you enjoy your camping trip. Getting a proper night's sleep is essential, and it is important to stay warm and dry at night.

There are two main decisions to make when it comes to choosing a sleeping bag. One is the type of filling, and the other is the warmth factor.

FILLING

Sleeping bags have an outer nylon shell stuffed with a filling of either synthetic fibres, or the down feathers of geese or ducks. Down-filled sleeping bags are lighter, warmer and more hard-wearing. However, they usually cost more and take longer to dry out if they get damp. Synthetic fillers, such as Hollofill, are bulkier, heavier and not so soft, but they are easier to clean, dry fast and will still keep you warm if they get damp.

WARMTH

How warm a bag is depends on its filling, bulk, weight, and will affect the price. Some bags are designed for summer use only, while others will keep you warm on a polar expedition – it's all a question of where and when you are most likely to use it, and whether or not you are carrying it. Decide how low a temperature you are likely to sleep out in and find a bag suitable for that level and a little bit more – just to be on the safe side.

Manufacturers often give sleeping bags a season rating. If you intend to camp mainly in the spring and summer in a country like the UK, for example, a two-season bag would probably be adequate. However, some people feel the cold more than others, in which case a three-season bag may be better as it is suitable from spring through to autumn.

SAFETY CHECK : Sleeping bags are not waterproof and should be kept as dry as possible. In wet weather it may be advisable to put your bag inside a waterproof bivi bag – see page 95.

COMPRESSION PACK

SLEEPING MAT

OTHER POINTS TO CONSIDER

Sleeping bags come in a variety of widths and lengths. Most are 'mummy shaped', meaning they are wider at the shoulders than the feet, so make sure you have enough room and don't feel too restricted. A raised hood helps keep your head, neck and shoulders warm.

Check that the zip is long enough to give you easy access in and out of the bag, and that it can be worked from the inside of the bag as well as the outside. The zip should have a flap over it to prevent heat loss.

Think about the weight and the size when packed. Most bags are stuffed inside a compression pack – or stuff sack – which uses straps to squash your bag down to the smallest possible size.

Most bags use a 'breathable' fabric for their outer shell to avoid too much condensation building up inside. If this is a problem, you may want to use a cotton, silk or fleece liner, which will keep your bag clean and is easier to wash.

A foam sleeping mat beneath your sleeping bag provides an extra layer of insulation between you and the ground and keeps you warmer and dryer. However, although lightweight they can be bulky to carry.

TOP TIPS

+ In dry weather, give your sleeping bag a good shake to fluff up the filling and air it out. If the weather is wet, keep it in its sack until needed so it does not absorb moisture from the air.

+ Cover the stuff sack with a plastic bag to keep your sleeping bag extra dry while carrying it.

+ Wear extra layers for extra warmth at night, including dry socks, long underwear, a hat and a fleece.

+ Fill the stuff sack with spare clothing to make a pillow.

OTHER EQUIPMENT

How much other equipment you need depends largely on how you are carrying it and whether you will be staying in a fixed camp, or moving from place to place.

WHAT TO TAKE

If you are staying in one spot, you can afford to be a bit more generous with your equipment on the basis that even if you carry it there yourself, you only have to do one trip in and one trip out. However, if you are moving from place to place and travelling under your own steam, you will want to keep your equipment to a minimum.

Start with a checklist and go through it with all the members of your group, agreeing who will supply what and how it will be carried. Separate the checklist into two parts: personal kit and shared kit. Obviously each person is responsible for their personal kit, whereas shared kit should be divided between you.

PERSONAL KIT

See Chapter 3 for information on clothing and basic equipment for walking. In addition, you may need:

▶ **Spare clothes – including extra socks, underwear and a spare pair of trainers.**

▶ **Sleeping clothes – keep a top and bottom just for sleeping in. Pack them inside your sleeping bag.**

▶ **Wash bag – a waterproof wash bag with toothbrush, flannel, biodegradable soap, comb, etc. Limit the weight by keeping products such as soap and toothpaste to the bare minimum.**

▶ **Antibacterial handwash gel.**

▶ **Tissues and/or toilet paper.**

▶ **Towel – as small or lightweight as possible. Camping shops now sell absorbent ultra-light towels that fold into a small pack.**

▶ **Eating equipment – a plastic bowl, plate and mug, plus a knife, fork and spoon. However, you could get by with just a mug, bowl and spoon, or one of the combined utensils that are sold in specialist camping stores – like a spork.**

▶ **Pocketknife – a good quality pocketknife with one or two blades and various tools, such as a can opener, screwdriver, bottle opener and so on, is an invaluable all-purpose tool. For more information on knives see pages 104–105.**

SHARED KIT

How many tents do you need? Rather than everyone carrying their own tent it may be better to share tents and carry the tenting equipment between you. The same can be said for food, stoves and other cooking equipment. Much will depend on the amenities at the campsites you are planning to use. Will you be allowed to build a campfire, for example? Will there be on-site toilet facilities or will you need to organize your own?

The following is a list of equipment for you to consider:

TENTAGE

▶ Extra tarpaulin – useful in all sorts of ways, including making a shelter for cooking, eating, or protecting your kit in bad weather.

▶ Rubber mallet – for securing tent pegs, or building shelters.

▶ Spare pegs and peg extractor.

▶ Lamps or torches for lighting – wind-up ones save carrying fuel or extra batteries.

SAFETY

▶ A fully equipped first aid kit – see Chapter 9, page 212.

▶ Fire blanket.

COOKING

▶ Collapsible water carriers.

▶ Cooking stove, plus fuel – lightweight camping stoves are convenient, easy to carry, and more environmentally friendly than a campfire – see Chapter 6, pages 130–133.

▶ Matches and disposable lighters.

▶ Cooking pans – at least two saucepans and a frying pan. You can buy cooking pans as a set that slot inside each other.

▶ Cooking utensils – a heat-resistant large spoon, ladle and spatula.

▶ Chopping knives.

▶ Folding colander, or perforated spoon.

▶ Tin opener.

▶ Vegetable peeler.

▶ Plastic boxes and/or zip-lock bags for storing food.

FOOD

▶ Snacks for hiking.

▶ Dried or tinned provisions for cooking – see Chapter 6, pages 134–137.

CLEANING

▶ Tea towels.

▶ Washing-up bowl.

▶ Cleaning sponge or cloth.

▶ Biodegradable washing-up liquid.

▶ Biodegradable washing powder.

▶ Recyclable plastic bags for packing and for rubbish.

MISCELLANEOUS

▶ Hand axe and wire saw – see pages 106–107.

▶ Folding shovel, or hand trowel – for making or covering a firepit and/or toilet pit.

▶ Duck tape – for all sorts of uses, including temporary repairs.

▶ Nylon rope.

▶ Mending kit – for clothes, rucksack, tent, sleeping bag, etc.

For information on building a temporary camp toilet, see pages 116–117 in this chapter.
For information on campfires, stoves and ovens, see Chapter 6, pages 120–133.

CUTTING TOOLS

A sharp knife is a useful tool when camping, particularly if you are intending to stay in a remote area with few amenities. A strong, multi-tooled pocketknife can be used to cut, chop or carve most things, as long the blades are clean and sharp. However, even a pocketknife can cause accidents if misused, and a larger or longer-bladed knife should never be carried or handled by anyone who does not know how to use one safely.

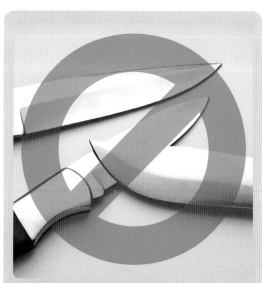

MULTI-TOOLED POCKETKNIFE

SINGLE–BLADE FOLDING KNIFE

KNIVES AND THE LAW

In the United Kingdom, the following laws apply to carrying knives in public:

▶ **It is an offence to carry a knife in public without good reason or lawful authority.**

▶ **The maximum penalty for an adult carrying a knife is four years in prison and a fine of £5,000.**

▶ **Knives where the blade folds into the handle, such as a Swiss Army Knife, are not illegal as long as the blade is less than 7.62 centimetres (3 inches) long.**

▶ **It is illegal for any shop to sell a knife of any kind (including cutlery and kitchen knives) to anyone under the age of 18.**

For more information, go to:
www.direct.gov.uk
and click on 'Crime Prevention'.

SAFETY CHECK

▶ Never throw a knife of any sort, even if you are aiming at a tree or the ground. You could miss your target or it could bounce off it and hit something or someone else, including you.

▶ When using a knife to chop or carve, always aim the blade away from your body.

▶ A sharp blade is much safer to use than a blunt one. There is a tendency to put too much pressure on a blunt blade to make it cut something and this can cause the blade to slip.

▶ Carving and whittling is best done with a small blade so you can control it more easily.

SHARPENING A KNIFE

To sharpen a knife blade you need a whetstone or sharpening stone. Wet the stone with water and place it on a flat surface.

Hold the knife handle in your right hand and lay one side of the blade flat on the stone. Pressing lightly on the blade with the fingertips of your left hand, slide it around in a circular clockwise direction. Don't push too hard and keep the angle of the blade flat.

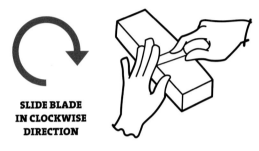

SLIDE BLADE IN CLOCKWISE DIRECTION

After half a dozen or so circles check the edge of the blade. The aim is not to get the sharpest edge possible, but to get one that will last. If the edge is too fine it might chip.

When you are happy with the edge, do the same thing on the other side, but this time move the blade in a counterclockwise direction.

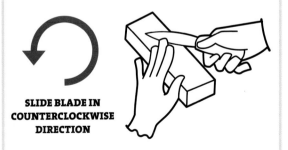

SLIDE BLADE IN COUNTERCLOCKWISE DIRECTION

Always wipe the blade of your knife clean and dry when you have finished using it. If you are not going to use it for a while, rub a little oil onto it.

AXES

If it is possible to build a campfire at your camping site and you are planning to do so, or you are intending to build a bivouac or some other structure, you may want to consider taking a small hand axe or a camping hatchet.

As with a knife, an axe is both useful and dangerous, and requires experienced handling. However, if you are hiking you will also need to consider the additional weight in your rucksack. Even a lightweight steel camping hatchet can weigh more than half a kilogram.

CARING FOR AN AXE

An axe should never be left in a damp place or outdoors overnight as the blade will soon get rusty. Keep the axe head greased, and if it has a wooden haft, oil this with linseed oil.

An axe blade is sharpened in much the same way as a knife (see previous page), but you will need both a coarse-grade stone and a fine stone. The stones should be moistened with oil, not water.

Hold the back of the axe head and angle the blade so that the edge, or bit, is flat on the stone.

Move the stone in small circles, being careful to keep the fingers of your other hand away from the bit. Start with the coarse stone and finish off with the fine stone.

As before, be careful not to over-sharpen the edge. When you have finished one side, turn the axe over and do the same on the other side.

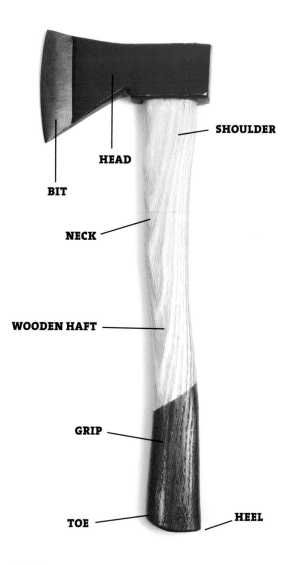

SHOULDER

HEAD

BIT

NECK

WOODEN HAFT

GRIP

TOE

HEEL

USING A FELLING AXE

SAFETY CHECK

The best way to learn how to handle an axe is from an experienced instructor. However, there are some safety rules that everyone should be aware of.

▶ **Never leave an axe lying around where it could be trodden on. Store it somewhere dry and out of sight.**

▶ **Always keep the axe head covered by its mask when not in use.**

▶ **When using an axe, make sure you are wearing strong leather boots to protect your feet.**

▶ **Do not wear scarves, lanyards or loose clothing that could get tangled with the axe.**

▶ **Never use a blunt axe – it might slip or bounce off the wood and could cut you.**

▶ **Make sure that the axe head is firmly fixed to the haft and that the haft is not damaged in any way.**

▶ **When using an axe, make sure there is plenty of room around and above you, with no obstructions such as branches or ropes to get in your way. Also make sure there are no people nearby.**

▶ **Never ask anyone to hold the wood you are cutting.**

▶ **Don't use an axe when you are tired, as this is when accidents are more likely to happen.**

▶ **When chopping logs, always do it on a chopping block, never directly on the ground.**

A WIRE SAW

A twisted wire saw is small, light and can be used instead of an axe to cut through tree branches. It is razor sharp and must be handled with care. Most wire saws have finger rings on the ends, as here, but it is safest to tie string or cloth handles to these to protect your hands. Pull the saw steadily back and forth across the wood. Do not press too hard as this could damage the wires. Clean the saw carefully after use to prevent moisture from the wood rusting the wires.

USING A BOW SAW

PACKING A RUCKSACK

Once you have your equipment sorted out, the next stage is to decide how to transport it. If you are carrying it on your back, you will need a fairly sturdy rucksack.

THE RIGHT SIZE

Depending on your height and build, it is best to choose a rucksack in the 50- to 75-litre range. Unless you are an expert packer, you will probably find it difficult to get everything you need into anything much smaller than this, while anything larger will be too heavy to hike with.

Apart from size, the main difference between backpacks is in the quality. It may be worth spending a little bit more to ensure that the straps and seams are sturdy and well-sewn and the pack material is lightweight but strong.

ORGANIZING YOUR LOAD

A golden rule when packing a rucksack is 'think light'. Ask yourself if every piece of equipment you want to take is really necessary, and if it is, how can you make it lighter. Could you take a half-used or small tube of toothpaste, for example, instead of a full, big tube? Can you get rid of packaging and put things in small plastic bags? Every gram counts when you add it all up.

The way in which you pack your rucksack is also important. A badly-loaded pack will affect your balance and your posture, and is far more uncomfortable to carry. Ideally, you want to put lighter things in the lower part of the rucksack, and heavier things in the middle to upper part, centred between your shoulder blades. This helps to balance the weight of the pack.

When you have everything you need, spread it all out on a bed or the floor and divide it into three piles:

▶ **Things you will need easy access to throughout the day or in an emergency.**

▶ **Things you will need at some point that day.**

▶ **Things you won't need until that night or on following days.**

Broadly, the idea is to pack the last pile first, then the second pile, then the first. Once you have the main compartments packed, try your rucksack on to make sure that the weight is comfortable. Also check that the straps fit correctly and adjust them as necessary. If the pack feels heavy, think how much heavier it will get after a few hours' walking, then ask yourself what you can leave behind.

For more information on choosing a rucksack, see Chapter 3, pages 68–70.

BOTTOM COMPARTMENT

Put your sleeping bag in the lowest compartment. (If you don't have a separate compartment at the bottom, put your sleeping bag in the bottom of the main compartment.) Make sure it is inside a fully waterproof bag. Some people also put their stove and fuel in this compartment so that if the fuel leaks it will leak out of the bottom of the bag. Or you could put it in a side pocket. You could also use the bottom compartment for bags of wet or dirty clothing.

MAIN COMPARTMENT

Line the whole of the main compartment with a waterproof sack. This can be a special rucksack liner, or a plastic dustbin bag or rubble sack. (Remember, rucksacks are not waterproof.)

First, put in spare clothing, your wash bag and anything light that you do not need ready access to. Fold clothes neatly so they take up less space. Group them inside separate plastic bags, such as underwear, socks and T-shirts in one bag; towel and sleeping clothes in another, and so on. This will keep them dry, easier to find, and neater to repack.

Next, load the heavier items, such as cooking and cleaning gear, spare shoes, containers of food, eating equipment, and so on.

The tent, spare groundsheet or parts of a tent should go next. Poles or pegs can be slid down the sides of the pack. Or strap your tent on the outside, in which case it should go on the top of your pack.

Slide small items down the sides and use every available corner. If you think you will need wet-weather gear or a warm fleece during the day, put it near the top.

MAIN COMPARTMENT

SIDE POCKETS

BOTTOM COMPARTMENT

DUSTBIN BAG FOR USE AS LINER

TOP AND SIDE POCKETS

Put emergency equipment and anything you may need ready access to in the top and side pockets. This could include water, navigation equipment, snacks, phone, first aid kit, any medication you take, and so on. Make sure the side pockets are evenly loaded.

If you have a sleeping mat, this can be rolled up and strapped to the outside. Remember to put it in a waterproof bag first.

A WELL-PACKED RUCKSACK

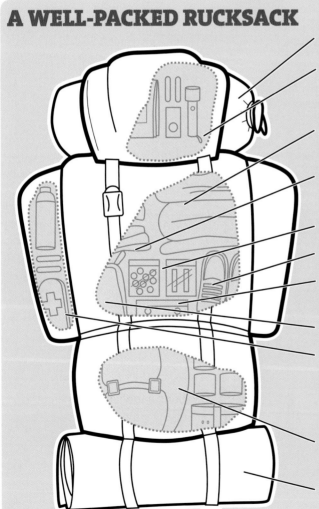

Tent bag strapped on top

Top pocket – a good place to put emergency items, torch, spare maps, snacks, etc.

Middle compartment – warm fleece or waterproofs at the top

Extra tarpaulin, bivi bag, hand axe or other tent items

Food provisions in plastic containers

Spare trainers

Cooking, eating and cleaning equipment

Washbag, towel, spare clothes

Side pockets – water bottle, first aid kit, phone, pocketknife, or anything you may want to get at regularly or in a hurry

Bottom compartment – sleeping bag, small stove, fuel

Sleeping mat – rolled up and tied onto rucksack

As well as keeping your pack dry in the rain, a rucksack cover will protect your pack at night if you cannot fit it into your tent.

HOISTING A HEAVY PACK

Once you have your rucksack fully packed, practise lifting it off and onto your shoulders a few times.

Make sure the shoulder straps are loosened. Bend one knee slightly and grip the shoulder straps to hoist the pack so that its weight rests on your knee. Slide one arm through a shoulder strap and swing the pack onto your back, slipping your other arm into the other shoulder strap at the same time.

Lean forward a little and adjust the pack so that it sits comfortably on your back, then do up the hip belt and tighten the shoulder straps. When you stand up straight, the main weight of the pack should sit against your back and rest on your hips.

KEEPING YOUR BALANCE

Walking with a loaded rucksack changes your sense of balance and puts extra strain on your feet and knees. Always do a few stretches to warm up your muscles before putting a heavy pack on your back, and do not expect to walk as far or as fast as you would without it. Take particular care when walking up or down slopes.

If anything inside the pack presses uncomfortably on your back as you walk, stop and rearrange it. Try to put something soft on the side closest to your back.

If you are walking a long distance and the straps start to rub, adjust them to change the way the pack sits on your back, or use a folded towel or spare bits of clothing as padding.

TOP TIPS

+ Pack sooner rather than later. This way if you are missing something you still have time to get it.

+ Use differently coloured plastic bags to group similar items together – for example, snacks in a green bag, documents in a red bag and so on, so you can find them more readily.

+ Use the compression straps to tighten your load and hold everything firmly in place.

+ Carry a couple of extra straps, buckles and safety pins for emergency repairs in case a strap breaks or a zip gives way.

+ If the weather could be wet, consider taking a cover to put over your rucksack.

+ Keep your compass and walking map in a plastic bag on a loop around your neck, and also your whistle if you have one, so that they are always easy to get to.

THE CAMPSITE

There are lots of campsites all over the UK, and plenty of websites that will give you information about them. You just have to decide where it is you want to go.

FINDING A SITE

If you are camping on a maintained site, check what amenities it offers and any rules and regulations before you go. Some sites do not allow you to light campfires, for example, or dig trenches or make other structures. Some are open only at certain times of year, or only to certain types of users.

If you are planning to camp in the wild, you will need to get permission from local landowners. In most parts of the UK, you are likely to be trespassing on someone's land or contravening local by-laws, even if you are on common land.

However, wild camping is often tolerated in remote areas as long as there are not too many of you, you do not stay more than a few nights, and you leave the area exactly as you found it – see pages 118–119. There are exceptions to this, however, especially in some National Parks and other areas of outstanding beauty where any form of camping is forbidden, so be sure to read any signs that are posted, or check with the local Tourist Information Office.

THINGS TO CONSIDER

Wherever you are camping, before you pitch your tent there are some factors that are always worth taking into account.

▶ Make sure you have a reliable source of safe drinking water within a reasonable distance of your site. Trekking backwards and forwards with heavy water containers can soon become a major trial. But don't pitch your tent too close to water as it attracts insects – as well as other campers.

▶ Avoid low-lying areas where the ground may be wet, boggy, or liable to flooding.

▶ Look for a dry, well-drained site, comfortably above any high-water mark, if you are near to a river or stream.

▶ Valley bottoms or hollows tend to be colder and can accumulate frost or damp mist.

▶ On the other hand, avoid open hilltops where you will be totally exposed to wind and rain.

▶ Look for level ground, preferably with some protection from the prevailing wind, such as a wall, shrubs or trees, but avoid pitching your tent directly beneath trees in case of falling branches.

▶ Check there is vehicle access of some kind to or near to the site in case of emergency.

▶ Find out where the nearest shop or source of food is. If there is nothing nearby, you will need to carry sufficient food stores with you or replenish them en route.

▶ Look out for well-used animal tracks – you will not want to wake up surrounded by cattle or sheep.

▶ In practice you are unlikely to find the perfect campsite, so be willing to compromise.

CAMP LAYOUT

Decide which way your tent will face. If the ground slopes, the tent should face downhill to prevent rainwater flowing in through the entrance. It should also have its back to the wind – unless it is very hot, in which case a breeze blowing into the tent may be helpful. If you want sun in the morning, aim to pitch your tent facing south-east.

The direction of the prevailing wind is also important if you are planning to build a campfire and do not want smoke and embers blowing into your tent.

If there is an established fireplace already on the site, place your tent at least 2 metres away and make sure the fireplace is downwind from you. If there isn't a fireplace, decide where to put your campfire, then clear the area around it of any dry grass, leaves or other debris. For more on campfires, see Chapter 6, pages 120-129.

You will also need to find a place for your woodpile and your wood chopping area. It's best to site them on the edge of your camping area but within fairly easy reach. Always chop wood in one place, both for safety reasons and to make it easier to clear up the woodchips when you leave.

If the campsite has toilets, make sure they are well away from your tent and downwind from you. The same applies if you have to dig your own toilet – see pages 116–117.

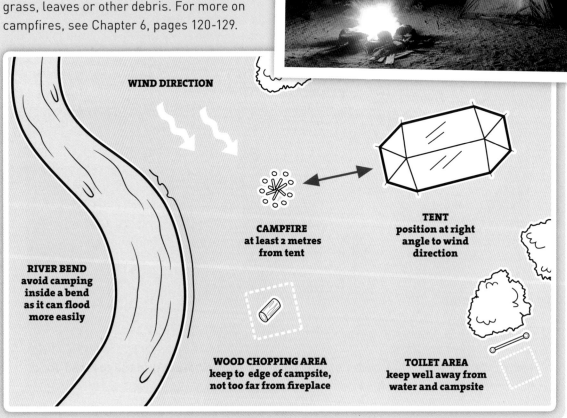

WIND DIRECTION

CAMPFIRE
at least 2 metres
from tent

TENT
position at right
angle to wind
direction

RIVER BEND
avoid camping
inside a bend
as it can flood
more easily

WOOD CHOPPING AREA
keep to edge of campsite,
not too far from fireplace

TOILET AREA
keep well away from
water and campsite

CAMP LIVING

On dry days, open up the tent as much as possible to allow the air to circulate and dry out any moisture that may have accumulated.

Shake out your sleeping bag and give it an airing too. It will keep the filling evenly spread and stop it getting musty. However, on damp days keep it rolled up.

If possible, avoid keeping wet clothing and damp towels inside the tent. If you must do so, store them in plastic bags to prevent moisture building up inside the tent. Do not hang damp clothing over the tent itself or its guylines. Instead, spread wet things over bushes or tree branches to dry. Or string up a line between two trees or two sticks pushed into the ground.

Keep the inside of the tent as neat and tidy as possible, and make sure that nothing touches the tent walls as this could damage your tent and make it less watertight.

Keep shoes and boots at the entrance to the tent, just inside the porch area if you have one. On dry days you can leave your boots outside. Put them upside down on a stick stuck in the ground. This will air them out, keep them dry, and keep any insects and other small creatures from crawling inside.

It is important to keep the groundsheet clean and free of mud, food crumbs or litter. Do not leave dirty dishes or food inside your tent. They will attract vermin and other small animals. Ideally, food should be kept in a separate shelter (this is where a spare tarpaulin comes in handy), in tins or lidded plastic containers so that animals cannot break into them. Food is best stored off the ground, either on some kind of raised structure made from stones or pieces of wood, or hung in bags from a tree branch. For more information on storing and cooking food at camp, see Chapter 6.

SAFETY CHECK : Never light a candle or cook inside a tent. Tent material will burn very rapidly and any live flame will reduce the oxygen inside the tent. If the weather is extremely bad, use a small cooking stove and place it in the covered porch, and keep the outer flaps open.

CAMP HYGIENE

Good hygiene is very important in a campsite. It will help keep you healthy and free of food poisoning or other illness. Eating and cooking utensils should be kept clean, and washed straight after use. Leftover food should be stored away or disposed of. Rubbish and waste of any sort must be dealt with responsibly and not left behind to pollute the site (including those 'biodegradable' banana skins or apple cores) – see pages 118–119.

PERSONAL WASTE

If you are camping on farmland or in a remote area where there are no toilet facilities, you will need to dispose of your own waste. If you are staying on a site for a night at a time and then moving on, it is not worth building a toilet pit. One solution is to dig a cathole.

Look for a sheltered spot at least 70 metres from the campsite, public paths or trails, or any stream, river or other water, and dig a hole about 20 centimetres (one and a half to two hands) deep. Put used toilet paper in a sealed, biodegradable plastic bag to take away with you and dispose of properly later. Any used sanitary products should also always be taken away and put in a sanitary bin (never flushed down a toilet). Fill in the cathole with soil, and spread leaves, small stones and other ground cover over the top.

If you are unable to dig a cathole – because the ground is too hard or stony, for example, or the landowner has asked you not to – you will have to take your waste with you. Collect the waste in a biodegradable plastic bag (like the ones used to collect dog poo), and store it in a container with a tightly fitting lid. A handful of cat litter will help reduce the smell. Do not put it in the first litter bin you see after you leave the campsite, but wait until you can dispose of it properly.

Never urinate near open water such as rivers or lakes, or near public trails.

BUILDING A TOILET

If you intend to stay on a site for a few days and the landowner does not object, the best solution is to build a toilet pit. Site your pit downwind and well away from your tent and any source of water. Screen it from view of the rest of your campsite behind a convenient group of bushes or construct a screen of some kind using sticks and leafy branches.

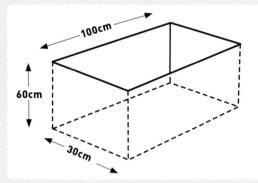

Make your toilet pit about 100 centimetres long, by 30 centimetres wide, by 60 deep. Pile the excavated soil nearby and sprinkle a layer of soil into the pit after every use. Do not put bleach or other chemicals into the pit as this will interfere with the natural degrading process – and make it smell worse.

Place a sturdy log in front of the pit as a position guide for the back of your legs. Mark the edges of the pit with posts and string or some logs to help you find it in the dark, and to prevent the unwary falling in. Always carry a torch at night

Do not urinate in your toilet pit: it's best to do this in a separate spot, or dig a smaller pit nearby – about 100 centimetres square and 20 centimetres deep. Line the bottom with stones or twigs and leaves to help with drainage.

When you leave the site fill in the pit completely.

For more information on building camp gadgets, see Chapter 7, pages 170–172.

SAFETY CHECK

The single most important way to keep yourself and others healthy is to always wash your hands with soap or antibacterial gel after going to the toilet, and before handling any food or drink.

LEAVE NO TRACE

As more and more of us make use of and enjoy the countryside, it is increasingly important that we protect and guard it against environmental pollution or damage.

The Countryside Code (see Chapter 2, pages 48–49) outlines a range of considerations to keep in mind, but when camping and hiking we should take these responsibilities even more seriously.

In particular:

▶ **Aim to use existing campsites wherever possible.**

▶ **Always keep to trails and footpaths.**

▶ **Avoid climbing walls and fences if possible; if not, do so with care, replacing any stones you may have dislodged in the process.**

▶ **Leave plants, rocks and other natural objects as you find them.**

▶ **Avoid disturbing or interfering with wildlife.**

▶ **Leave no waste – whatever you bring in, you should take out.**

For more information, visit the Leave No Trace website on: **www.lnt.org**

REMOVING RUBBISH

Leaving behind litter and other rubbish spoils the landscape, endangers wildlife and can pollute soil and water. Aim to leave home with as little packaging as possible, and plan your meals to avoid food waste and leftovers.

Always check with the landowner or campsite manager about what to do with your rubbish. There may be a specific area for waste disposal, or a particular system they would like you to use. Or they may prefer you to take all your rubbish with you when you leave. Always abide by their wishes.

If you are able to build a campfire you can burn combustible rubbish, such as paper and food waste. If not, put the dry items in one bag and wet in another and carry them out when you leave. Put food waste in a double bag and store it out of reach of animals.

Tin cans, plastic bottles and other waste items should be rinsed out and squashed flat if possible. Then collected in a waste bag and carried away when you leave.

WASHING-UP WATER

Filter dishwater to remove food particles, using a strainer or colander. Or make a filter using a tin can or other container with holes in the bottom. Stuff the container with straw or grass and suspend it over a bucket.

Pour the waste water through the container to filter it. You will need to change the grass or straw at regular intervals, and carry out the soiled filter material in your wet waste bags when you leave.

Spread the filtered dishwater and other washing water on the ground, well away from your campsite or any open source of water. Use as little soap and detergent as possible, and make sure they are biodegradable.

CLEARING CAMP

When you leave your campsite, make sure any toilet pits are filled in and the ground cover replaced. Set up a marker post on the spot, with the date that you used it, so that other campers will know to avoid it. The usual 'foul ground' marker is a small cairn of stones or a cross made of sticks, either laid horizontally on the ground or stuck upright on a post.

Make sure the campfire is completely out and the ashes removed and scattered or taken away – for more on campfires, see Chapter 6, pages 120–129. Clear away the woodpile and woodchips and dismantle and remove any camp gadgets or structures you may have made.

Take pride in the fact that when you leave the campsite, it will look as if you have never been there.

CHAPTER 6:

FIRES, FOOD & COOKING

So you've chosen your campsite, pitched your tent and shaken out your sleeping bag. It's time to light the fire and get cooking!

CAMPFIRES

A campfire is a wonderful thing. It warms your body, dries damp clothing, turns raw food into a feast, keeps insects and animals away, and cheers and comforts everyone's spirits.

Knowing how to build and light a campfire is an important skill – and a vital one in a survival situation. But campfires can also be dangerous to people and property, and can scar and destroy the ground. They need to be handled with care and attention. If you are camping on someone else's property, always make sure you have their permission to build a campfire first.

WHAT YOU'LL NEED

 MATCHES – the trick to lighting a fire with just one match is in the way that you build it.

 TINDER – small bundles of dry material such as shredded paper, dead leaves, dead moss, dry grass, frayed tree bark, bits of rotten wood or wood chippings, even frayed twine or bits of wool. The fluff from tumble-dryers can work well too.

 KINDLING – lots of small pieces of dry wood, such as pencil-thin twigs, sticks or pine cones.

 FUEL – thicker twigs, sticks and pieces of wood of various sizes, including some logs if you want to keep your fire going for a long time.

 OXYGEN – in order to burn, a fire needs oxygen from the air. However, if the wind is too strong, the flames must be shielded to prevent them from being blown out.

 **STRONG KNIFE OR A SPADE** – used for cutting away turf if you need to.

BUCKET – of water, sand or fine soil in case you need to put the fire out quickly.

FINDING A FIREPLACE

Set up your campfire in an open spot away from trees, hedges, fences, tents or anything that could catch fire. Fires built directly on the ground damage the soil, so it is best and most environmentally friendly to use an altar fire (see page 123), or look for a spot where fires have been lit before.

If this is not possible, find a patch of clear ground and brush away any leaf litter or debris that could accidentally catch fire. If the ground is grassy, lift away a section of the turf and put it to one side, grassy side down, so that you can replace it later.

BUILDING THE FOUNDATIONS OF A CAMPFIRE

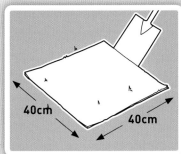
40cm   40cm

1 Using a spade or a strong-bladed knife, cut through the turf to mark the outline of your fireplace. Then divide the area into smaller squares.

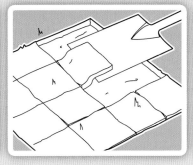

2 Slide the spade or knife under each small square and lift it away. Store the squares away from the fire, grassy side down, and water regularly to prevent them drying out.

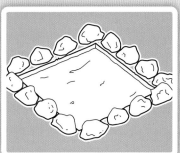

3 Edge the cleared area with large stones, logs or bricks to keep the fire from spreading. Space them out a little so that air can be drawn into the base of the fire.

CHOOSING YOUR WOOD

Not all wood burns in the same way and it is hard to make green (living) or damp wood burn at all. Never damage living trees or shrubs – it is wasteful and the wood will not burn well; instead, pick up fallen dead wood – as dry as possible. Don't collect too many large, heavy pieces of wood unless you want to spend time chopping them up. Large logs will only burn on a hot fire.

Thick sticks that can be easily broken make good fuel wood. If they do not snap easily the wood is green. Once your fire is hot enough, it is possible to burn green or damp wood and it will slow your fire down and make it last longer. Damp wood gives off lots of smoke, but this can be useful if there are mosquitoes or midges about.

TOP TIPS

+ Before you light your fire, make sure you have a good supply of extra firewood near (but not too close) to the fire.

+ If possible, protect your woodpile with plastic sheeting to keep it dry.

+ It can be useful to carry a small bag or tin of dry tinder with you.

+ If the earth is damp, lay a sheet of aluminium foil on the ground before you build your fire.

SPOTTERS' GUIDE: WOOD TYPES

Quick burning

Some types of wood flare up brightly and burn quickly to a fine ash. These include softwoods – conifers, such as fir, larch, pine and spruce – and some hardwoods such as apple, birch and hazel. These woods make good kindling for getting a fire going quickly, but they burn so fast the wood is soon used up. Also, conifers are full of resin, which makes the wood spit and give off sparks when burned.

PINE   **BIRCH**   **HAZEL**

Slow burning

Hardwoods are broad-leaved or deciduous trees, and most, such as ash, beech, cherry, hawthorn, holly, oak and maple, burn slowly and evenly, leaving embers that retain heat. These woods work less well as kindling (although dry holly leaves make great kindling), but will keep a fire going for hours and give off a great deal of heat. They are ideal for slow-cooking stews or pot roasts. But avoid chestnut, elm, poplar, sycamore and willow as these woods smoulder rather than burn.

ASH   **BEECH**   **HAWTHORN**

OAK   **CHERRY**   **MAPLE**

TYPES OF FIRE

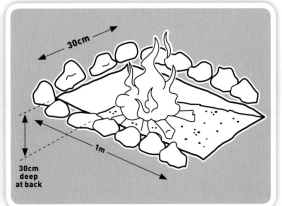

ALTAR

An altar fire is built on a raised platform. Place logs at right angles to each other and lash them firmly together. Cover the top with a row of logs pushed tightly together, then add a thick layer of earth on which to build the fire.

✦ **Protects ground from fire.**

✦ **Ideal fire for cooking.**

TRENCH

A trench fire can be built up on three sides to support a metal grate for cooking. Remember to always face the open side of your trench into the wind to help funnel oxygen into the fire.

✦ **Works very well in windy conditions.**

– **Requires quite a bit of digging to construct.**

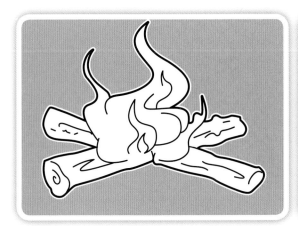

STAR

A star fire is begun by making a small fire. When it is hot enough, three or four long logs are placed with their ends facing into the centre of the fire. As the logs burn they are slowly pushed further in.

✦ **Fire is small but burns for a long time without having to continually add fuel.**

WIGWAM OR TEPEE

A wigwam or tepee fire is shaped much like a Native American tepee tent. The shape creates a chimney which draws the fire upwards. It is the commonest and simplest way to build a fire.

✦ **High flames give off plenty of light.**

– **Burns rapidly and needs lots of fuel.**

For more information on using campfires for cooking, see pages 142–151.

LAYING AND LIGHTING A TEPEE FIRE

1 Stand the first twig upright into the ground and surround it with a handful or two of tinder. Build a tepee shape around the tinder by leaning pieces of kindling against the central twig.

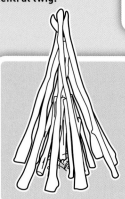

2 Use thicker twigs on the outside to make the tepee larger, but don't pack them too tightly. Make sure there are gaps around the base and in the middle to let in oxygen to feed the fire.

TOP TIPS

+ Firesticks make great kindling and really help to get your fire going. Take a dry, dead wood stick and use your knife to carve shallow cuts all around it so that the shavings curl outwards creating a feathered effect. If you cannot find a dry stick, carve the outer bark away first and you will probably find that the wood is dry underneath.

+ Dry wood shavings also make great tinder.

3 Light the tinder and pieces of kindling in the centre of the fire. (If it's difficult to reach the centre with the match, use it to light a longer strip of kindling and use this as your 'match'.)

4 Poke small pieces of kindling into the centre of the fire, as necessary, to keep the flames alight until they spread to the thicker twigs.

5 If the wood smoulders but does not burn, blow gently into the base of the fire. When the flames catch, they will quickly burn away the sides of the tepee. Add larger twigs and sticks until the fire is firmly established.

6 Lay thick logs or bricks on two sides of the fire, parallel with the direction of the wind. This helps to funnel air into the fire while protecting it from the wind. Add more sticks and logs as needed, but be careful not to smother it.

Once you have a good bed of hot embers you are ready to use the fire for cooking.

USING MATCHES

In the wild, wooden matches that will strike against any rough surface are more useful than safety matches. The cardboard 'book' matches are best avoided if possible, as they often bend and fail to strike.

All matches have to be dry to work, and must be struck against a dry surface. Always keep your matches in a waterproof container of some sort, whether it's a small plastic bag, tin foil or a metal film canister. You can also 'waterproof' the match head by dipping it in

melted candlewax and letting the wax harden in a protective coating. Scratch the wax off before using the match.

In windy conditions, strike the match into the wind, keep your hands cupped around it and make sure it is fully alight before trying to light the fire. Hold the match to the tinder in the same direction as the wind is blowing, so the match flame is blown into the tinder.

OTHER FIRE LIGHTERS

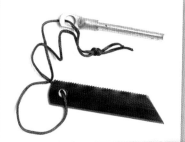

CANDLES – use your match to light a small candle, as this can be used many more times than the match. If you have some night lights, you can get a fire going in bad conditions by placing a lit night light in the centre of the tinder and kindling.

LIGHTERS – especially the disposable kind, can be tricky to light a fire with directly, but are useful to light a piece of kindling to act as a fire lighter.

FLINT AND STEEL – this traditional method of lighting a fire works by striking a steel rod against a flint block to produce sparks. Make the sparks directly over a small bundle of tinder. When it catches, blow gently on the tinder until you see a flame then place it in the centre of your prepared fire. Flint and steel fire lighters can be bought as kits from most camping suppliers.

MAGNIFYING GLASS AND SUNLIGHT – works well if there is enough sunlight. Use the magnifying glass (or other lens) to focus the sunlight into a point and direct it at a bundle of tinder. Blow gently on the tinder when it starts to smoulder.

FRICTION – this method is tricky and needs lots of practice. See next page.

FIRE BY FRICTION

This involves creating heat by rubbing two pieces of wood together. It requires patience and practice, but can be vital in a survival situation. The fire bow, or bow drill, is the easiest method for a beginner to use, although making the equipment takes a little time.

A fire bow consists of:

SPINDLE – a straight hardwood stick about 30 cm long, and 4 cm thick. Round off the ends of the spindle, and make one end more pointed. Give the middle of the spindle a 'waist' by making it a little less thick.

BASEBOARD – a roughly rectangular block of softwood, about 2–3 cm thick and at least as long as your foot. One surface of the baseboard should be fairly flat. Cut a v-shaped notch in one end of the baseboard. Then carve a small circular depression around the inner point of the notch to fit the sharpened end of the spindle.

BOW — A hardwood branch about as long as your arm and as thick as your index finger, and a length of strong string or cord at least one and a half times longer than the bow. Tie

TOP TIPS

+ Make sure the wood you use for your spindle and baseboard is dead wood, as dry as possible.

+ PIne or balsa wood works well as a baseboard.

+ If the powder you make is light brown, there is not enough heat being generated so try rotating the spindle faster.

+ If you need to carry your lit tinder to the fireplace, put a piece of bark or a thin strip of wood beneath it before you start the fire bow.

+ Keep practising.

the string to the bow at both ends. Make sure there is enough slack to wind the string once around the spindle.

HANDHOLD — a small hardwood block that fits comfortably into your hand. Carve a small depression in the centre of the handhold, to fit the top of the spindle.

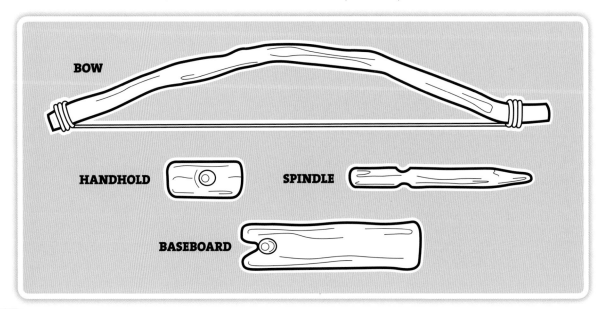

BOW

HANDHOLD

SPINDLE

BASEBOARD

USING A FIRE BOW

1 Place a small amount of tinder under the baseboard notch. Kneel down and place one foot on the other end of the baseboard to hold it steady.

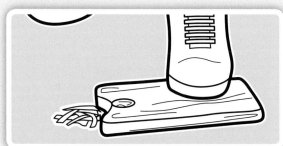

2 Wrap the bow string once around the spindle waist, making sure to keep the string between the spindle and the bow.

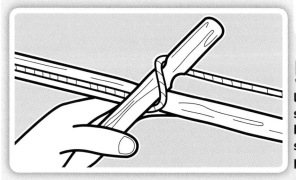

3 Place the sharpened end of the spindle into the depression above the notch and keep it in there, pushing down on the spindle with the handhold.

4 Use your other hand to push and pull the bow backwards and forwards to rotate the spindle.

FIRE DRILL

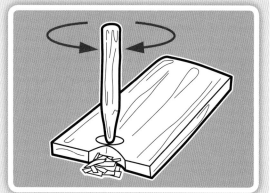

A hand drill is a simpler version of the fire bow but is trickier to use. The spindle is rolled backwards and forwards between your hands while also applying a downward pressure.

5 Keep going until you see smoke coming from the notch. You may have to push a little harder on the handhold, or rotate the spindle faster. (If smoke comes from the handhold, rub a little grease into it.) You should also see some ashy black-brown powder begin to build up in the notch.

6 When the notch starts to fill with powder, increase the speed of the spindle until there is lots of smoke. Remove the spindle, and if the notch continues to smoke it is likely that the heat of the powder has ignited the tinder. Gently blow on it until it begins to glow, then remove the baseboard and add more tinder.

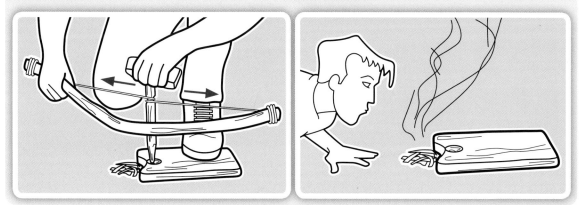

PUTTING OUT A FIRE

Always make sure that your fire is well and truly out before leaving it. Even when a fire appears dead, embers can continue to smoulder beneath the ashes and could set fire to undergrowth, fields and forests.

To put the fire out completely, let it die down then stir the embers with a stick to help them cool. If you have plenty of water, pour it over the embers. If you are camping on a managed campsite, find out what the rules are regarding disposal of ashes and embers. If you are in the wild, rake up the cold ashes and embers and scatter them over a wide area. (Note that embers are only truly cold when you can hold them in your bare hand.) Do not bury them in a pile as they could heat up again and set fire to underground roots.

BANKING A FIRE

If you want to keep your fire going safely overnight so you can use it again in the morning, bank it up before you go to bed. Let the flames die down so you have just a bed of ash and hot embers. Pile up stones around the fire and cover it with ash or dry soil. If you have aluminium foil, put a double layer of that over the embers, then pile on earth and stones. In the morning, lift off the covering layers and you should find hot embers underneath. Coax them back to life by feeding them gently with tinder and kindling.

For more information on clearing up a campsite, see Chapter 5, pages 118–119.

CLEARING AWAY A FIREPLACE

If you are leaving the campsite altogether you must clear the fireplace away. In a countryside or wilderness area, try to leave as little trace of it as possible. Dig over the base of the firepit to make sure there are no ashes left on the surface. Scatter it with fresh soil, then smooth it down and water it well. Replace any cut turf and fill in gappy edges with soil, grass and leaves to look as natural as possible.

SAFETY CHECKLIST

☑ Never leave a fire unattended.

☑ Be aware of the time of year and any regulations for the area in which you are camping. Is the area prone to bush fires in dry summers, for example? Or are there protected species of trees or plants nearby?

☑ Never use methylated spirits, paraffin, petrol, or other chemicals to start or rekindle a fire. These liquids are very volatile, and if the vapour from them catches alight, you could be caught in the flames.

☑ Do not build a bigger fire than you need and be aware of the direction and strength of the wind. Wind can make a fire flare up and blow sparks which could set light to other areas.

☑ Do not use riverbed rocks or flint to line or edge your fireplace as they have been known to explode when they get hot.

☑ Take care when using a fire within or near to a shelter. Sparks or exploding embers could burn you or your clothing.

CAMPING STOVES

It's not always possible to build a campfire and sometimes you won't have the time to wait until the fire is hot enough to cook on. A lightweight camping or backpacking stove is a quick and easy way to get hot water or a hot meal within minutes.

Plus, camping stoves also have far less impact on the environment as they do not damage the ground or require burning wood. The one big disadvantage is that the stove and its fuel have to be carried with you.

CHOOSING A STOVE

There are a variety of camping stoves on the market, so it's worth giving some thought to how much cooking you will be doing, what sort of food you will want to make, and how you will carry the stove, or stoves. A single-ring burner stove is fine for one or two people making simple one-pot meals, for example, but for groups or families it may be better to take a double or triple burner.

Apart from size and the number of burners, stoves vary according to the fuel they use. Different fuels have different properties, and deciding which fuel to use will help narrow down your choice of stove.

GAS STOVES

Liquid Petroleum Gas (LPG), such as butane, propane and isobutene, is sold in metal cartridges or cylinders. These are easy to use, work instantly with no need for preheating or priming, and burn cleanly without leaving sooty marks on pots and pans.

There is a huge range of gas stoves, but each make often requires a specific type of cartridge or cylinder, so check the availability of refills. Also, it can be hard to judge how much gas is left in a partly-used container, so you can end up carrying more fuel than you need – or take the risk of running out. Gas stoves also work less well in extremely cold conditions.

LIGHTWEIGHT, SINGLE BURNER CARTRIDGE STOVE

Cartridges

Gas cartridges are smaller, lightweight and attach to a single burner either directly or via a flexible hose. They are easily packed and carried, but do not last long and are not usually refillable or recyclable so can be expensive to run. Small burners can be unstable and may not support a very large cooking pot, although some single burner stoves come complete with supports and a 1–1.5 litre pot with lid and handle, and the whole thing packs away inside the cooking pot.

SINGLE BURNER CARTRIDGE STOVE

Cylinders

Cylinders last longer and some are refillable, but they are heavier. They may slot into the stove or are attached to it by a flexible hose. They work with single, double or triple burners, or a burner and grill combination. Some cannot be disconnected until empty, which can make packing them more of a problem.

DOUBLE BURNER CYLINDER STOVE

WARNING : Gas cartridges and cylinders can explode – always treat them with care and follow the instructions on the container.

LIQUID FUEL STOVES

Many liquid fuel stoves burn multi-fuel, which means they run equally well on different types of liquid fuel, whether it's kerosene, petrol, paraffin or methylated spirits. The stoves are efficient, reliable and hardwearing, but they can be slow to start and slow-burning.

Methylated spirit stoves are particularly economical and popular. They are sold in sets of various sizes, most of which include 2 saucepans, a frying pan, the burner, a windshield and an optional kettle.

THE FUELS

Liquid fuels are usually cheaper to buy and easier to carry than the equivalent quantity of gas. They burn well in cold conditions, are widely available and the containers are usually refillable. However, they can leave sooty residues on pots and pans.

WARNING : Never burn liquid fuel in a poorly ventilated space as the fumes can be dangerous. These fuels are more volatile than gas so care must be taken to avoid spills and leaks.

SOLID FUEL STOVES

This is the simplest form of fuel and ranges from firewood to small tablets of a compound called hexamine, such as Esbit. Solid fuels require little more than a metal tray of some sort on which to burn them, and supports to balance your pot.

A large metal or aluminium tray or fire pan with raised sides can be used as a base for a wood-burning stove large enough to cook on, and if it is raised off the ground on logs or stones, it will protect the soil from damage. But as with a campfire it will need time to build up enough heat.

A metal can with the top cut off and some holes in the sides for ventilation will make a very basic stove to use with the tablets, or you can buy ready-made versions. Solid fuel tablets are easy to carry and simple to light, but give out a low heat, so it's hard to do more than boil water with them. The tablets can be hard to find and some of the chemicals in them are toxic and can give off fumes. They are best kept as an emergency back up.

SOLID FUEL BURNER (CARRICOOK)

METHYLATED SPIRIT STOVE (TRANGIA)

MULTI FUEL BURNER AND FUEL CANISTER

FIRES, FOOD & COOKING

SAFETY CHECK

- ☑ Make sure the stove is placed on a flat, stable surface.
- ☑ Never use a stove inside a tent.
- ☑ Do not leave a lit stove unattended.
- ☑ Never try to refuel a liquid fuel stove when it is hot.
- ☑ Store all fuels and containers out of the sun and away from food stores, fires and sleeping areas.

TOP TIPS

- ✚ With any new stove, read the instructions carefully and practise using it beforehand.
- ✚ Test your stove to make sure it is working properly before setting off.
- ✚ Always carry a backup supply of fuel in case you run out in the middle of a meal, or in the middle of nowhere.
- ✚ Find out how to maintain your stove and where to get spare parts.
- ✚ At the end of a trip, clean the stove carefully before packing it away.

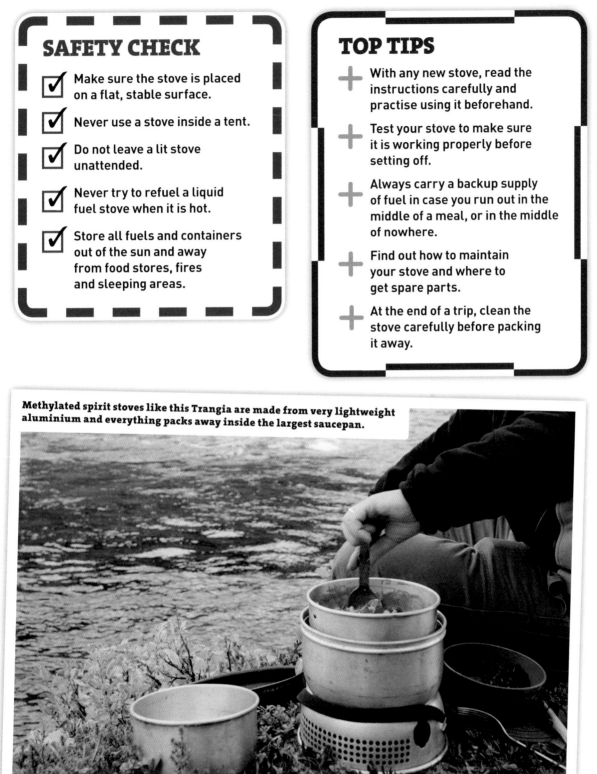

Methylated spirit stoves like this Trangia are made from very lightweight aluminium and everything packs away inside the largest saucepan.

FOOD SUPPLIES

Good food and a well-balanced diet are vital when you are living outdoors and being active.

FOOD PLANNING

To make sure you have the right kind of ingredients and equipment, it's best to plan your meals before you leave. Don't forget that you will also need plenty of water – for drinking, cooking and cleaning – so be sure to check where your nearest water supplies will come from.

How much food you take with you will depend on how long your trip will last and where you are going. If you are away for a weekend, for example, you can probably take most of the food you will need with you. If you are planning a longer trip and know you can buy fresh produce along the way, then it is better to concentrate on packing dried foods, seasonings and staples for cooking. Canned foods are useful too, but are heavier to carry if you are hiking.

BREAKFAST

A good breakfast will warm you up and give you plenty of energy for whatever activity you have planned that day. Porridge made with fresh or powdered milk, or plain water, is a quick, easy one-pot hot breakfast, and you can add chopped fresh or dried fruit, seeds and honey for taste and an extra boost of energy. If you are short on time in the morning, have cereal or cereal bars, a piece of fruit and a hot drink. Or if time is no object, try scrambled egg on toast, with or without bacon, or pancakes with honey.

LUNCH

Lunch is likely to be eaten on the move, so think about high-energy foods that can be easily prepared and packed. Wholemeal rolls or pitta breads can be easier to carry than sandwiches. Keep fillings tasty and fairly dry so they don't make the bread too soggy during the day. Or forget the bread and take chunks of cheese and some cleaned and sliced raw carrots, celery and red peppers.

Alternatively, cook up some thin dried noodles, rice, or bulgur wheat the night before. Let it cool, then mix with chopped onion, cucumber, peppers, tinned corn or raisins, dried tomatoes, fresh or dried herbs, and a little olive oil and lemon or soy sauce and put it in an airtight container. Other high-energy snacks for lunchtime or during the day could include fresh fruit, trail mix made from dried fruit and nuts, and chocolate.

DINNER

The evening meal can be a high point of the day. Plan dinners that are filling but simple to prepare. If you are not much of a cook, don't fancy making the effort after a long day's hike, or are limited to what you can carry, take some ready-made convenience foods that are lightweight and easy to pack, such as boil-in-the-bag rice or pasta meals, or dehydrated or freeze-dried stews.

Check the contents before you buy as some are full of additives and flavours rather than real food, and if you are unfamiliar with them you might like to test a few beforehand. Freeze-dried food tends to cost a bit more, but does have the advantage of looking and tasting more like the real thing once it has been cooked.

Otherwise, try to make sure your evening meal contains a carbohydrate, such as pasta, rice or potatoes, some protein such as eggs, meat, fish, beans or tofu, and some vegetables or fruit, which can be dried or fresh. See pages 142–151 for cooking methods and some suggestions for recipes.

FOOD LIST

Your list of staples might include some of the following, for example:

- ✔ Plain flour
- ✔ Rice
- ✔ Pasta
- ✔ Bulgur wheat
- ✔ Couscous
- ✔ Noodles
- ✔ Lentils
- ✔ Porridge or cereal
- ✔ Salt and pepper
- ✔ Stock cubes or powder
- ✔ Garlic powder
- ✔ Dried mixed herbs
- ✔ Chilli powder or other spices
- ✔ Tomato paste (concentrated)
- ✔ Sugar or honey
- ✔ Dried milk powder

- ✔ Hot chocolate, cocoa powder
- ✔ Instant coffee
- ✔ Tea bags
- ✔ Margarine – but won't keep very well, so may be better to put peanut butter, jam or mayonnaise on your bread instead and cook only with oil
- ✔ Vegetable/olive oil
- ✔ Jam/marmalade
- ✔ Peanut butter
- ✔ Mayonnaise
- ✔ Marmite
- ✔ Mustard
- ✔ Tomato sauce
- ✔ Grated or hard cheese, or small cheeses in their own wrapping
- ✔ Bacon bits

- ✔ Packets of frankfurters, or dried sausage like chorizo or salami
- ✔ Dried eggs, or a few fresh eggs will keep for a day or two if packed in an empty biscuit or crisps tube with scrunched-up paper between them for protection
- ✔ Dried mushrooms, carrots, leeks, onions
- ✔ Packets of freeze dried/dehydrated soups, stews, pasta meals, chilli or curry meals, and sauces you can use for cooking
- ✔ Dried fruit
- ✔ Nuts
- ✔ Mixed seeds
- ✔ Chocolate
- ✔ Cereal/energy bars
- ✔ Tinned food – if you have space and can carry them, you might consider adding some small tins, such as:
  - Tinned tomatoes
  - Tinned tuna or salmon
  - Baked beans

HOW MUCH TO TAKE

Work out how many meals you will need while you are away, and decide on a menu for each meal. List the ingredients for each meal and roughly estimate how much one person will eat, then multiply the ingredients by the number of people. Allow a little bit extra, just in case.

If you are hiking and it is all adding up to too much weight, look for ways you can cut down on ingredients without cutting down on nutrition. See Chapter 1, pages 18–19 for more information on diet and nutrition.

If you know you will be able to buy fresh produce along the way, or at the campsite, you can obviously cut down on the dried or canned foods. However, it is still worth taking a few general staples such as grains, cereals, flour, seasonings, drinks and so on, as otherwise you could end up buying some of these foods in greater quantities than you will need or be able to carry home.

TOP TIPS

+ Break down packets of dried food into sufficient quantities for one meal and store them in resealable plastic bags. Remember to keep the cooking instructions.

+ Look for liquids and sauces in small, squeezable tubes rather than jars, or decant them into small plastic screw-top bottles.

+ Make your own trail mix from chopped dried fruit and nuts, seeds, chocolate raisins, dried coconut pieces, or whatever you fancy.

+ Crackers and crispbreads last longer than fresh bread.

+ Get creative – think of meals you can make in one pot: see pages 143–145 for some ideas.

FOOD SAFETY

Food safety is especially important when you are camping. There are plenty of opportunities for coming across harmful bacteria in the countryside, and the ground and open water may contain residues from agricultural pesticides and fertilizers as well as organic matter from animals. It's best to avoid putting food products, or cooking or eating utensils, directly onto the ground.

However, the single most important thing to remember is to always wash your hands before touching food.

FOOD STORAGE

Food is best stored in tightly lidded plastic or metal containers to keep out insects and other animals. If possible, keep food off the ground and in the shade, and store it away from cleaning chemicals or fuel. When transferring food from one container to another, or when storing leftover food, always make sure the new container is clean. For more information on camp living, see also Chapter 5, pages 114–115.

Perishable foods, such as meat, dairy and pre-cooked foods, have a very short shelf life when not stored in a refrigerator – even if you have a cool box. Raw meat and fish should be bought and used on the same day, and most dairy food should be kept out of the sun and eaten within a few days.

Fresh fruit and vegetables are long-lasting (except for soft fruit), but should be rinsed before use. Vacuum-packed and canned products last for months, as long as their packaging has not been pierced or opened. Once opened they must be used within a day or two.

Most sauces and jams with a high vinegar or sugar content are long-lasting, but their container lids and mouths should be kept clean and lids should not be placed on the ground. Freeze-dried and dehydrated foods are the most stable food source of all, but should be kept in sealed plastic bags until required and handled with clean hands.

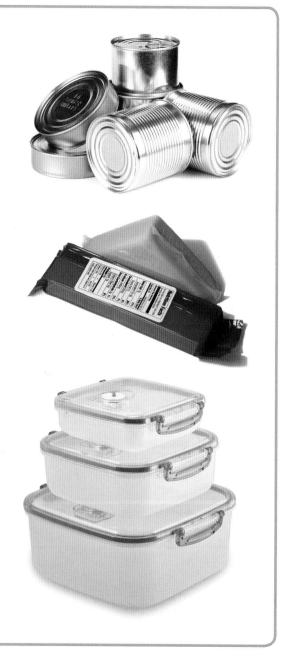

WATER

It's amazing how much water you need when camping, so a reliable source is an important consideration.

If you have easy access to a clean mains water supply, your only problem will be carrying the water to your campsite. There are various types of plastic water carriers on sale, ranging from sturdy 25-litre containers to 5-, 10- or 15-litre collapsible water 'bags'. Whichever version you use, make sure the carrier itself is regularly cleaned out and sterilized, and never drink directly from the spout unless you are sure you will be the only person to use it.

Keep your personal drinking water in a separate container. Many health experts recommend that adults drink 2–2.5 litres of water a day. Water is heavy to carry, especially when you are hiking, but you should make sure you have at least 1 litre of water with you when you set off each day, and refill your water bottle whenever you get the opportunity.

PURIFYING WATER

If you are in a remote area and need to use water from a stream, spring, or well – or even if you are unsure of the water supply – always treat the water before drinking or brushing your teeth with it, or using it to wash food.

The most reliable way to purify water is to boil it. Keep the water on a rolling boil for at least 5 minutes, then let it cool. This will kill most germs that may have been in it. Cooking with it is fine as long as you are boiling the water with the food in it.

Alternatively, you can use water purification tablets and follow the instructions given. You may get a slight taste of chemicals in the water, but this can be masked by adding other ingredients to your drink. Or buy a portable water filter system.

A portable water filter pumps dirty water through a strainer.

KITCHEN HYGIENE

 Wash your hands with soap or antibacterial hand gel before touching food. Make sure that knives, chopping boards or chopping surfaces are clean, and rinse fresh food before using it. Put spoons, ladles and other cooking utensils on a plate while you are using them – never on the ground.

 Thoroughly clean all your cooking pans and utensils after every meal. Leaving dirty pans lying around attracts insects and animals, and using equipment that has not been properly cleaned is a sure way of ending up with a bad stomach.

WASHING UP

 Heat a pan of hot water for washing up while you are eating your meal. Have one pan of hot water to wash in and a pan of cold water for rinsing. Some people recommend putting a sterilizing tablet into the cold rinse, and having a third pan of hot water for a final rinse, but if your fuel is limited you can stick to just one pan of hot water.

 Stack your washed dishes and utensils on a clean cloth to air dry, or hang them up in a net bag. Remember to strain your cooking and washing-up water when you have finished and dump it well away from any natural water source – and well away from your campsite.

 Hang up dishcloths and tea towels to dry and boilwash them when they get dirty, or use disposable cloths.

For a basic list of cooking and cleaning equipment, see Chapter 5, pages 102–103. For more information on waste food and water, see Chapter 5, pages 118–119.

TOP TIPS

+ If you are using a campfire or liquid fuel stove, wipe detergent or soap on the outside of your cooking pans before using them. It makes any sooty marks on them much easier to clean.

+ Put water in your pans immediately after using them, so food particles don't harden and become difficult to clean.

+ If food burns and sticks to a pan, put a layer of salt and water on the bottom and let it stand for an hour or two, then boil the water. You should find this makes it easier to clean.

+ If you are infested by ants, stand open food containers in bowls of water while they are in use. Closed food containers should be completely clean on the outside so that there is nothing to attract the ants.

OUTDOOR COOKING

The key to outdoor cooking is a hot fire, as few pans as possible, and patience – especially if you are cooking on a wood fire. Always get your campfire going well before you begin to cook.

COOKING BY FIRE OR BY STOVE?

Wood fires are best:

▶ **when there are lots of people**

▶ **for fixed camps lasting more than two nights**

▶ **when you have lots of time**

▶ **when you have permission and there are supplies of dead wood available**

Make sure you have plenty of hot embers that give a constant heat, not lots of smoke and flames.

Portable stoves are best:

▶ **when there are just a few people**

▶ **when you are hiking and moving on each day**

▶ **when you want a quick hot drink or hot meal**

▶ **in poor weather conditions**

▶ **in places where campfires are not allowed or there is no fuel available**

Make sure you have enough fuel before you start, otherwise you have to let the stove cool before you can refuel.

PREPARING TO COOK

There are lots of ways of cooking food, even when you are camping. Decide beforehand which method or methods you are going to use and in what order – some types of foods and methods need more time than others.

Work out what pans you will need. The fewer pans you have the more inventive you can be in using them – there is a lot you can do with one-pot cooking. Make sure you have everything to hand before you start, including plenty of fresh water and fuel.

Begin by cleaning and chopping any fresh vegetables or meat and measuring out any dry ingredients so they are ready to use as you need them.

ONE-POT COOKING

This can be one of the simplest and most satisfying ways of preparing a meal. The trick is to add the ingredients in the right order. One-pot meals can be boiled, stewed or pot-roasted. Many ready-made, boil-in-bag or dehydrated meals are also prepared in one pot.

BOILING

This simply involves bringing a pan full of water to the boil, adding vegetables, rice, pasta or other grains and keeping the water on or just below boiling until the food is cooked, which can take anything from 5 to 30 minutes. Root vegetables take longer to cook than other types of vegetables, although the smaller you chop them the faster they will cook. They can be put in the pan while the water is still cold. Green vegetables cook fast and are best added once the water is boiling. Be careful not to overcook the food, or let the pan boil dry.

If you are adding a ready-made sauce to the cooked food, you will need to drain the cooking water away, then put the food back in the pan and add the sauce to heat it through.

If you are making a soup, start with the root vegetables (potatoes, onions, carrots, parsnips) and a stock cube or powder, and cook for 15 minutes. Then add a handful of rice, pasta or lentils, seasoning, herbs, mushrooms or green vegetables, or anything you like for extra flavour and cook for another 15–30 minutes. The great thing about soup is that you also eat the cooking water with all the nutrients from the food still in it.

SAFETY CHECK

☑ **Make sure grills or pan supports on wood fires or stoves are stable and will take the weight of the cooking pans.**

☑ **Metal cooking utensils and containers get very hot. Always use a tea towel or oven pad to lift them.**

STEWING

Stewing usually involves cooking minced or chopped meat, or fresh or dried fruit. Once the water has come to the boil, the heat is lowered to a simmer so that the ingredients cook gently. But make sure that the heat is not too low and the liquid is still bubbling. With a campfire, this will mean moving the pot carefully from the hot embers in the centre to one side of the fire, or raking some of the embers away.

For a meat stew, it's best to put a little oil in the bottom of the pan and brown the meat and then the onions before adding the water. If you are adding cold water, take the pan off the heat and let it cool first, otherwise the hot oil will make the water spit and steam. Of course, you can just put the meat straight into cold water and bring it to the boil. Add some stock powder or herbs and root vegetables (but not potatoes). Bring it back to the boil, put a lid on the pot and let it simmer for about 40 minutes. Then add potatoes and any other vegetables, canned beans, lentils, rice or pasta and cook for another 20 minutes or so.

To cook fresh fruit you will need very little water – just enough to cover the fruit. Dried fruit may need soaking before you cook it: check the instructions on the packet.

POT HOLDER

Use a moveable pot holder to adjust the cooking temperature of your stewpot over a campfire. Push a forked stick into the ground and rest a longer stick inside the fork so that one end hangs over the fire. Link the other end of the long stick to the upright stick with a loop of string. Tighten or loosen the loop to raise or lower the pot, or gently swing the long stick to one side to move the pot off the fire.

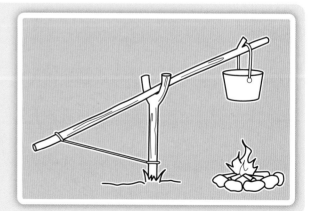

POT-ROASTING

This is a way of cooking a single large piece or joint of meat (preferably boneless) without using an oven. You will need a large sturdy pot with a tight-fitting lid. An aluminium or cast iron Dutch oven pot (if you can carry one) is perfect for this type of cooking, but any largeish pot will do. It is a very delicious but very slow way of cooking and best used with a campfire unless you have a plentiful supply of stove fuel. Depending on the size of your piece of meat, this method can take anything from 1 to 3 hours.

Heat some oil in the bottom of the pan and brown the meat on all sides. Remove the meat and put it to on side. Pack a layer of large chunks of root vegetables (carrots, onions, swedes, turnips) into the bottom of the pan with just enough stock or water to cover them.

Add herbs, seasoning or cloves of garlic. Lay the meat on top of the vegetables. Bring the liquid to the boil, then lower to a simmer. Make sure the lid is on firmly so the meat will cook in the steam from the liquid.

Check the pot every 30 minutes or so to make sure it has not boiled dry, and add more liquid if necessary. It is ready when the meat is tender and cooked right through.

DUTCH OVEN A Dutch oven is a traditional campfire cooking pot. The original design has a metal handle for hanging the pot over a fire, and legs for standing it in hot embers. The lid may also have a raised rim so that hot coals can be piled on the top. It is very tough and versatile and can be used for boiling, stewing, pot-roasting, baking and frying – but it is also heavy to carry, so not much used by hikers. Flat-bottomed versions can also be used on a sturdy gas ring.

FRYING

Frying is a quick way of cooking food such as eggs, bacon or sausages, mushrooms or slices of bread in a flat-bottomed pan, coated with oil. However, most lightweight camping frying pans do not heat evenly, especially over a single burner, so the pan must be moved around all the time to make sure all the food is cooked to the same degree. This is often made more difficult by the fact that the frying pan handle is usually detachable and has to be held in place by the cook, using a clamping device.

A frying pan or shallow pot can also be used to stir-fry thin strips of meat or fish and sliced vegetables with a small amount of oil. As all the ingredients, including pre-cooked rice or noodles, are eventually added to the same pan, this is a quick and economical way of cooking. However, as above, the pan must be moved about and the food stirred throughout the cooking process.

ROASTING AND GRILLING

Pieces of meat and whole or large pieces of vegetables can be roasted over a campfire on long skewers or spits, or placed on a metal grill which is supported over the fire on metal legs, large stones or logs. For example, chunks of sausage, bacon, or chicken, mushrooms, peppers or onions can be brushed with oil and then threaded onto skewers to make kebabs.

Cook whole sausages by threading them lengthways on a skewer. Support the skewers over a fire with two forked sticks pushed into the ground at either end. Or grill them. Fish is best cooked on a grill as it can fall off a skewer. Or cook it in the embers, see opposite, or in a mud case, see page 148.

If you are using a grill, brush the bars with oil before you start cooking so the food is less likely to stick to the metal. With both roasting and grilling, the food should be turned regularly to make sure it is cooked on all sides. If you are cooking quite fatty food on a grill, such as sausages or beefburgers, the fat will drip into the fire and make flames flare up, so take care that the food does not catch fire.

COOKING IN FOIL

With a campfire some foods can be wrapped in packets made from double layers of aluminium foil and placed directly on the hot embers to cook. This method works best with foods such as sausages, burgers, fish, corn on the cob, onions, tomatoes, mushrooms, potatoes, apples, oranges and bananas. It's best to avoid using very large chunks of meat as they may not cook evenly.

Cooking times will vary depending on the food and how hot the embers are. Potatoes will take about 40 minutes, sausages around 30 minutes, fruit about 15 to 20 minutes. It helps to grease the inside of the foil with a little oil or margarine before wrapping up the food. Use sticks or tongs to turn the packets once or twice while cooking.

Try mixing foods together inside the packet. Put a layer of onion and pepper slices in with the burgers or fish, for example, and add a few herbs or spices. You could make a kebab and wrap it in foil rather than grilling it. You could cut the top off a potato, scoop out some of the insides, break an egg into it, and put the top back on before wrapping it up in the foil. Put the potato in the fire so it stands with the lid uppermost. Or cut the core out of an apple and fill it with dried fruit, honey, sugar or chocolate.

Remember that your fire needs time to burn down in order to give you plenty of hot embers.

BACKWOODS COOKING

Backwoods cooking is all about cooking a meal without using the usual pots, pans or other utensils – not even aluminium foil. Instead you use sticks, stones, leaves or even the food itself as your utensils.

LEAVES AND GRASS

As with the aluminium-foil method described on the previous page, the same sorts of food can be wrapped in layers of large leaves, such as cabbage leaves, which are then pegged shut with peeled and sharpened slivers of green wood. You can also use kale leaves, 'greens', or romaine lettuce for this, but be sure to wash all leaves before using them. Potatoes and onions can also be 'baked' just in their skins

Alternatively, lay three or four layers of leaves flat on top of the embers and place the food on top of the leaves. After 10 minutes or so, lift the food off the fire using sticks or forked twigs, turn it over and replace the leaves at the same time. Keep doing this until the food is cooked.

Bake a whole fish – make sure it has been cleaned and gutted – by wrapping it in leaves and binding long grass stems around it to make a tight package. Then completely cover the package with mud to seal it and put it on a bed of hot embers. Scrape more embers over the top of it. Depending on the size of the fish it should be done in about 30 minutes to one hour.

SAFETY CHECK : Do not wrap food in rhubarb leaves as they are poisonous.

CLEANING FISH

If you buy a whole fish from a shop it will usually have been cleaned and gutted, although it may still have its head. If you catch a fresh fish (see page 242) you will need to do this yourself.

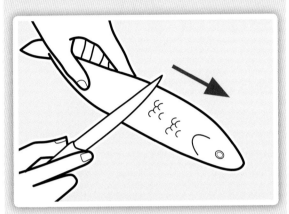

It's not always necessary to scale a fish, but if the scales are large, use a knife to scrape from tail to head to remove them. Cut open the belly of the fish from its anus to its throat. Scoop out all the entrails from inside.

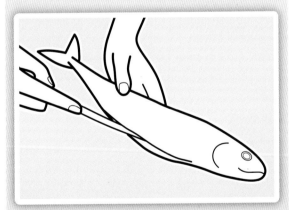

Cut off the head just behind the gills, or cook with the head on if you prefer. Thoroughly wash the fish inside and out. If you are wrapping the fish in foil or leaves, put fresh or dried herbs, seasoning and chunks of lemon or orange or onion inside the fish for extra flavour.

Try cooking a fish held between a split cane or two sticks tied together.

To grill a fish on a skewer, push a sharpened stick beneath the head, under the gill flaps.

TWIGS AND STICKS

Green twigs and sticks with the bark stripped off and one end sharpened can be used for spits and skewers, but the wood must be green otherwise it will burn. Pierce the middle of each piece of food with the tip of a knife first, so it will thread onto the stick more easily.

A 'grill' can be made from pliable green sticks. Peel the sticks and lash four of the sticks together to make a frame. Then place one row of sticks across the frame and a second row at right angles to it to make an open grid. 'Weave' the sticks in and out of each other and the frame to hold them in place. Soak the lashing and the sticks so they will not burn in the heat.

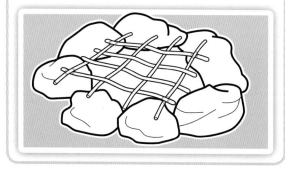

HOT STONES

Scrub a flat stone and place it directly on top of the fire. Support it on each side by smaller stones or logs to make a small altar. Once the stone heats through it can be used as a frying stone or griddle.

If you cannot find a large flat stone, use a pile of fist-sized smaller stones instead. Lay the stones closely together to make a flat bed. Build a fire on top of the stones and let it burn. When the fire has burned down, brush away the ashes and the rocks will be hot enough to cook on. You can lay food directly on top of the stones, or place a low spit or twig 'grill' over them.

MAKING CAMP BREAD

Camp bread is also known as 'twists' or 'dampers'. Make a thick dough from flour and water (you can add milk or a beaten egg to the water if you like). Knead the dough until it is pliable, then roll it into a long sausage shape. Wrap it around a peeled green stick and toast it over a fire until it is lightly browned.

FIRES, FOOD & COOKING

TOP TIPS

+ Stretch a double thickness of aluminium foil around the end of a forked stick to make a triangular-shaped frying pan.

+ Slice the top off an orange. Scoop out and eat the insides. Chop up a few pieces of chocolate, or use chocolate buttons, and put in the bottom of the orange. Make up a cheap packet of sponge-cake mix and spoon it into the orange until half full. Put the top back on the orange and pin it in place with small green-wood splinters. Place the orange carefully in the embers and wait for the sponge to bake and rise.

+ Cook sausages on a stick. Make camp bread dough and wrap it around the cooked sausages then toast slowly over the fire – campfire sausage rolls.

SAFETY CHECK

☑ Do not make spits or skewers out of yew, holly, elm and laurel wood as these are poisonous.

☑ Do not heat slate or any flaky stones or rocks in a fire as they might explode.

☑ Be careful to avoid lifting large containers of boiling water. Use a jug or a ladle to transfer boiling water from one container to another.

CHAPTER 7

KNOTS, LASHINGS & GADGETS

There are many situations in which a length of string or rope can be a lifesaver, especially when it is used to create an essential piece of equipment.

ROPES AND KNOTS

Whether you are mending a strap on a rucksack, or swinging down the side of a cliff, it's important to use the right kind of rope and the right knots.

TYPES OF ROPE

String, twine, cord and rope are pretty much the same thing. They are all made by twisting fibres together. The main difference is in their thickness and strength, and the material from which they are made, which may be natural fibres or synthetic fibres.

Natural ropes use plant fibres such as hemp, sisal, coir, manila, jute and cotton. They are flexible, soft, and fold more easily than synthetic ropes. Synthetic ropes, made from nylon, polyesters and polythene, tend to be lighter, stronger, and last longer than natural ropes as they are less likely to rot or be damaged by rodents or insects.

LAID OR BRAIDED

Most ropes are made in one of two ways:

Laid ropes use three strands of fibres twisted around each other. The fibres may be natural or synthetic. This is the traditional way of making rope and gives it more strength because if one fibre snaps, the other two may still hold.

Braided rope is usually made of synthetic material. It has an even number of strands, often eight or twelve, which are braided or plaited together into a circular tube. The centre of the tube may be empty, or filled with an inner core of more twisted or braided strands.

COILING A ROPE

Laid rope naturally prefers to fold one way rather than another, depending on how it was made. It's best to allow it to do this as it avoids putting unnecessary stress on the fibres.

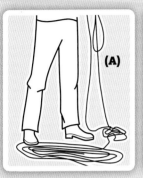

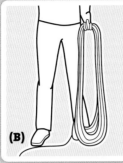

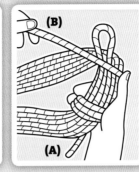

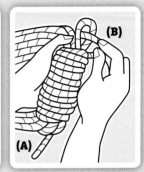

1 Leave a length of rope (A) free before starting the first coil. Rope can be coiled flat on the ground or hanging from one hand. Make each coil about the length of your forearm.

2 Give the rope a little shake as you coil it so that it does not twist or kink. Leave a length free at the end of the rope (B) and hold the coil firmly in one hand.

3 Fold length A into a loop and lay it along the coil. Wrap length B around the loop a few times to bind it in place. Make sure the top of the loop and the end of length A are still showing.

4 Feed the end of length B through the end of the loop and pull length A to tighten the loop around length B. Tie the two ends together with a reef knot – see page 157.

CARING FOR ROPE

No rope lasts for ever, but careful handling should help to ensure it does not fray or break at the worst possible moment. Always:

▶ store it somewhere dry and shady. Wet rope should be allowed to dry naturally and the ends should be bound or fused to prevent fraying – see page 154.

▶ keep it as clean as possible and avoid stepping on it. Dirt and grit may get into the rope and damage the fibres.

▶ coil rope when not in use. This prevents it from becoming tangled or kinking. It also makes it easier to handle and carry.

▶ check rope regularly for kinks, fraying or other signs of wear and tear. Do not use damaged rope for load bearing.

HANKING A ROPE

1 Fold the rope in half. Hold the middle of the folded rope and fold it in half again.

2 Continue folding the rope in half until it is between 30 cm and 60 cm long, depending on the thickness of the rope. Secure all the strands together by tying them into an overhand knot (see page 156).

ROPE REPAIRS

If a rope does become frayed or damaged it may be worth cutting away the damaged section and continuing to use the remaining lengths.

However, unless you are sure that the rest of the rope is completely undamaged, it is best not to use it for weight-bearing purposes.

The cut ends will need to be sealed to prevent them from unravelling. Ropes made of plastic fibres can be heated to melt the ends and fuse them together. Natural fibres will need to be bound or 'whipped'.

BINDING A ROPE END : COMMON WHIPPING

This is also known as 'whipping' a rope.

 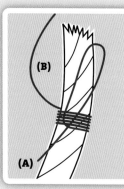 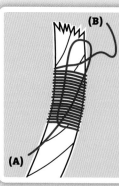 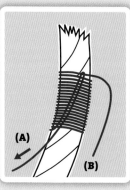

1 Use strong twine or cord, thinner than your rope. Fold one end of the twine into a loop. Lay it along the side of the rope so the top of the loop meets the end of the rope and one end (A) hangs free.

2 Bind the other end (B) tightly around the rope, working towards the rope end. As you wrap the twine round, you will start to cover the loop. Wrap the circles of twine tightly and keep close together.

3 When the twine is near to the end of the rope, thread the binding end (B) through the end of the loop.

4 Pull end (A) to tighten the loop and draw end (B) underneath the binding to hold it securely. Then trim off both ends of twine.

MAKING A ROPE

It is possible to make rope out of many everyday plant fibres, such as grasses, rushes, nettles or other long plant stems, strips of willow bark, long fibrous leaves that can be torn into strips, or even stringy, pliable roots. The easiest way to make rope is to plait it. Test your material for strength and pliability before you start. Most plant materials are best used while still green, and some stems or leaves may need to be soaked and then pounded to separate the fibres from the soft parts. If you want to practise making rope, do make sure you have permission to gather your plant material first.

To make rope from nettle stems, for example:

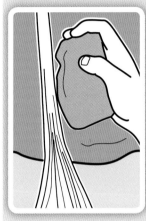 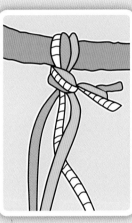 

1 Gather the longest stems you can find and soak them in water for a day. Then pound them with a stone to separate the fibres from the rest of the stems. Tease out the stringy fibres and leave them to dry.

2 Gather a bunch of fibres and knot one end to a twig or nail hanger to hold it in place. Split the bunch into three equal groups or strands. Bring the right-hand strand over the centre strand and hold it in place. This is now the centre strand.

3 Bring the left-hand strand over the new centre strand and hold it in place. Then bring the new right-hand strand over the centre strand. Carry on plaiting the strands in this way. Twist the strands lightly as you fold them over and keep the plait tight and even.

4 As one length of strands starts to come to an end, lay another length on top of it and feed this into the plait. Don't introduce new lengths to all three strands at the same place as this will weaken the rope. When the rope is the required length, knot or bind it at the ends and trim.

To make a stronger rope, make three plaits as above then plait these together.

BASIC KNOTS

It's important to use the right knot for the right purpose, whether it's for climbing, sailing, fishing, weaving, or simply tying something up. Of course, learning every knot there is could take a lifetime, but it is extremely useful to know how to tie a few essential ones.

The following pages give instructions for a range of widely used knots which will suit a great many purposes. Practise tying and untying them until they are so familiar you could tie them in the dark.

USEFUL TERMS

When learning about different ways to knot and use rope, you may come across the following terms:

WORKING END – the end you are using to tie a knot.

STANDING END – the opposite end to the working end.

STANDING PART – any part of the rope between two ends.

LOOP – a loop made by folding the rope back on itself and crossing the standing part.

BIGHT – a loop made by folding the rope back on itself without crossing the standing part.

A BEND – a type of knot used for tying one rope to another.

A HITCH – a way of fastening a rope to another object such as a post, log or rail.

OVERHAND KNOT AND LOOP

This very basic knot is a simple 'stopper knot' for temporarily securing the end of a piece of rope to prevent it fraying, or to make an end-stop on a rope. Doubling the rope and then tying the knot will make a quick non-slip loop.

A) OVERHAND KNOT

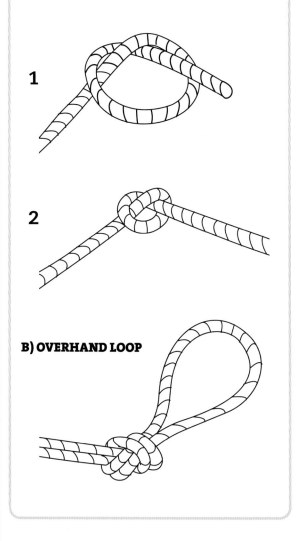

1

2

B) OVERHAND LOOP

FIGURE OF EIGHT

This is a stronger stopper knot. It is unlikely to work loose and can be doubled to create a strong loop.

A) SIMPLE FIGURE OF EIGHT

If the knot is tied correctly, it will look like a 'figure of eight'.

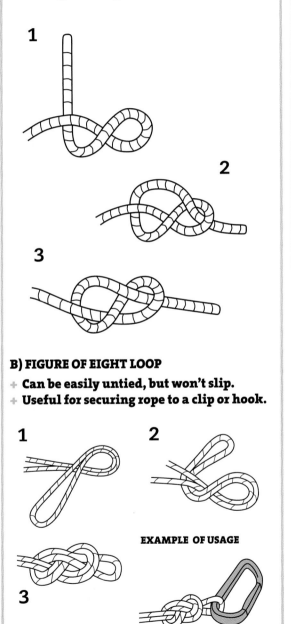

1

2

3

B) FIGURE OF EIGHT LOOP

+ **Can be easily untied, but won't slip.**
+ **Useful for securing rope to a clip or hook.**

1   **2**

EXAMPLE OF USAGE

3

REEF KNOT

A common knot for joining together two ends of the same thickness or material. It is often used to tie bandages as the knot lies flat.

1

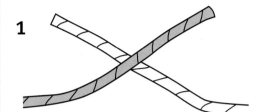

2

3

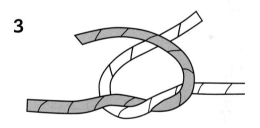

4

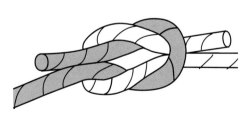

One way to remember this knot is: 'Left over right and under, right over left and under'. Although it can also be tied the other way.

FISHERMAN'S KNOT

This is another useful joining knot, mainly for tying thin, slippery materials such as wire or lengths of fishing line.

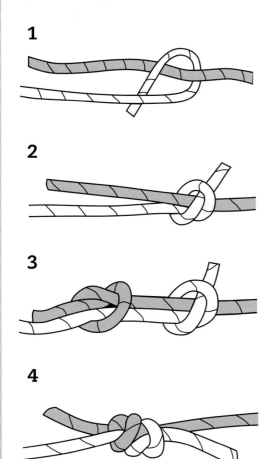

1

2

3

4

This is a difficult knot to untie and not good to use with thick ropes.

SHEET BEND

This is used for joining together two ropes of the same or different thickness.

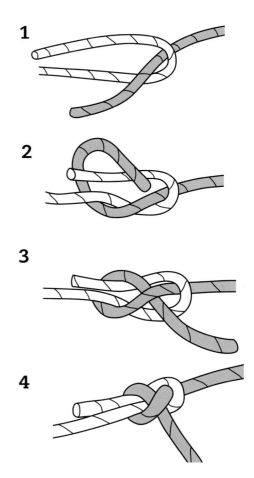

1

2

3

4

Tighten the knot by holding the bight in one hand and pulling the standing part of the other rope with the other hand.

If one rope is much thinner than the other, or is slippery, it may be necessary to secure the knot by wrapping the working end twice around the bight before threading it under itself and tightening the knot. This is called a Double Sheet Bend.

ROUND TURN AND TWO HALF-HITCHES

This is used to attach a rope to a fence, post, or tree, such as when mooring a boat. If tied correctly it won't slip when pulled.

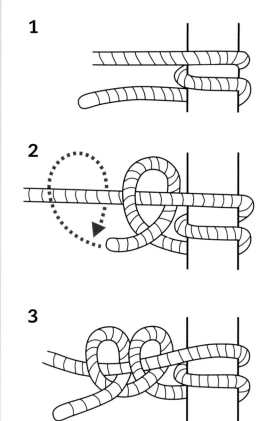

CLOVE HITCH

This is another way of attaching a rope to a post, but is not as secure as the Round Turn and Two Half-Hitches. It is most often used to fix rope to a pole to start a lashing (see pages 164–167).

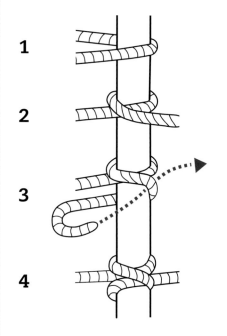

Once you are familiar with this knot, it can be 'ready-made' by forming two loops in the right order and slipping them on to a pole, then tightening. This method can be used to tie a clove hitch in the standing part of a rope without using the ends.

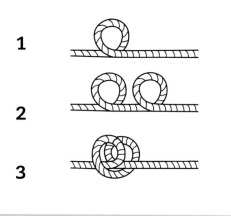

HIGHWAYMAN'S HITCH

This is a quick-release knot, supposedly used by highwaymen to tie up their horses so they could make a quick getaway.

1

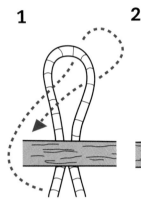

2

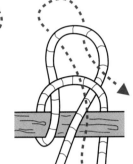

3

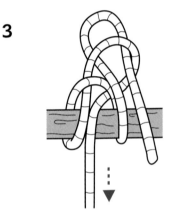

4

The hitch is released by tugging sharply on the loose end.

TIMBER AND ANCHOR HITCHES

The Timber Hitch is used for dragging or lifting heavy logs or other objects. It tightens when the rope is taut, but will come undone when the rope is slack. Adding a Half Hitch further along will make an Anchor Hitch to hold an object more securely.

A) TIMBER HITCH

1

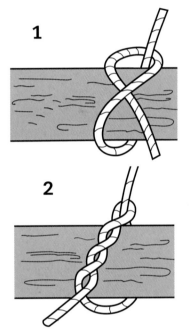

2

B) TIMBER HITCH WITH HALF HITCH

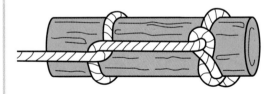

The Timber Hitch can also be used for starting a lashing (see page 165).

(see page 165)

KNOTS, LASHINGS & GADGETS

MARLIN SPIKE HITCH

This is a useful knot for lashing, or to link the standing part of a rope to a post.

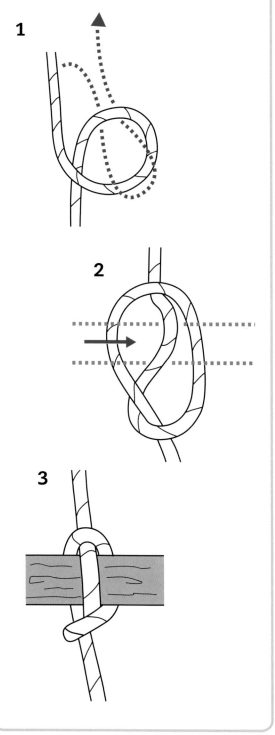

1

2

3

SHEEPSHANK

This knot is used to shorten a length of rope, or to make a bridge across a piece of damaged rope without cutting it.

1

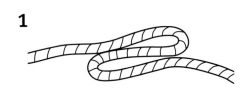

2

3

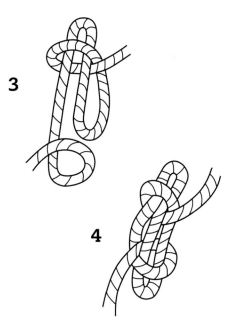

4

This knot can be tied in the standing part of the rope, without using the ends.

BOWLINE

This is a simple way of making a loop of rope that does not slip or tighten. It is often used in climbing and as a lifeline.

MANHARNESS HITCH

This knot makes a non-slip loop that can be tied along the standing part of a rope without needing working ends.

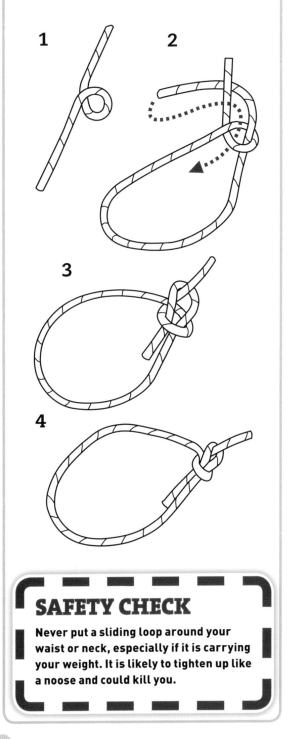

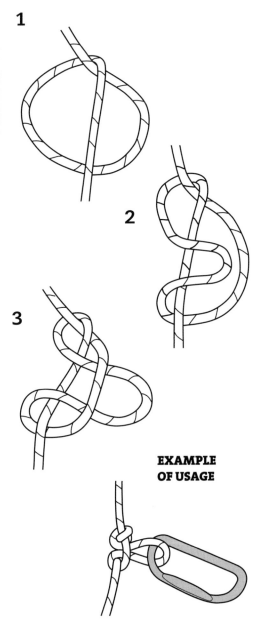

EXAMPLE OF USAGE

SAFETY CHECK

Never put a sliding loop around your waist or neck, especially if it is carrying your weight. It is likely to tighten up like a noose and could kill you.

Make sure the loop is pulled into shape and the knot eased tightly together. Test before using to ensure that the loop does not slip.

KNOTS, LASHINGS & GADGETS

PRUSSIC KNOT

The Prussic Knot is a way of attaching a loop to another piece of rope. It is used to attach climbing ropes, and also for making netting – see pages 168–169.

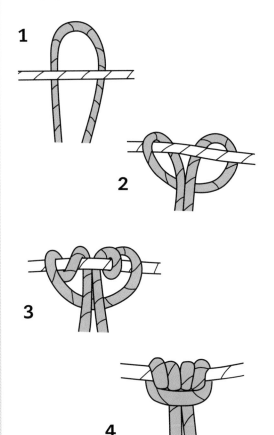

1

2

3

4

EXAMPLE OF USAGE

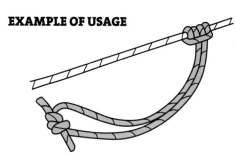

This knot will not slide when the loop is pulled tight, but will slide when the pressure is released.

A ROPE LADDER

Manharness hitches can be used to make a climbing rope. Tie equally spaced loops along a length of rope big enough to slide your hand or foot into.

If you use two lengths of rope, or double a length and make matching loops on both sides, you can feed lengths of wood through the loops to make rungs. Do this before tightening the knots. Make sure the pieces of wood are strong enough to take your weight and extend beyond the knots on both sides so that they do not slip out.

LASHINGS

Ropes and knots can be used in a number of ways to lash together sticks, logs, branches or poles to make any number of useful structures, from shelters and rafts to simple camp gadgets.

DIFFERENT LASHINGS

As with knots, there are different lashings for different purposes, depending on what you are making. Most lashings use quite basic knots, mainly the Timber Hitch and the Clove Hitch.

The trick to making strong and secure lashings is to do them as neatly and as tightly as possible. Practise with lengths of cord and a selection of staves, broom handles or garden canes.

SQUARE LASHING

Square lashing is used to bind together two poles that cross each other. It works best when the poles cross at right angles – when making a frame, for example.

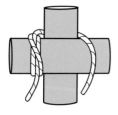 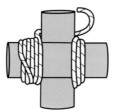 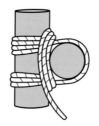 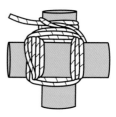

1 Begin by tying a Clove Hitch on one of the poles. Wrap the rope under the crossed pole, over the top pole, and back under the crossed pole on the other side to make a complete circuit.

2 Continue wrapping the rope under and over the poles, pulling the rope tightly each time.

3 After three or four circuits, change direction and wrap the rope between the two poles, circling the previous turns to make them even tighter. This is known as 'frapping'.

4 Finish by tying a Clove Hitch on the opposite side to where you began.

DIAGONAL LASHING

This is used for binding together two poles that are not at right angles to each other, or have to be pulled towards each other.

  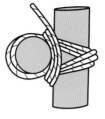 

1 **Start by tying a Timber Hitch** across the middle of both poles. Pull the knot tight and wrap the rope three times around the poles in the same direction as the Timber Hitch.

2 **Change direction and wrap the** rope three times over the opposite diagonal.

3 **Make two or three frapping** turns between the poles to tighten the wrapping.

4 **Finish by tying a Clove Hitch** on one pole.

SHEER LASHING

Sheer lashing is used to join two poles together to make one longer one. For strength, the two poles should overlap each other by a least a quarter to one third of their original length, and have a lashing near each end of the overlap.

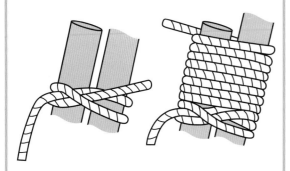

1 Start by tying a Clove Hitch around both poles near one end of the overlap. Wind the rope tightly eight to ten times around both poles (for about 10–15 cm).

2 Finish with a Clove Hitch around both poles.

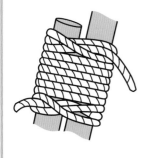
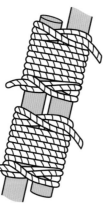

3 To make the lashing tighter, push small wedges under the lashing.

4 Add a second lashing at the other end of the overlap.

SHEER LEG LASHING

A similar style of sheer lashing can be used to join two poles of the same size that will be opened out at the bottom to make an A-frame. In this case, only one lashing is required.

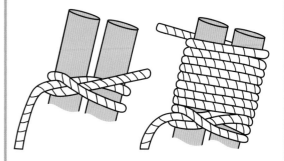

1 Line up the two poles and tie a Clove Hitch around the end of one of them. Put a small wedge between the two poles so as not to wrap them together too tightly.

2 Make eight to ten turns around both poles.

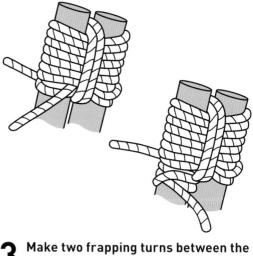

3 Make two frapping turns between the poles to tighten the lashing.

4 Finish with a Clove Hitch on the opposite side to the first one. Open out the bottom ends of the two poles.

FIGURE OF EIGHT OR TRIPOD LASHING

Figure of eight or tripod lashing joins together three poles to make a three-legged structure.

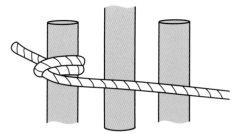

1 Three poles are laid together so that the centre one points in the opposite direction to the outer two. Start with a Clove Hitch on one of the outside poles.

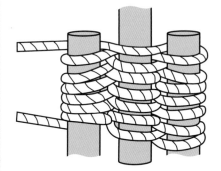

2 Wrap the rope six or seven times over and under each of the poles. (Do not make the wraps too tight, otherwise you will not be able to open out the poles into the tripod shape.)

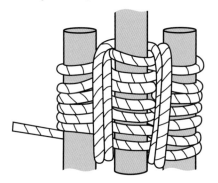

3 Make two frapping turns between the outer poles and the centre pole.

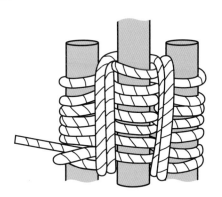

4 Finish with a Clove Hitch on the opposite side to the first one.

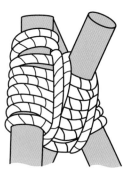

5 Position the tripod by turning the centre pole 180 degrees and opening out the two outer poles.

An example of a square lashing

GADGETS AND STRUCTURES

Once you are familiar with making knots and lashings, the only limits to the things you can construct will be the materials you have to hand and your imagination.

Here are some ideas to get you started. It's useful to build up a store of different types and thicknesses of cord and rope, and a range of poles and sticks. If you don't have the space or materials to practise on full-sized structures, make smaller models instead using small sticks or even straws.

MAKING NETS

Nets have any number of uses: as bags, hanging storage, for fishing, or as a hammock for sleeping. There are two basic ways of making netting – the knotting method and the weaving or knitting method. The simplest is the knotting method shown here.

You will need:

▶ a thicker cord to use as an edging or 'outer' line

▶ thinner cord for the netting

▶ two upright poles or posts to support the outer line

▶ a piece of wood to use as a spacer. Depending on how fine or tight you want your net to be, the spacer could be from 1–5 cm long

1 Decide how wide you want the net and position the poles accordingly. Tie a length of outer cord between the two poles.

2 Cut equal lengths of netting cord. As a general guide, the depth of your finished net will be just over a third as long as the lengths you start with. The number of lengths you need will depend on how many you can fit across the outer cord, using your spacer.

3 Fold the lengths of netting cord in half. Using the bight end, attach each length to the outer cord with a Prussic Knot. Use your spacer to spread them evenly along the cord. The lengths are now hanging in pairs from the outer cord.

4 Begin from the left, leaving the first strand hanging (the outer half of the first pair). This will become one end of the net. Take the second strand of the first pair and the first strand of the second pair and knot them together using an Overhand Knot. Position the knot one spacer length below the outer cord.

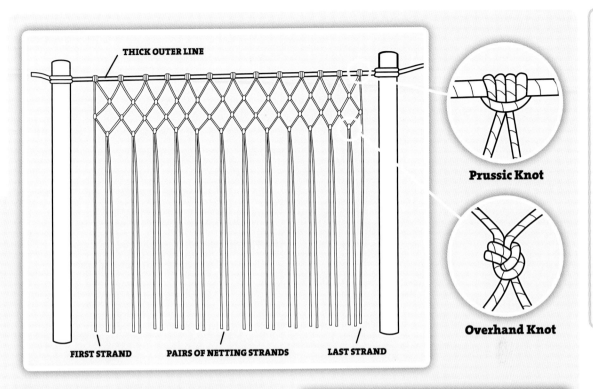

THICK OUTER LINE

Prussic Knot

Overhand Knot

FIRST STRAND   PAIRS OF NETTING STRANDS   LAST STRAND

5 Work your way along the line, knotting the second strand from each pair with the first strand of the next until you come to the end of the line and leave the last strand hanging. Use the spacer to keep the row of knots even.

6 Start the second row, but knot the first strand to the second strand this time, to make a diamond pattern. Continue all the way along to the end, also knotting the last strand.

7 Continue repeating the first and second rows until you are near to the end of your lengths.

8 Tie a second length of outer line between the two poles. Loop the ends of each pair of strands twice around the bottom line, separate the pair and tie off like a frapping to tighten the loops on the outer line.

9 Untie the outer lines from the supporting poles and knot the four corners to prevent the net sliding off. Leave any excess on the ends of the lines to attach your net to other things.

MAKING A HAMMOCK

Place the two support posts about 2 metres apart so that your hammock will be long enough. Make the net about 1 metre wide. Use strong cord for the net and a thicker rope for the outer lines. Leave plenty of length at either end to hang the hammock. Put poles at each end to hold the hammock open. Make a deep notch in the ends of each pole to hook onto the outer lines.

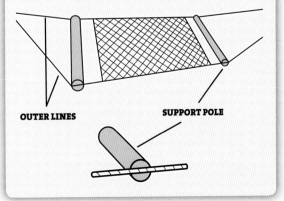

OUTER LINES   SUPPORT POLE

CAMP GADGETS

Camp gadgets are any kind of object or structure that makes life easier when you are living outdoors. This might be simply two sticks lashed together into a cross and stuck in the ground for your clothes to hang on, or a dining table and chairs.

There is no fixed design or way of building these gadgets; it's a question of adapting your knowledge of knots and lashings to the materials you have available, and learning by experience. Here are a few examples of different structures to give you some ideas.

TRIPOD POT HANGER AND HOOK

Tripod stands can be used in any number of ways. One of the most useful is to construct a pot hanger to support a cooking pan over a fire. Add an adjustable pot hook and you can raise and lower your pot over the fire to control the temperature at which the food is cooked.

1 Use a Figure of Eight (Tripod) lashing to make the stand.

2 For the variable pot hook, you will need a strong piece of wood with several branches. Strip the bark off the wood to make sure there is no rot to weaken it. Cut the branches to about 10 cm stumps. Lash the hook to the stand. Test the hook for strength before lighting the fire and hanging a pot full of food on it.

SAFETY CHECK

Remember to protect your hands before touching the hot pot handle.

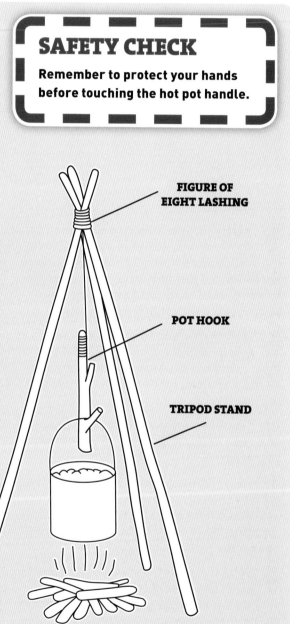

FIGURE OF EIGHT LASHING

POT HOOK

TRIPOD STAND

TOP TIP

➕ If you cannot find a suitable branch, look for two or three different lengths of forked wood. Hang a loop from the tripod and switch pot hooks as required.

BOWL STAND

Make a tripod stand with the lashing further down the poles, and you have a simple washstand that will support a washing-up bowl.

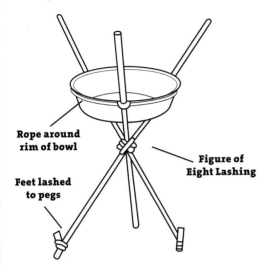

Rope around rim of bowl

Feet lashed to pegs

Figure of Eight Lashing

1 Lash the three sticks in the middle.

2 Tie a rope around the rim of the bowl to secure it to the stand.

3 For extra stability, lash the feet to wooden pegs pushed into the ground.

LOG SEAT

Make a simple seat by resting a sturdy log on a pair of low, crossed log supports.

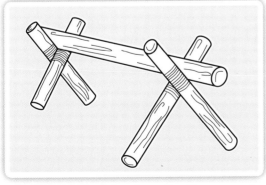

Use Sheer Leg lashing to make the supports.

WALLS AND SCREENS

Walls and fences of sticks and poles make useful shelters, windbreaks or privacy screens for a toilet or washing area. Or build one behind a campfire to reflect the heat of the fire back towards you.

HEAT REFLECTOR

1 Push two pairs of sticks into the ground a stick-width apart. Fill the gap between them with a row of sticks and lash the upright poles together to hold everything in place.

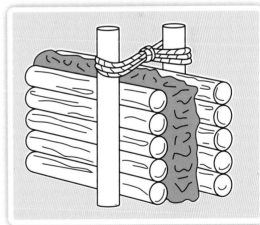

2 To give the wall extra strength, or to make a sturdy base for a platform, widen the space between the uprights and line it with two rows of poles with earth piled between them.

CAMP TABLE

A basic table can be made to any size or height. You will need:

▶ **9 poles or sticks of the same length**

▶ **2 short poles for bracing the side frames**

▶ **A number of staves, sticks or planks to make the tabletop**

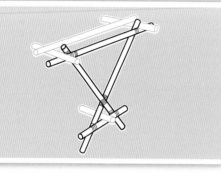

1 Make two side frames by lashing three same-sized poles together, plus a smaller bracing pole at the bottom. Make sure both frames are the same height and width.

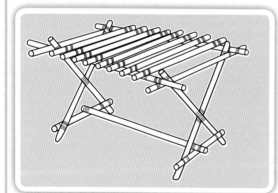

2 Join the two side frames with two horizontal poles at the top – one each side – and one at the bottom, lashed to the centre of the two bracing poles. Add extra bracing by running two diagonal rope ties from the top cross bars to the opposite end of the bottom horizontal bar. Lash the tabletop staves or sticks to the horizontal bars. They can be laid close together or spread apart, as required.

TRAVOIS

A travois is a way of carrying heavy loads, like firewood or camping gear. It is also useful for carrying an injured person. The travois is pulled at the narrow end and the wider end drags along the ground, so it needs a relatively smooth surface, such as grass, to work well.

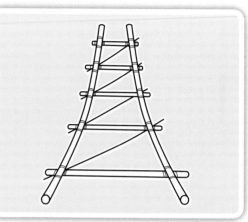

1 The poles should be about 2 metres long and sturdy but not too rigid. Trim off any branches to make them as smooth as possible.

2 Lash a series of sticks between the poles. Make them long enough to extend a little on either side.

3 For extra strength, add diagonal cross pieces.

4 Allow room at the narrow end to walk between the poles, holding one pole in each hand to pull the travois.

5 Alternatively lash a stick across the end and tie shoulder straps to it (B). For short distances, lash the two narrow ends together to make a hand grip (A).

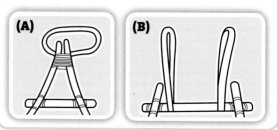

(A)   (B)

MAKING STRUCTURES

Building larger or more complicated structures is often called 'Pioneering' or 'Scout engineering'. Using knots, lashings, poles or spars, ropes and sometimes pulleys it is possible to build a tower, a tree house, or even a bridge.

BASIC SHAPES

Most structures are formed using different combinations of the same few basic shapes – shown below. Once you have decided which shapes to use and how many, they can be linked together by additional poles and ropes. It is usually better to build your structure from a number of smaller components than to build fewer but larger sections. The bigger the section, the heavier and more difficult it is to move.

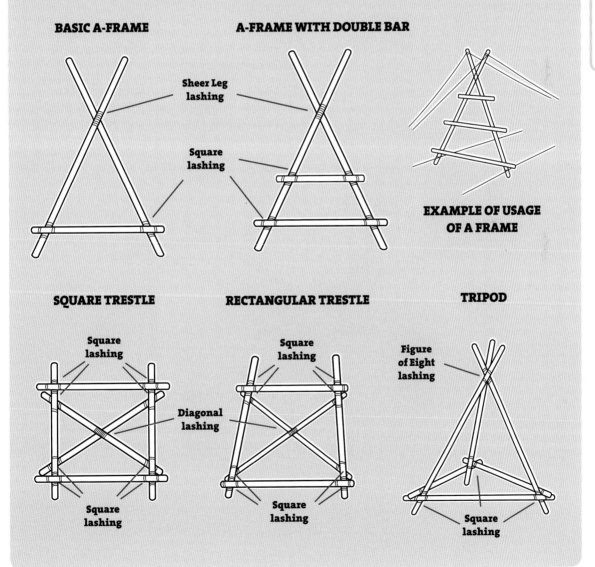

BASIC A-FRAME

Sheer Leg lashing

Square lashing

A-FRAME WITH DOUBLE BAR

EXAMPLE OF USAGE OF A FRAME

SQUARE TRESTLE

Square lashing

Diagonal lashing

Square lashing

RECTANGULAR TRESTLE

Square lashing

Square lashing

TRIPOD

Figure of Eight lashing

Square lashing

LOOKOUT TOWER

You will need:

- ▶ 4 x 3.6m–5m poles (sides)
- ▶ 8 x 2.5m poles
  (bottom rails and braces)
- ▶ 6 x 2m poles (top rails)
- ▶ approx. 24 x 2m light poles
  (platform floor and rails)
- ▶ 4 x 1.5m light poles
  (platform uprights)
- ▶ lashing lengths
- ▶ rope ladder
- ▶ large pegs or pickets

Optional:

- ▶ 3 x 3.5m poles (tripod)
- ▶ 3 x ropes approx. 20m long
  to lift the tower
- ▶ 1 pulley

1 Construct the sides from 2 trestles made with the longest poles, a 2m pole for the top rail and a 2.5m pole for the bottom rail. Brace each side with a single 2.5m pole.

2 Lay the trestles on their sides and join them using 2 x 2m poles and 2 x 2.5m poles. Make sure the joining poles at the top are on top of the existing side rails, as they will form the supports for the platform. Brace these sides with two more 2.5m poles.

3 Lash the two remaining 2m poles across the top of the tower to strengthen the base for the platform.

4 Put aside 4 x 2m light poles and lash the rest to the top of the tower to make the platform floor.

5 Use 4 x 1.5m poles as uprights for the platform handrail and join them with the 4 x 2m light poles you put aside to make the handrail. Brace the spars if necessary.

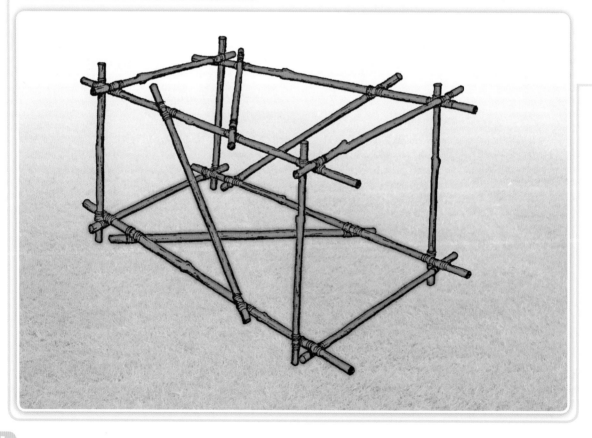

6 Tie the rope ladder to one of the poles at the base of the platform.

7 To lift the tower upright, make a tripod and hang the pulley from the centre. Position the tripod about 10m from the base of the tower. Tie two long ropes to the back corners of the tower (not the handrail). Fix the third rope to the middle of the front of the tower and feed it through the pulley. Use this rope to raise the tower while it is steadied by others using the back ropes.

8 When the tower is upright, peg the bottom of the rope ladder to the ground. The tower should be stable enough to be free standing, but if you are in any doubt at all, knock in large pegs or pickets by each foot and lash the legs to them.

MONKEY BRIDGE

SIMPLE LADDER BRIDGE

CHAPTER 8:

OUTDOOR SKILLS & SPORTS

Along with all the other activities in this book, there are some sports that bring you into direct contact with the outdoors and enhance and increase your understanding of it – as well as being fantastic fun.

WATER SPORTS

SWIMMING

Swimming is a great form of exercise at any age or stage of life. It's good for your heart and lungs, takes the weight off your body if you need low-impact exercise, allows you to move around in ways that are otherwise impossible, and is a great way to relax. It is also an important life skill and means that you can safely take part in all kinds of other water activities, including canoeing and kayaking.

However, as with many sports, there are risks involved with swimming outdoors, and it is sensible to be aware of the dangers. For example:

▶ The water may be colder than you are used to.

▶ The banks or sides may be slippery and it may be difficult to get out.

▶ The water could be deeper than you thought.

▶ There may be rocks, rubbish or other objects under the water.

▶ There may be strong tides or currents.

▶ The water could be polluted.

WATER SAFETY

▶ Choose somewhere safe to swim, preferably an area patrolled by a lifeguard. Know what dangers to look out for and learn the water safety signs and flags – see below.

▶ Don't swim alone, whether you are in a swimming pool, a lake or the sea. No matter how well you can swim, it is always possible to get into difficulties. It's best to swim with a 'buddy', but always make sure there is someone to help you or get help for you if necessary.

▶ Don't overdo it – always stay within your own range of abilities, regardless of what your friends are doing. Don't be tempted to try to swim too far, or for too long, or out of your depth.

▶ If you are a good swimmer, be considerate towards those who are less experienced.

▶ Consider taking a lifesaving course and learn what to do in an emergency. The Royal Lifesaving Society UK **www.lifesavers.org.uk** have information about courses.

WATER SAFETY FLAGS

May be used on beaches

RED AND YELLOW STRIPES – indicates that lifeguards are on patrol. Two flags near the water's edge show the area in which it is safe to swim.

RED – indicates that it is dangerous to bathe or swim and you should not go in the water.

BLACK AND WHITE SQUARES – indicates that an area has been separated off for water sports and craft and is not safe for swimmers.

WATER SAFETY SIGNS

May be used near any water

RED AND WHITE CIRCLE WITH RED STRIPE ACROSS BLACK SYMBOLS

These signs mean that you SHOULD NOT do something or go somewhere.

NO SWIMMING · NO SNORKELLING EQUIPMENT · NO SUB-AQUA EQUIPMENT · NO DIVING · NO SAILING · NO WINDSURFING · NO ROWING

NO MOTORISED CRAFT · NO PERSONAL WATER CRAFT · NO WATER SKIING · NO SURFBOARDING · NO INFLATABLES IN THE WATER · NO RUNNING · NO FISHING

BLACK AND YELLOW TRIANGLE WITH BLACK SYMBOLS

These signs warn you of potential dangers that could be hard to see.

BEWARE DIVING AREA · BEWARE STRONG CURRENTS · BEWARE THIN ICE · BEWARE SAILING AREA · BEWARE SLIPWAY · BEWARE WINDSURFING AREA · BEWARE ROWING AREA

BEWARE MOTORISED CRAFT AREA · BEWARE WATER SKIING AREA · BEWARE SURFBOARDING AREA · BEWARE DEEP WATER · BEWARE SHALLOW WATER · BEWARE SUDDEN DROP

SOLID BLUE CIRCLE WITH WHITE SYMBOLS
These signs tell you what you SHOULD do to stay safe.

MANDATORY ACTION - life jackets to be worn

BLACK AND WHITE SQUARES

These signs are for general information.

SUB-AQUA · FISHING · SWIMMING · SNORKELLING

IF SOMEONE IS DROWNING

▶ Do not put yourself in danger. If you can, get someone to call for help straight away.

▶ If the casualty is still conscious, get their attention and let them know that help is on the way. Do not try to pull them out of the water directly unless you are trained in lifesaving. A drowning person might panic and push you under the water.

▶ Instead, try to reach them with something you can use to pull them to safety, such as a lifebelt and rope or an oar.

▶ If they are too far out and enough people are available, tie a safety rope to the waist of the strongest swimmer, who can then swim out with a rope or pole that will reach the casualty without making direct contact.

▶ If the person is unconscious, take a boat out and pull them on board, or tie a safety rope to the strongest swimmer who can swim out and pull them back to shore.

▶ When they are out of the water, check that they are breathing; if not, immediately administer CPR – see Chapter 9, page 215. Keep trying even if they do not seem to respond.

▶ If they are breathing, get them to put on dry clothing and treat them for shock and possible hypothermia – see Chapter 9, pages 214 and 218.

OUTDOOR SWIMMING

No matter how strong a swimmer you are, keep in mind that open areas of water are usually much colder than swimming pools. Cold water can be a problem in two ways:

SHOCK – if you suddenly jump into very cold water, the shock to your body could cause a heart attack. Or it could make you gasp and gulp air. This could mean that you inhale water, faint or suffer muscle cramps. Always enter open water gradually, and try to control your breathing. Wearing a wetsuit or extra clothing also helps, although extra clothing will weigh you down further so you may tire more quickly.

HYPOTHERMIA – if you are in cold water for too long, your body can begin to suffer from hypothermia (see Chapter 9, page 218). This can result in death or loss of consciousness. If you think the water will be cold it is best to wear a wetsuit or some kind of thermal swimwear – see pages 184–185.

Most people are only likely to stay in cold water for any length of time if they are in an emergency situation, in which case they should conserve their energy as much as possible – see panel below. **You should always wear a buoyancy aid if you are taking part in any activity on open water.**

COLD WATER SURVIVAL

If you are wearing some kind of lifejacket or buoyancy aid, you can adopt the **HELP** posture. HELP stands for Heat Exposure Lessening Position. Raise your knees as close to your body as you can and cross your ankles. Cross your arms over your chest. This will protect the areas of greatest heat loss: your head, neck, sides and groin.

If you are not wearing a buoyancy aid, you must try to stay afloat using as little movement as possible. The more you move about, the more energy you lose and the faster your body will cool down. Conserve your body heat by keeping your head out of the water and your arms and legs as close to your body as you can. If there is any debris floating in the water, use it to help you stay afloat.

If you are with other people, adopt the **HUDDLE** position. Form a circle, linking arms above and below each other's shoulders and keep as close together as possible. Put the smallest or youngest people in the middle. This position protects the sides and lower parts of the body. It also gives everyone emotional support and makes you more visible from above.

Unless it presents a danger, stay close to any overturned craft as it may give you something to hold onto and will make you more visible from above.

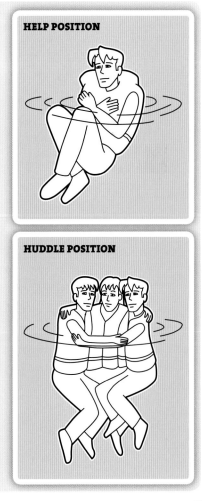

HELP POSITION

HUDDLE POSITION

RIVER SAFETY

Rivers and streams can be more dangerous than they appear. The current may be stronger than you imagine, there could be unexpectedly deep pockets in the riverbed, or large rocks or debris hidden beneath the surface. In areas where the water is slow moving, the river could be deep and choked with underwater plants.

If you need to cross a river on foot, always study it carefully before you set off. If the river is wide, try moving further upstream to a narrower point. Check the water surface for disturbances that may indicate hidden obstacles. Do not cross on a bend, as currents tend to flow faster on the outside edge. Avoid steep banks that may make it difficult to climb out of the water. Remember that handy-looking stepping stones may not be stable when you stand on them, and the surface will probably be slippery.

WADING ACROSS A RIVER

Never underestimate the currents in a river. Find a strong stick that you can use to help support you and keep your balance. You can also use it to feel ahead for any sudden drops in depth.

Roll up your trouser legs if the water is deep, as this will offer less resistance to the current. Keep your boots or shoes on to protect your feet and give you a better grip on the river bed. If you are carrying a backpack, undo the hip belt and loosen the shoulder straps so you can easily slip out of the pack if you lose your balance. Try to keep hold of it, though, as it will probably float and will give you more buoyancy.

Cross facing the direction of the current, with your body turned towards it but at an angle so that the current will help push you in the direction you want to go. Do not try to walk in strides, but shuffle sideways in small steps, putting your weight on your stick as you move.

If you are in a group, link arms and cross in a line, with the strongest person leading and the smallest or weakest in the middle. Cross facing the opposite bank, so that the first person breaks the current for the others, who will help support each other and the leader.

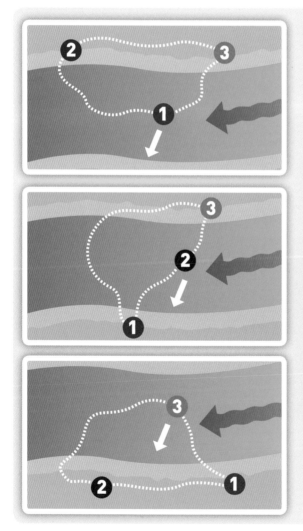

USING ROPES

If there are three people or more, and you have a piece of rope three times as wide as the river, you can use it to make your crossing safer. Tie the ends of the rope together to make a loop.

1 The strongest person should be the first to cross and clips or ties him or herself onto the loop. The other two stand some distance apart along the bank and feed the rope along as the first person crosses. The rope should be kept out of the water as much as possible, so that if necessary the two supporters can pull on the rope and prevent the crosser from being washed away.

2 Once the first person reaches the other side, he or she unclips the loop and the second person ties it on and wades across, supported by the first and third person. If there are more people to cross, they follow the second person in the same way.

3 Finally the third person ties him or herself onto the loop and wades across supported by the first and second person.

CANOES AND KAYAKS

The best way to explore a river is by paddleboat – either a canoe or kayak. But managing a boat, especially a small one, is not as simple as it looks. It requires skill and training.

WHERE TO START

One of the best and most enjoyable ways to learn about canoeing is to join a club. Many canoeing clubs run some kind of introductory or beginners classes which are open to the public. A good way to find out about clubs near you is to visit the British Canoe Union website on **www.bcu.org.uk** – see also Useful Addresses, pages 244–247. A number of leisure, water sport or adventure activity centres also offer courses or classes.

Most people start with recreational canoeing, which is any non-competitive activity, including touring, whitewater rafting, open-canoe sailing and sea kayaking. If you like something more challenging, however, there are plenty of race events too.

You don't have to be especially fit or strong to enjoy canoeing, but you should be able to swim at least 50 metres in clothing.

BUOYANCY AID

Any area of open water, whether it is a lake, canal or river, has the potential to be dangerous. Whenever you go out on any kind of craft you should always wear a buoyancy aid or lifejacket, and keep it on at all times, even while you are tying up or loading gear. It is also sensible to attach an emergency whistle to one of the loops on your lifejacket.

Check that the lifejacket is the right size for you and fits correctly. It should be comfortable and allow you to move and stretch your arms, but tight enough so that it will not slip off if you fall out of the boat or are tumbled about by currents. When you have finished using your lifejacket, always hang it up to dry. Do not leave it lying on the ground or in the bottom of the canoe.

If you are canoeing on fast water, it is best to wear a canoe helmet as well as a lifejacket.

CLOTHING

Whatever you wear when you are in a canoe, you can be certain that it will get wet. Therefore wear clothing that will dry quickly and help you to stay warm even when it is wet, such as nylon or micro-fleece. Avoid cotton, especially denim, as it soaks up water and is cold when wet. It's best to wear lightweight layers – see Chapter 3, page 62. Always take a waterproof jacket (even if the weather is good), and a spare set of clothing. Make sure they are in a watertight bag, so they do not get wet.

Always wear something on your feet. An old pair of lace-up plimsolls or lightweight trainers is ideal. They will not fall off as you move around or get in and out of the canoe, the rubber soles will give your feet more grip on the boat and when you are wading, and they will protect your feet from anything sharp on the riverbed or shoreline.

SAFETY CHECKLIST

☑ Always wear a lifejacket or some kind of buoyancy aid.

☑ Never canoe on your own.

☑ Always make sure that someone on shore knows what you are doing and where you are going.

☑ Check that you have the right clothing and equipment for the weather conditions. Remember that the water may be much colder than the air above it.

☑ Do not go out on fast rivers, estuaries or the sea until you have enough experience.

☑ Take a first aid course and know what to do in an emergency.

☑ If you capsize, stay with the boat – you can use it as an extra buoyancy aid and it is easier to spot from the shore or from above.

WETSUITS

If you know that the water will be cold, or if you are likely to capsize or be soaked with waves or spray, you should consider investing in a wetsuit.

Wetsuits are made of a stretchy, rubber material called neoprene. The suit traps a thin layer of water between the material and your skin. Your body heats up the layer of water to a comfortable temperature, and the wetsuit prevents that heat escaping – as long as the suit fits properly with no loose, baggy areas.

A wetsuit will make an amazing difference to your ability to cope with cold water, but can become uncomfortable to wear for long periods of time. If this is a problem for you, try wearing a rash vest, or 'rashie' underneath your suit.

Choosing a suit depends on what you are doing, and when. Neoprene comes in different thicknesses, so a suit that is mainly for summer wear is usually only 2 mm or 3/2 mm thick. (The 3/2 mm thickness means that the body is 3 mm thick, while the legs and arms are 2 mm thick.) Year-round suits range from 5 mm thicknesses to 7/5 mm.

LONG OR SHORT?

FULL SUIT – this usually has full-length sleeves and legs, although may have short or even detachable sleeves. The thicker the suit, the more it can withstand the cold, but thicker material is also less flexible. Some suits separate the top from the trousers.

SHORTIE – this has short sleeves and short legs, usually finishing just above the elbow and the knee. It gives the wearer maximum freedom of movement, but is intended mainly for summer wear

IF YOUR CANOE CAPSIZES OR SINKS

Do your best to stay in your canoe: even if it is filling with water, you may be able to paddle it to shore and it will give you some protection against obstacles in the water. Use your emergency whistle to attract the attention of other canoeists or people on the shore.

If you are tipped out, try to hang onto your canoe. It will stay afloat even upside down and will help you stay afloat and make it easier for you to be seen. Try to work your way around so that the canoe is between you and any oncoming obstacles.

If you lose contact with your canoe and the water is cold or you are approaching rapids, try to swim to the shore. Do not swim directly across the current; if you can, aim for a spot further down and work your way across to it at an angle.

If you are swept towards rapids, aim your body feet first so that you can use your feet and legs to push yourself away from rocks. Use a backstroke to move yourself around obstacles.

Do not try to stand up in very fast flowing water, even if it is shallow. The current could push you over.

Look out for a rescue rope and do your best to catch it – see page 186. When you do, take hold of the line, not the bag on the end – there may still be a lot more rope inside it.

DRYSUITS

Alternatively, drysuits maintain body temperature by keeping the water out. They cover your body from neck to ankles. They are loose-fitting, but have tight seals around the neck, wrists and ankles. Drysuits work as a watertight barrier, but do not have much warmth in themselves. They are best worn over a layer of fleece thermal clothing.

Because they are baggy, drysuits are comfortable to wear for long periods of time, although they can become sweaty in warm weather. They also need careful handling, as wear and tear can cause them to leak.

A RESCUE ROPE

A rescue rope or throw line is a strong, lightweight rope about 20–25 metres in length that will float on water. It is usually brightly coloured to make it clearly visible. The most useful type of throw line is stored in a throw bag. The rescuer pulls out an arm's length of rope with one hand and, keeping firm hold of that end, throws the bag with the other hand. As the bag travels through the air, the rest of the rope is paid out.

Using a throw rope takes practice. The weight is different to throwing a ball, and your target is likely to be moving. Before you throw, shout or blow your whistle so that the person you are throwing to knows which direction the rope is coming from. Ideally, you want to aim directly at the person in the water, but if in doubt, aim a little upstream of them so at least they have a chance to swim to the rope before the current pushes it back to the bank.

You must also take care to secure your end of the rope, but without wrapping it around your body. The force of the current and the weight of the person on the other end could pull you in.

Always dry and carefully repack a throw rope after use.

CANOEING KIT

Whenever you go out in a canoe or a kayak, check that you have the following:

▶ **BUOYANCY AID** – see page 182.

▶ **HELMET** – for whitewater canoeing or kayaking.

▶ **WHISTLE** – in case you need help, or need to get the attention of someone else who does. The sound of a whistle will carry much further than your voice.

▶ **PERSONAL FIRST-AID KIT** – see Chapter 3, page 66.

▶ **BAILER AND SPONGE** – for scooping out water from inside the boat. A small plastic jug is ideal, as it can be tied to the boat. Do not make the line too long. (A small hand pump can be useful in a kayak.)

▶ **PORTAGE YOKE** – see page 192.

▶ **THROW LINE** – preferably in a throw bag so it can be stored safely in the canoe without getting tangled up. Each group should have at least one throw line.

▶ **RESCUE (OR SAFETY) KNIFE** – with a serrated blade and rounded tip. An essential tool for cutting lines if you or your boat get tangled up. Most have a small hole in the handle so they can be tied to the boat or to a loop on your buoyancy aid.

▶ **EXTRA ROPE** – for tying up the canoe and for securing all your kit to the boat.

▶ **DRY SACKS** – or strong plastic bags securely tied at the neck – for keeping your spare clothes and other belongings dry. If there is room in the canoe, you could use a plastic barrel, but it is still best to put your kit inside a dry sack first.

▶ **KNEE PADS** – kneeling to paddle a canoe gives you better control than sitting, but is painful on the knees after a while.

▶ **FOOD AND WATER** – for energy snacks.

▶ **A HAT** – to keep the sun out of your eyes in summer or to keep your head warm and dry in winter.

▶ **SUNGLASSES** – to protect your eyes from sunlight glinting on the water.

▶ **HEAVY-DUTY WATERPROOF TAPE** - will repair most things and can also be used to wrap around your fingers and palms to prevent paddle blisters.

OPEN CANOES

The canoe most commonly used is the open (or Canadian) canoe. Open canoes are wide-bodied and flat-bottomed with an open top and pointed ends. Traditionally made of wood, the earliest canoes in the world were open dug-outs carved from a tree trunk. Some modern canoes still have a wooden frame and a canvas or wood-panelled body, but most are made of lighter, synthetic materials such as fibreglass.

Open canoes are usually propelled with single-bladed oars, with the canoeist sitting on a plank stretched across the boat or kneeling on the bottom. Most canoes are paddled by one or two people, but there are larger canoes for carrying more passengers.

Open canoes have a wide range of uses, from touring (day trips or longer), to whitewater canoeing, racing and canoe sailing. Some whitewater canoes are covered, which makes them look more like kayaks, but the canoeist still uses a single-bladed paddle and kneels in the middle of the canoe.

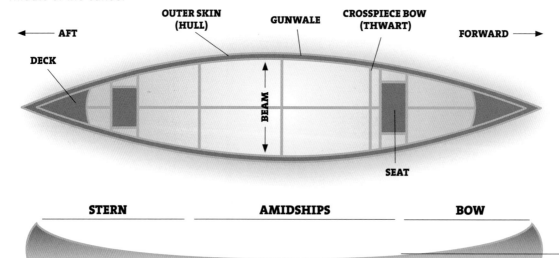

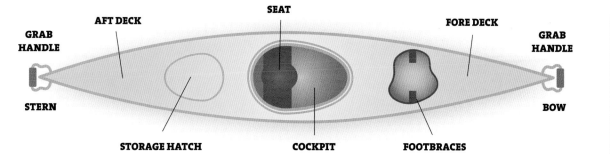

GRAB HANDLE

AFT DECK

SEAT

FORE DECK

GRAB HANDLE

STERN

STORAGE HATCH

COCKPIT

FOOTBRACES

BOW

KAYAKS

The shorter, stubbier hybrid kayak is used for whitewater kayaking.

Kayaks are usually slimmer and lighter than open canoes and have a covered deck with a hole in the centre (the cockpit) for the canoeist to climb in and out. The hole is covered with a waterproof skirt (or spraydeck) that fits around the paddler to prevent water from flooding the hull. It is this skirt that allows kayaks to flip over and come upright again without filling up.

Kayakers use a double-bladed paddle and sit in the centre of the boat with their legs stretched out in front of them. Most kayaks are for single use, although some carry two or three people.

Kayaks are more manoeuvrable than canoes, and are easier to handle in fast, shallow, whitewater rivers. Although longer, flatter versions are also used for touring and sea kayaking.

A CANOE PADDLE

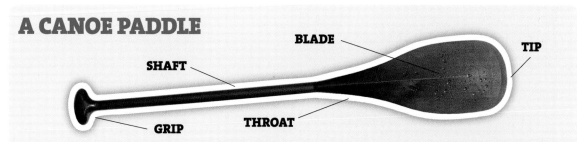

BLADE

TIP

SHAFT

GRIP

THROAT

Paddles vary in length and the material from which they are made – which might be wood, aluminium, fibreglass, plastic or a mixture. The shaft may be straight or bent, and the blade may be long and thin, short and wide, or somewhere in between.

Choosing a paddle is a very personal decision. It depends on your height, strength, type of canoe and how you are using it. A lightweight paddle is always a good starting point, but otherwise try as many different types as possible until you find one that you like.

GETTING INTO A CANOE

When launching a canoe, always place it fully in the water so that it floats – do not position it with one end on the shore and the other in the water. Keep the canoe parallel to the shore while you load it. Store your kit in the bottom of the boat, towards the centre, and make sure it is securely tied down.

Keep the canoe parallel while you climb in. Put one hand on the nearside gunwale and one foot in the centre of the canoe. Bend down to keep your weight low, transfer your balance to the foot in the canoe and grab the gunwale on the other side, lifting your other foot into the boat as you do so.

Immediately kneel or sit in the middle of the boat to keep it stable. Keeping your centre of gravity low in the canoe will make it less likely to flip over. Standing up or leaning too far to one side will unbalance it.

PADDLING FORWARDS

Hold the paddle with one hand on top of the grip and the other hand as far down the shaft as is comfortable. Hold your top arm straight out at about eye level. Extend your lower arm as far forward as it will reach, put the paddle in the water and pull the canoe towards it. You should feel as if the canoe is moving and not the paddle.

Once you have moved past the paddle, lift it up, swing it ahead of you and dip it cleanly into the water again. Try to keep the paddle vertical: if you hold it out at an angle, the canoe will begin to turn rather than move forward. Every five or six strokes, switch your paddle to the other side to ease the strain on your muscles, and keep you going in a straight line.

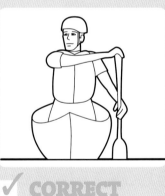

✔ CORRECT

✗ INCORRECT

MOVING FORWARDS AND BACKWARDS

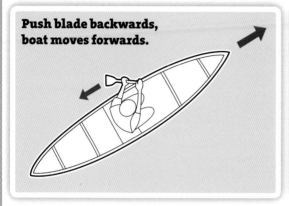

Push blade backwards, boat moves forwards.

Push paddle forwards, boat moves backwards.

Paddle forwards as described (left). To slow a canoe down, stop it, or move it backwards, put the paddle blade into the water next to your hip and push it forwards. Once the paddle is at full stretch, lift it up and bring it back alongside your hip again.

CHANGING DIRECTION

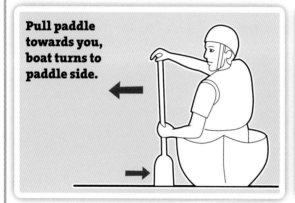

Pull paddle towards you, boat turns to paddle side.

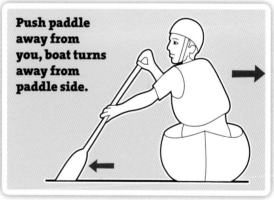

Push paddle away from you, boat turns away from paddle side.

To turn the canoe towards the paddle side, use a draw stroke. Hold the paddle with the blade facing the canoe. Keeping the paddle in line with your body, reach out and dip the blade into the water, then pull the canoe towards the paddle. Lift the blade out before it gets carried under the canoe.

To move the canoe away from the paddle side, you basically reverse the draw stroke (known as a pry). Keeping the paddle in line with your body, dip it into the water close to the side of the canoe and push it away.

TOP TIP Try to keep your hands dry when you paddle. Having wet hands means you are more likely to get blisters.

DOUBLING UP

If there are two people in the canoe, you paddle on opposite sides, one sitting in the bow and one in the stern, and try to synchronize your strokes so that they happen at the same time. To switch sides, the stern paddler calls out to let the bow paddler know to switch on the next stroke.

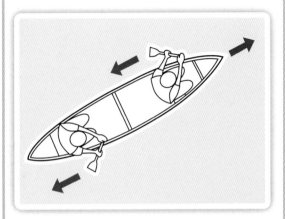

When two people are paddling, the stern paddler's strokes will tend to push the canoe slightly off course. To compensate for this, the stern paddler can use something called a 'J stroke'. This is the same as the forward stroke, but as your body comes level with the paddle in the water, you turn the paddle blade 45 degrees and push it away from the canoe to form the loop at the end of the 'J'.

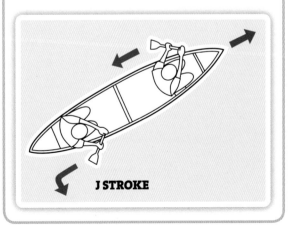

J STROKE

CARRYING A CANOE

If you are canoeing on an unknown stretch of river and think there may be rapids or falls ahead, tie up the canoe and scout ahead on foot. If you are at all uncertain about paddling through what lies ahead, it is far better to portage your canoe – lift it out of the water and carry it downstream.

The best way to portage a canoe is with one person balancing the middle of the boat upside-down on their shoulders. To do this you will need a yoke. Some canoes have a yoke built into the centre thwart, or have a detachable yoke clamped to the side.

Get your boat partner or another canoeist to help you to lift the canoe and position it over your head. Begin by balancing the canoe on its side so the hull rests against your legs. Reach across it and grab the gunwales on both sides, then lift and flip it together.

Once you have the canoe lifted, your partner holds it steady while you move towards the yoke in the centre, keeping both hands on the gunwales on each side. When you have the yoke comfortably positioned on your shoulders, your partner can duck out and walk ahead to lead the way and warn you of any obstacles on the path.

GETTING INTO A KAYAK

Kayaks are light and mobile, and move with your movements. This makes them lots of fun to use, but can be tricky until you get the hang of them.

First, fix the skirt around your waist. Slide your kayak into shallow water so it is parallel to the shore. Keep one hand on it at all times and hold your paddle in your other hand. Position yourself next to the cockpit and place your paddle across the back of the cockpit, up against the rim.

CARRYING A KAYAK

Carrying a kayak is usually a lot more manageable than carrying a canoe. As with a canoe, turn the kayak on its side and rest the hull against your legs. Take hold of both sides of the cockpit and hoist it up so that the edge of the cockpit rests on your shoulder. Move it around a bit until the kayak is well balanced.

Facing the front, lean across and put the hand nearest the boat on top of the paddle on the far side of the cockpit, so that your palm is pressing down on the paddle shaft and your fingers are holding onto the cockpit rim. With your other hand holding the paddle and cockpit on the other side, ease your bottom onto the back of the boat so that you can carefully swing your legs into the cockpit – one at a time.

Take a moment to adjust your balance, and when you feel steady, slide into the cockpit. Lift the paddle over your head to the front of the kayak and secure your skirt to the cockpit rim.

PADDLING A KAYAK

The two blades on a kayak paddle are slightly curved. The concave, or inward-facing, curve is the front of the blade, and the convex (outward facing) curve is the back of the blade. You paddle with the fronts of the blades facing towards you. Think of them as scooping through the water. Hold the paddle with both hands, keeping them a little more than shoulder width apart. Do not grip the shaft too tightly.

FORWARDS AND BACKWARDS

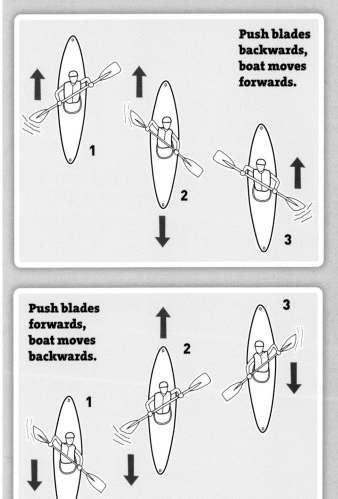

Push blades backwards, boat moves forwards.

1

2

3

Push blades forwards, boat moves backwards.

1

2

3

To move forwards, sit upright and turn your upper body to the left and extend the right blade as far forwards as it will go. Dip the blade into the water close to the bow. Pull your right arm back and push your left arm forwards, turning your upper body to the right.

As the kayak moves past the blade in the water, keep turning your body until the left blade is fully extended to the front. Then lift the right blade and dip the left, pulling your left arm back and pushing your right arm forward.

To slow down or move backwards, use the reverse of the forward stroke. Turn to the right and dip the right blade into the water behind you. Push forwards with your right arm and pull your left arm backwards, turning to the left as you do so. Lift the right blade and dip the left blade into the water behind you.

Sweep right blade backwards, boat turns to left.

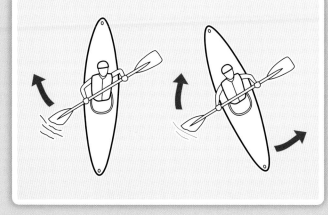

Sweep right blade forwards, boat turns to right.

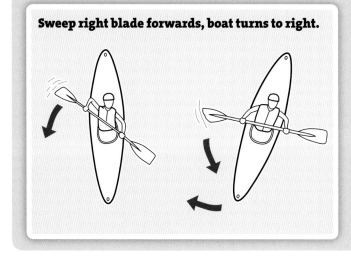

TURNING SIDEWAYS

To turn to the left you use a sweep stroke to the right. Bring the paddle level across the front of the cockpit. Make sure the blades are facing you. Extend the right blade as far forward as possible before dipping it in the water. Sweep the paddle in a wide arc towards the stern, turning your body as you do so. By repeating the stroke you can turn the kayak in a complete circle.

To turn the bow to the right, use the sweep stroke to the left. Alternatively, you can use a reverse sweep. This stroke is exactly how it sounds, instead of dipping the blade to the front and sweeping in an arc to the back, you dip the blade at the back and sweep towards the front. This slows the boat down and turns it in the same direction as the side on which the stroke is being made.

ROLLING OVER

Kayaks capsize a lot; when whitewater kayaking, it's part of the experience. The technique for climbing out of a capsized kayak under the water, and getting back into it from the water, is best learned from an experienced instructor. An instructor will also teach you how to perform an Eskimo roll. This allows you to stay in a capsized kayak and turn it the right way up from a seated position. You need to practise these manoeuvres in very calm water – instructors often use a swimming pool – and be quite proficient before testing them out on a river. You will also be taught how to help another kayaker who gets into difficulties when capsizing.

CLIMBING

All forms of climbing, whether indoors or outdoors, involve risk, but learning the skills and techniques of climbing can give you an incredible sense of achievement and confidence in your own abilities.

TYPES OF CLIMBING

There are a range of activities that come under the heading of climbing:

Rock climbing with ropes can be done indoors on artificial climbing walls, or outside on the rock face. It requires a minimum of two people – the climber, who is tied to a rope, and the belayer, who holds and controls the rope in case the climber should slip or fall.

Bouldering is a style of climbing limited to short routes over large boulders or low rock faces. Its focus is on individual moves or short sequences, and often involves a degree of problem-solving. It does not use ropes, so most climbers use crash pads to land on. It can be used as a form of training to build up strength for rock climbing, but is also a recognized sport in its own right.

Scrambling is a mixture of rock climbing, bouldering and hill walking. It often takes place in high or mountainous terrain, including some traversing of steep ridges.

Ice climbing is a more extreme version of rock climbing as you are climbing on ice, or rock and ice. Some indoor climbing centres have ice walls that allow people to experience ice climbing in a more controlled environment.

Mountaineering or Alpine climbing involves all the elements of hill walking and climbing.

HOW TO START

Most people begin climbing on an artificial climbing wall at an indoor centre. There are around 500 or more indoor centres in the UK and they will usually have instructors on hand who will give advice and offer regular training sessions to those who want them.

Alternatively, there are a large number of climbing schools and clubs around the UK. However, climbing clubs are often formed by groups of enthusiasts, and although some of their members may be very experienced climbers and will give advice and help, they do not necessarily give formal instruction. To find a centre, club or school near you, try the British Mountaineering Council website at **www.thebmc.co.uk**, or UK Climbing at **www.ukclimbing.com**. There are also climbing holidays that will teach the basics – for example, see the National Mountain Centre website at **www.pyb.co.uk**.

WHAT YOU WILL NEED

As with most sports, climbing requires specialist equipment – see next page – particularly ropes. It is extremely dangerous to climb with damaged or inadequate ropes. Most of this equipment, including climbing shoes, can usually be hired at indoor and outdoor climbing centres, and should be supplied on any training course or holiday.

If you intend to take climbing seriously, it may be worth buying a helmet and a pair of climbing shoes, and eventually your own harness. It is generally not a good idea to buy second-hand climbing equipment as there is no way of knowing how much 'wear and tear' it has had.

Climbing is like any other outdoor activity, in that you will also need to take a certain amount of personal kit with you. This should include extra clothing for warmth and protection from rain, high-energy foods, water, a mobile phone and a first aid kit – see Chapter 3, pages 64–66.

CLIMBING EQUIPMENT

Basic climbing equipment includes:

▶ **ROPES** – these must be specially certified climbing ropes. There are two types: static and dynamic. Dynamic rope will stretch under pressure, which means that it will absorb some of the impact of a fall. Most climbing is done with dynamic rope. Static rope does not stretch and is used for carrying equipment or in rescue situations.

▶ **HARNESS** – this wraps around your waist and legs and has a central loop that attaches to the belay and other safety ropes. If you fall, the harness holds you securely to the ropes. It also has thinner loops for attaching other equipment you might need.

▶ **BELAY DEVICE** – to help the belayer control the belaying rope.

▶ **KARABINERS** – strong metal clips that are used as links to connect ropes and equipment to the rock or to the climber's harness.

▶ **PROTECTION DEVICES** – various pieces of equipment inserted into rock to help prevent a climber from falling.

▶ **CLIMBING SHOES** – are close-fitting and lightweight, with moulded rubber soles. They are designed to give your feet maximum grip on the rock.

▶ **HELMET** – a properly fitting safety helmet is vital for any rock-climbing activity.

▶ **CHALK** – powder is used on your hands to absorb sweat and prevent your hands from slipping on the rock.

TOP ROPING

Most people learn to climb using top roping. This means that they are attached to one end of a belay rope, which is threaded through a strong anchor point at the top of the climb. The other end of the rope is fed through a belay device and controlled by a belayer at the top or bottom of the climb.

As the climber climbs, the belayer takes in the belay rope, allowing the climber room to move but staying alert and ready to hold the rope if the climber slips. When the climber reaches the top, the belayer will lower them to the ground again. A climber's safety depends on their belayer. Belaying requires as much skill and training as climbing, and most climbers form partnerships that allow them to take it in turns to climb and belay.

Climbing requires a thorough knowledge of a few specific knots, especially the Figure of Eight, for tying the climbing rope to a harness, and the Clove Hitch and Prussic Knots – see Chapter 7, pages 159 and 163.

LEAD CLIMBING

Indoor centres generally have pre-fixed top ropes, but on an outdoor climb you will need to set up a top rope anchor. This is done by an experienced lead climber. The lead climber is roped to the belayer below. While climbing, the lead climber places protection devices into cracks and crevices in the rock face and clips the belaying rope to these so as to break their fall if they slip. On arrival at a suitable anchoring point, the lead climber establishes a series of anchors to spread the strain should the second climber fall, and becomes the belayer while the second person climbs.

CLIMBING SKILLS

Climbing requires not just a good head for heights, but strong hands and feet. As you climb, your fingers are continually searching for reliable handholds. These can vary from fingertip ledges to pocket crevices or outcrops you can wrap your whole hand around.

At the same time, your feet and legs are taking most of your body weight and providing most of the power to push you up the rock face. You need to keep your body vertical – holding yourself out from the rock face rather than clinging to it. There are various techniques and ways of using your feet when climbing which you can only learn by doing it. As with all sports, the key is to practise.

Narrow, fingertip holds are also called crimp holds. They are not the best holds to take as they put a lot of strain on the fingers.

SAFETY CHECK : Any form of climbing is a high-risk activity and should not be undertaken without the correct training and equipment. Anyone who climbs must be prepared to take absolute responsibility for themselves, and the safety of their equipment and of their climbing partners. If you are ever in doubt about any aspect of a climb, do not do it.

ABSEILING

Once you have reached the top of your climb, the easiest way to get down is usually to be lowered down by your belaying partner. Another way is by abseiling or rappelling.

Although many non-climbers see abseiling as an exciting adventure sport, many climbers view it as a high risk. This is because non-climbers abseil under tightly controlled conditions, whereas on a rock face abseiling relies entirely on the strength of the anchor, the rope, and the skill of the climber. However, anyone who intends to climb outdoors needs to know how to abseil correctly as it may be the only way to get off a cliff face safely.

How it works . . .

Abseiling involves lowering yourself down a cliff (or from any other height) using a rope with one end securely attached to an anchor and the other reaching the ground at the bottom. The anchor for an abseil may be a natural feature, such as a tree trunk or a boulder, or a climber's device fixed into a rock face.

The rope is fed through a belay or abseiling device linked to your harness. Keeping hold of the rope, you gradually feed it through the device to lower yourself down.

Depending on how you feed the rope through it, the abseiling device applies greater or lesser friction to the rope to slow down or speed up the rate at which the rope slides through it – and therefore the rate at which you travel. The skill is in keeping control of the rope. At the same time, you lean away from the rock face and use your feet and legs to keep yourself horizontal and maintain your balance. Most people learn to abseil by lowering themselves down a gentle slope, before moving on to higher and steeper structures.

And how it doesn't

In movies, it is common to see abseilers leaping and swinging down the side of a rock face, but in practice this is rarely done unless you are absolutely certain of the strength of your anchor and your rope. Leaps and swings place additional stress on the ropes and anchors and few climbers are willing to risk the possibility of a break when there is nothing else between them and the ground to break their fall.

OTHER SPORTS

There are a great many ways of exploring and enjoying the outdoors, from cycling to sailing. There is not enough space to cover them all in this book, but there are many organizations and websites that will give you lots of information about them – a selection is included in 'Useful Addresses' at the back of this book, pages 244–247. Here are a few ideas to get you started.

CAVING

If you like a challenge that's out of the ordinary, try caving. As with climbing, caving is a potentially dangerous sport that requires specific skills and training.

The best way to begin is to join a caving club or go on a course with a registered adventure centre. There are caving clubs all around the UK and you can find a list of them on **www.trycaving.co.uk**, which is a website run by the British Caving Association (BCA) specially for those interested in finding out about caving. The BCA's main website – **www.british-caving.org.uk** – also lists clubs that are members.

Clubs organize caving trips and share knowledge and equipment. Some clubs will only let you join if you are 18 and over, and some will accept 16 and over. For children and families, or to get an introductory 'taster', try an adventure centre. You will find some listed under 'Commercial Links' in the 'Links' section of the Try Caving websites, or to find an instructor offering courses in your area, go to the BCA website and click on 'Training' then 'New Caver'.

CAVING TECHNIQUES

Basic caving involves scrambling up and around piles of rock, sometimes crouching down and crawling on your hands and knees, or even on your belly, to squeeze through low-ceilinged passages, or using your hands and feet to push yourself up a narrow chimney.

To explore some caves you will need a certain amount of rope training. Single Rope Technique or SRT is a method used by cavers to lower themselves into and pull themselves out of vertical caves or potholes. The easiest way to learn SRT is at an indoor climbing centre. Using SRT to lower yourself is basically the same as abseiling but with slightly different devices that give you greater control over your rope. Learning to climb up the rope requires hand-held clamping devices.

WHAT TO WEAR

▶ **HELMET** – that fits properly, with a chinstrap and a light mounting.

▶ **CAVING LAMP** – that attaches to your helmet and leaves your hands free.

▶ **ONE-PIECE OVERALL OR BOILER SUIT** – or jacket and overtrousers, preferably waterproof. Caves are usually wet and muddy.

▶ **WELLINGTONS** – with non-slip soles are the best things to wear on your feet. Otherwise you can wear walking boots, but they should not have raised bootlace hooks as these can catch in crevices.

▶ **OLD CLOTHES** – that are warm and comfortable. It's best to wear two thin layers rather than one thick layer – a long-sleeved thermal T-shirt and fleece, for example, with thick walking socks and tracksuit trousers. Do not wear jeans: they get heavy and uncomfortable when wet. Remember that caves are cold, no matter what the temperature is outside.

▶ **KNEE PADS** – are useful for protecting your knees on long crawls.

▶ **HEAVY-DUTY GLOVES** – to protect your hands from sharp rock edges.

▶ **SPARE CLOTHING** – to change into at the end of your trip.

▶ **SUPPLIES** – of food and water to keep you going.

▶ **SRT KIT** – including a harness with a chest strap, and ascending and descending devices. This is usually supplied when you go on a caving course.

CYCLING

Instead of hiking and camping, why not cycle with a tent? As more and more people try to leave their cars at home, cycling is the obvious answer – it's healthy, virtually free once you have bought a bike, good for the environment, and fun to do.

Types of cycle vary, depending on what you want to do and where you want to go. A basic bike that rides equally well on roads and tracks is known as a hybrid bike. Hybrid bikes are good all-purpose bikes with decent gears for getting you up and down hills and flattish handlebars that allow you to sit fairly upright.

If you want something sturdier to carry more equipment, look at trekking bikes or touring bikes. These come with more accessories included, such as mudguards, bottle holders and luggage carriers. They may have stronger back wheels to take more weight, wider tyres and differently shaped handlebars that allow the rider to change hand positions.

EQUIPMENT

If you are planning to do mainly day trips, you will not need a lot of equipment – just a helmet, water bottle, snacks, a map, mobile phone, first aid kit, wind- and rainproof jacket, bike lock, pump and basic bicycle repair kit, and a small rucksack. It's uncomfortable to cycle far with a heavy rucksack, so if you are travelling any distance at all it is better and safer to fit a rear carrier rack and panniers.

If you are touring and camping out at night, racks and panniers are a must. It is best to get the strongest racks and panniers you can, as they do give out under the strain, especially when travelling on bumpy tracks. You will probably need front panniers as well as rear, but make sure they are fitted correctly as a badly fitted rack can cause an accident. A handlebar bag that you can easily unclip and carry is useful for personal items, such as keys and money.

Aside from personal and camping kit – see Chapter 5, pages 102–103 – you will need a full repair kit. This should include a puncture repair kit, tyre levers, a set of spanners, Allen keys, pliers, screwdrivers, a spare valve, inner tube, brake blocks and cables, gear cables, chain links and a few wheel spokes.

TOP TIPS

✚ Always ensure your cycle has front and rear lights and reflectors. You may not be planning to cycle at night, but you can easily be delayed or find yourself cycling in bad weather or through a tunnel when lights are a real safety issue. It is also illegal in the UK to cycle at night without lights.

✚ Make sure you know how to keep your bike in good repair, mend a puncture or replace a tyre, adjust the brakes and replace brake blocks or cable, repair a broken chain, adjust the gears, and so on. If possible, take a cycle maintenance course. Check CTC – the Cyclists' Touring Club on www.ctc.org.uk

✚ Always wear a helmet.

✚ Know the Highway Code, especially the section on Cyclists – for more information go to www.direct.gov.uk and click on Travel and Transport, the Highway Code.

CYCLE ROUTES

Organizations such as Sustrans www.sustrans.org.uk are working with local authorities to open up more and more cycling routes, and the National Cycle Network now has nearly 20,000 kilometres of routes and links around Britain. A map of the National Cycle Network can be downloaded from the Sustrans website, as can information and routes for long-distance rides throughout the UK.

FISHING

One of the other great outdoor sports is fishing. People fish for many reasons. Some see it as a form of relaxation and a way of enjoying a peaceful afternoon by a river. Others simply enjoy practising the skill that it takes and the insight it gives them into the natural world.

One thing is certainly true: it is not half as easy as it looks, yet anyone can do it using anything from a bent piece of wire on a line to the most expensive fishing tackle you can buy.

GETTING PERMISSION

The one thing you will need is a fishing licence. Anyone over the age of 12 must have an Environment Agency rod licence to fish for freshwater fish, salmon, trout or eels in England and Wales. If you are fishing on private land, you will also need a fishing permit from the landowner. In Northern Ireland you will need a local licence. The licence laws in Scotland are a little more complicated, as it depends on the type of fish and where you want to catch it. It's best to check with the local authorities before you start fishing.

A GUIDE TO GOOD ANGLING

☒ Never leave a fishing rod unattended with its line in the water – in fact, it is illegal to do so in the UK. Do not leave a baited rod lying on the riverside, either, as the bait will attract wildlife which could then be caught by the hook.

☑ Unless you need a fish you have caught for food, you should always release it back into the water – gently. For this reason it is best to use barbless or semi-barbed hooks as they are easier to unhook and cause much less damage to the fish and other wildlife, especially birds.

☑ When handling a fish you are going to release, always try to keep it in the water as much as possible. If you do lift it out, make sure your hands are wet and never put it on a dry surface (this will strip away the protective layer of mucus from the fish's body).

☑ A live fish is not easy to hold, so always kneel down or sit with it in your hands if you are having your picture taken, for example, then immediately put it back in the water. Never throw the fish back, but gently hold it upright just below the surface with its head upstream, until it regains the strength to swim away.

☒ Weighting your fishing line with lead weights of most sizes is illegal in the UK as it poisons the water, the fish and birds – especially water fowl such as swans, geese, ducks and others. However, although non-toxic, lead-free fishing weights are available, some types of lead weights are allowed and some anglers still use them, in spite of their effect on wildlife and the environment.

☒ Broken and discarded fishing line should never be left lying on the riverbank or thrown into the water. Waste fishing line causes a serious problem to birds, which may get tangled in it and starve or seriously damage themselves trying to get free. Tangles of waste line also cause problems for swimmers, boats and other anglers, and add to river pollution. Always take broken line home and cut it up into small pieces before disposing of it.

☑ The best way to learn how to fish well and responsibly is with an experienced instructor. The Professional Anglers Association, for example, and the Angling Trust will give you advice on finding a fishing club or qualified coach in your area. Contact: www.paauk.com or www.anglingtrust.net

CHAPTER 9:

IN AN EMERGENCY

Accidents happen – they are a fact of life, and we should not let fear of them unduly limit our actions. The best way to prevent accidents is not to stay at home, but to recognize and plan for potential risks, avoid or limit them where we can, and be prepared to deal with them when we must.

MANAGING RISK

Any sporting activity contains an element of risk, and the challenge this presents is part of the adventure. The key element in preventing a potential risk from becoming an actual danger is in the way that it is managed.

ASSESSING THE SITUATION

Whatever the situation or activity, the first thing to do is to carry out a risk assessment. This means looking at all the things that could possibly go wrong, and then working out how to prevent or reduce the likelihood of them actually happening.

Simple risk assessment is something most of us do without thinking in our everyday lives. Whenever you cross a road, for example, you instinctively stop and check for oncoming traffic. If the road is busy and the traffic is moving fast you might decide to go a different way and avoid crossing the road altogether. You might look for a pedestrian crossing and so lessen the potential danger, or you might wait until you feel there is a suitable gap in the traffic. Every time is different, and in each situation you use your experience, your knowledge of your own abilities and any previous training to help you decide what to do.

Carrying out any risk assessment draws on these same skills, although if the situation is unfamiliar you may also need to carry out some research in order to be fully aware of the potential problems or to find possible solutions to those problems.

HAZARDS AND RISKS

The following two terms are frequently used when carrying out a risk assessment:

A HAZARD – is anything that could cause harm. With outdoor activities, for example, this could include extreme weather conditions, difficult terrain, or fast-flowing water.

A RISK – is the chance, whether high or low, that someone will be harmed by a hazard.

An important part of a risk assessment is deciding a hazard's significance. In other words, the level of risk it could pose. This helps to determine the action you take in order to minimize that risk. For example, if you are likely to be hiking in severe weather conditions you would plan to take appropriate clothing and equipment. However, if the conditions include flood warnings you would probably change your planned route or even cancel the trip altogether.

SHARED RISK

There is a difference between managing your own risk, and taking part in a group activity where the potential risk is shared. In any risk assessment, the leader of a group must take into account the abilities of every member of the group. Different situations can present different levels of risk for each person. If canoeing, for example, some members of a group may be stronger swimmers than others.

At the same time, each member of the group has a responsibility to safeguard themselves and others, and not put anyone at risk by their behaviour. This may mean deliberately slowing down, watching out for less able members of the group, or letting others know that you are having difficulties or are concerned about something even if you are worried about what they might think of you.

REVIEW AND REASSESS

No matter how carefully you plan a trip, when you are outdoors events can happen that are unexpected and beyond your control. A part of risk management is understanding and accepting this and being ready to adapt and change your plans in response to new situations. Even to the extent of calling the trip off and heading back if that is clearly the safest option.

As situations present themselves, no matter how minor, consider the implications of your actions before you do anything. For example, if recent rain has made a steep track slippery, you might consider what could happen if someone slipped and fell. Determining factors could include the pitch of the slope and whether or not there are trees or shrubs to use as handholds; the weight of the packs you are carrying; and the strength and agility of everyone in the group. Also, whether there is an easier, alternative route.

Even if the decision is to carry on, the fact that you have all thought about and discussed it will make everyone aware of the potential hazard and take greater care.

ASSESSMENT CHECKLIST

The following diagram indicates some of the factors that should be continually reassessed during an outdoor activity. Bear in mind that some of these factors may change or new ones be added depending on the type of activity.

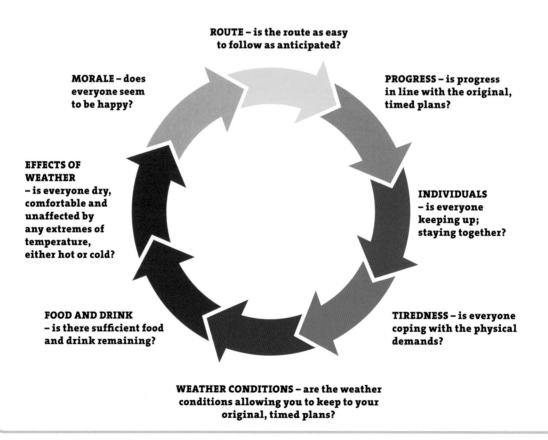

ROUTE – is the route as easy to follow as anticipated?

PROGRESS – is progress in line with the original, timed plans?

INDIVIDUALS – is everyone keeping up; staying together?

TIREDNESS – is everyone coping with the physical demands?

WEATHER CONDITIONS – are the weather conditions allowing you to keep to your original, timed plans?

FOOD AND DRINK – is there sufficient food and drink remaining?

EFFECTS OF WEATHER – is everyone dry, comfortable and unaffected by any extremes of temperature, either hot or cold?

MORALE – does everyone seem to be happy?

READY FOR RISK

Experience is a great teacher, but if a situation is unfamiliar to you it is usually a good idea to listen to your instincts. If you feel uneasy about something, even if you are not sure why, then it is wise to take the time to really think through your options.

Learning a few useful skills will also stand you in good stead in an emergency. Developing good navigational skills will give you confidence and help you avoid the many hazards that can result from getting lost. You should, of course, always travel with a fully-charged mobile phone, but if you are in an area with a very patchy network you will need your maps and compass to identify and find the quickest routes to get help.

Basic first-aid training is also important, especially if you are likely to be travelling in more remote areas. Some first-aid techniques are contained in this chapter, but it is best to complete a first-aid course with an organization such as the British Red Cross, St John Ambulance, or St Andrew's First Aid (St Andrew's Ambulance Association), in Scotland. All these organisations have good websites – see Useful Addresses, pages 244–247.

TOP TIPS

As an individual, the best preparation for managing your own risk is:

+ **Keep yourself in good physical shape.**

+ **Know where you are going and what to expect.**

+ **Make sure you have the right clothing for the conditions you will face.**

+ **Make sure you have the right equipment, in good working order.**

+ **Make sure you have sufficient food and water.**

+ **Find out beforehand where the nearest help points will be along your route.**

For more information on navigation, see Chapter 4, Finding the Way.

EMERGENCY FIRST AID KIT

For short journeys and day hikes, a basic first-aid kit should be part of everyone's personal kit – see Chapter 3, page 66. But for longer or more remote journeys one member of your team should carry a more extensive first-aid kit – and know how to use it. The organizations listed on the previous page, among others, sell a variety of first-aid kits and supplies (see Useful Addresses, pages 244–247 for website addresses).

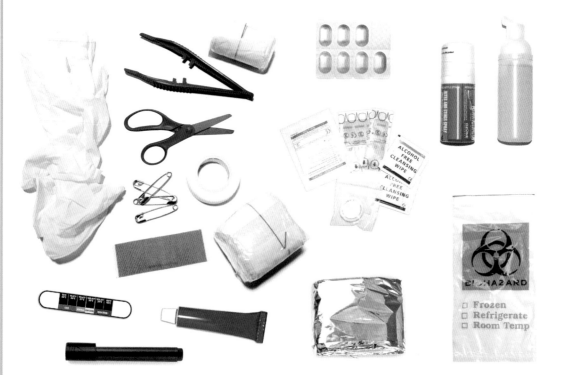

A larger kit might include:

- Foil/heat-retaining blanket for hypothermia.
- Resuscitation face shield.
- Disposable thermometer.
- Disposable pen light.
- Blunt-nosed scissors.
- Disposable gloves.
- Alcohol hand-cleaning gel.
- Biohazard waste bags for used dressings until they can be safely disposed of.
- Instant ice packs.

- Rehydration drink sachets.
- Burnshield dressings.
- Small phials of eyewash.
- Eye pad dressings
- Antiseptic cleansing wipes.
- Antiseptic cream.
- Safety pins, for securing bandages.
- Surgical tape.
- Steri-strips for closing wounds.
- Sterile gauze swabs.
- Large, medium and small

sterile dressing pads.
- Crepe bandages.
- Triangular bandages to support broken bones or sprains.
- Selection of plasters, waterproof and fabric, including blister plasters.
- Insect bite or sting pads.
- Paracetamol or other pain relievers (check for any allergic response to these or other medications beforehand).

IF AN ACCIDENT HAPPENS

The first thing to do is to stay calm. Do not make the situation worse by putting yourself or anyone else in danger in your attempt to help the injured person.

Assess the situation as quickly and carefully as possible to work out what has happened and what needs to be done. Check the site for any further danger, either to the injured person or persons, or to yourself or the rest of the group. Try to make the area safe or move away from the danger. Do not move the casualty if this could make his or her condition worse, unless it is more dangerous to leave them where they are.

Do your best to reassure the injured person. Talk to them calmly and explain what you are doing. Do what you can to find out how bad the injury is and give them whatever treatment you can. If more than one person is injured, deal with the most serious case first.

GETTING HELP

If the injury is serious it is vital to get medical help as soon as possible. If possible, call the emergency services (999 in the UK). Take a moment before you call to think about what you will say.

The emergency services will need to know precisely where you are and may want you to give them a map reference and grid co-ordinates, or direct them to a nearby landmark. If you are lost or are unsure of where you are, give them your last known location and briefly describe the journey you took from that point.

Explain what has happened and describe the physical and emotional state of the casualty or casualties as concisely and clearly as you can. Describe any difficulties or dangers at your location, such as heavy rain, or a steep incline, so they will know what equipment they will need to bring.

Stay on the phone until the emergency operator tells you to hang up.

If members of your group have to go for help, make sure they know which direction to go in and have all the information they will need to give to the emergency services. It is best to write down all the information you can about the situation, including a detailed description of where you are.

While you are waiting for help to arrive, keep the injured person and the rest of your group as warm and as dry as possible and treat your patient for shock – see page 214.

SAFETY CHECKLIST

☑ **Stay calm**

☑ **Assess the situation**

☑ **Make the area safe**

☑ **Administer reassurance and first aid**

☑ **Get help**

For more information on search and rescue situations and survival skills, see pages 226–243.

BASIC FIRST AID

The following first aid procedures describe some of the most common conditions that can happen as a result of an accident or other emergency. However, this section is only intended as a guide and is by no means comprehensive. Any group travelling in a remote region should ensure that at least one member of their party has received first aid training.

SHOCK

Shock is a physical response the body can have to pain, injury or other conditions. It may happen instantly or some hours after an injury. Shock can be life-threatening if not treated effectively.

Signs of shock include:

▶ **Pale, cold but sweaty skin**

▶ **Rapid heartbeat**

▶ **Shallow, fast breathing**

▶ **Feeling faint or dizzy**

▶ **Thirst**

Treatment:

1. **Treat any obvious injuries.**
2. **Lay the person down on a warm surface, such as a blanket or rug.**
3. **Prop their feet up to lift them above heart level.**
4. **Loosen any tight or restrictive clothing.**
5. **If necessary, cover them with a blanket to maintain their body warmth (but do not let them get too hot).**
6. **Talk to them calmly and reassuringly.**
7. **Do not give them food or liquid until help arrives or they have recovered.**
8. **Call 999 for help.**

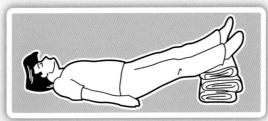

UNCONSCIOUSNESS

If someone is unconscious they may be having problems breathing, in which case you must act as quickly as possible.

1. Check the airway:

Place one hand on the forehead and two fingers under the chin. Gently tilt the head back. Remove any obstruction from the mouth and nose.

2. Check for breathing:

Can you see movement in the chest or abdomen? Can you hear them breathing? Can you feel their breath against the side of your cheek when you hold your face close to their mouth and nose?

▶ **If they are not breathing – resuscitate.**

▶ **If they are breathing – consider moving into the recovery position (page 216).**

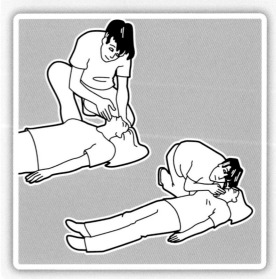

RESUSCITATION

If someone is not breathing, you must first call 999. Then you must give the casualty CPR – which stands for cardio-pulmonary resuscitation.

1. Make sure their chin is lifted and the head tilted back.
2. Place one hand on top of the other and put the heel of your hand in the centre of their chest, just above the end of the breastbone. Press the heel of your hand down firmly (4–5 cm), then release.
3. Do this 30 times, then give 2 rescue breaths.
4. To give rescue breaths, pinch the person's nose between your finger and thumb. Place your mouth completely over their mouth and blow steadily for about 2 seconds. Do this twice.
5. Repeat 30 chest compressions and 2 rescue breaths until their breathing restarts or help arrives. By continuing until medical help arrives you may manage to keep someone alive.

CPR FOR CHILDREN

Start with 5 initial rescue breaths, then continue with 30 chest compressions and 2 breaths as described.

CPR FOR DROWNING

Start with 5 initial rescue breaths, then continue with 30 chest compressions and 2 breaths as described. If you are on your own, give one minute of CPR before calling the emergency services.

SAFETY CHECK

You must not practise CPR on someone who is breathing. The best way to learn CPR is from a trained first-aid instructor.

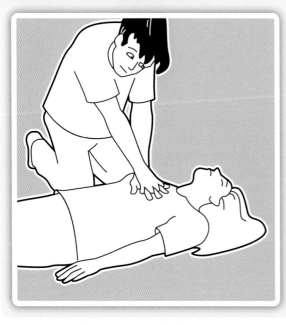
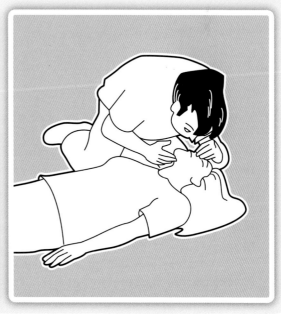

For more information on helping someone who is drowning, see Chapter 8, page 178.

RECOVERY POSITION

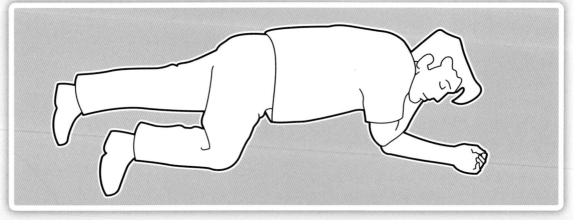

If someone is unconscious but breathing normally, they should be put into the recovery position. Important: DO NOT move them if you think they may have a spinal injury, unless there is a danger that they may vomit and choke.

1. Move the arm nearest to you at a right angle to the body – elbow bent and palm upwards.

2. Lift the other arm across the body and place the hand under the cheek nearest to you.

3. Straighten the leg nearest to you, and raise the knee of the other leg until the foot is flat on the ground.

4. Use one hand to keep the casualty's hand against their cheek and your other hand to pull the raised knee towards you, and roll the casualty onto their side.

5. Place their top leg so that the knee is bent and the thigh is at a right angle to the body. This will stop them from rolling onto their stomach.

6. Check that their head is tilted slightly back and the chin is at a right angle to the ground. This will keep their airways open. Make sure they are still breathing normally, and stay with them.

7. Call for help.

SAFETY CHECK

A spinal injury may be caused by a fall, a head injury, or any impact injury such as a car accident. It can damage the nerves in the spinal cord and lead to paralysis. Indications of a spinal injury may include any awkward twisting of the body or head, numbness, lack of feeling or paralysis in the limbs, headache or neck pain.

If you think someone may have suffered a spinal injury, you should advise them to keep still. Do not move them unless their life is in further danger, as movement could make their condition much worse. Get medical help, and while waiting kneel behind their head and support it with your hands while keeping it in the same position. Do not lift or try to reposition or straighten it. If they are wearing a helmet, do not try to remove it. Check that they are breathing and, if necessary, give them CPR (page 215), but in this case DO NOT tilt the head back. Cover them with coats or a blanket to keep them warm.

DIARRHOEA AND VOMITING

Diarrhoea and vomiting, or gastroenteritis, can be caused by a viral or bacterial infection, food poisoning or drinking contaminated water. However, there are other causes, such as a side effect of taking a particular medicine, anxiety, or a more serious condition. It may be accompanied by stomach pains and fever. Gastroenteritis does not usually last more than a few days. If it does, get a medical check up.

Treatment:

1. It is important to drink lots of fluids to avoid becoming dehydrated. If drinking makes you vomit, take small sips as often as possible.
2. If you have rehydration sachets, follow the instructions on the packet to mix them with water.
3. Rest as much as you can.
4. Eat starchy foods (bread, potatoes, pasta) as soon as you are able.

SAFETY CHECK

Gastroenteritis can be infectious and the best way to avoid reinfecting yourself or passing it on to other people is to thoroughly wash your hands, food utensils, soiled clothes or bedding with soap, detergent or an antibacterial cleaner. It is best to avoid food preparation if possible.

SUNBURN

If someone is suffering from sunburned or blistered skin, move them immediately into the shade. Drink cool liquids and cool the skin with tepid water. If the skin blisters, it should be protected by a light, dry dressing. DO NOT burst the blisters. Cover the skin or stay out of the sun until the sunburn has faded.

SAFETY CHECK

Always wear adequate sun lotion and protect your face and eyes with a sunhat and sunglasses.

NOSE BLEED

1. Sit down and lean forward with chin lowered.
2. Pinch the bridge of the nose, just below the hard, bony bit and breathe through the mouth until the nose stops bleeding. This could take at least 10–15 minutes.
3. Do not blow or rub the nose for the next few hours.

HYPOTHERMIA

Hypothermia is what happens when someone spends too long in a cold condition and their body temperature drops one or two degrees below the normal body temperature of 37°C. If the body temperature drops more than one or two degrees, it can cause death.

Signs of hypothermia include:

▶ Shivering, pale cold skin

▶ Apathy, confusion, unusual behaviour, disorientation

▶ Lethargy or hyperactivity

▶ Slow and shallow breathing

▶ Slow or erratic pulse

Treatment:

1. If outdoors, find shelter.

2. Make sure the casualty is dressed in warm, dry clothes, including a hat and gloves if possible.

3. Cover them with extra clothing, blankets, sleeping bag or a survival blanket, and make sure there is something warm between their body and the ground.

4. If they are fully conscious, give them a hot sweet drink or sweet food such as honey or chocolate.

5. Stay with them and do not let them sleep until you are sure their temperature is back to normal.

SAFETY CHECK

☑ If heat loss is rapid, warm up rapidly.

☑ If heat loss is slow, warm up slowly.

DEHYDRATION

About three-quarters of our body is made up of water, yet we cannot store water and are constantly losing it through breathing, sweating and passing urine. If we do not replace the water we lose, our body will begin to dehydrate and eventually die. People can become dehydrated under any conditions, simply by failing to sufficiently replace their natural fluid loss.

Signs of dehydration include:

▶ Feeling thirsty

▶ Dry mouth, eyes and lips

▶ Lack of appetite

▶ Impatience

▶ Lethargy and nausea

▶ Headache

▶ Tiredness

▶ Dizziness or light-headedness

▶ Inability to walk

▶ Delirium

Treatment:

1. Find a shady area to rest in.

2. Drink fluids slowly.

3. Keep cool and avoid sweating.

HEAT EXHAUSTION

Heat exhaustion is caused by a severe loss of water and salt from the body, through excessive sweating brought about by exposure to heat and humidity. It often affects people who are not used to very hot and humid conditions, but it can also happen to those who are already unwell, especially if they have been vomiting or had diarrhoea.

Signs of heat exhaustion:

▶ Muscle cramps, especially in the arms, legs and abdomen

▶ Headache, dizziness, confusion

▶ Sweating with cold, clammy skin

▶ Nausea and loss of appetite

▶ Rapid, shallow breathing

▶ Delirium or unconsciousness

Treatment:

1. Rest in shaded area, with legs propped up.

2. Drink plenty of cool liquids, preferably water.

3. Loosen clothing and cool skin with damp cloths or cool water.

4. Even after recovery the casualty should get a check up from a doctor.

HEATSTROKE

Heat exhaustion can lead to heatstroke. This is when someone's body overheats from too much exposure to the sun or working too hard in a hot environment, and they are no longer able to regulate their own temperature. Heatstroke requires immediate medical treatment to bring the person's temperature down.

Signs of heatstroke include:

▶ Hot, dry skin

▶ Face flushed and feverish but with no sweating

▶ High temperature and fast pulse (see page 21)

▶ Severe headache and vomiting

▶ Unconsciousness

Treatment:

1. Place casualty in a cool or shady area.

2. Remove outer clothing to allow body heat to escape.

3. Wipe down with tepid, not cold, water, around the head, neck and chest.

4. Use a fan to help cool the casualty down.

5. If fully conscious, give them plenty of cool, not cold, water to drink.

SAFETY CHECKLIST

☑ **DEHYDRATION**
Lack of body water.

☑ **HEAT EXHAUSTION**
Lack of body water and salts due to heat and excessive sweating.

☑ **HEATSTROKE**
Overheating and inability to lower one's body temperature.

WARNING

DO NOT lower a heatstroke victim directly into cold water. This could send their body into shock and cause them to stop breathing.

DO NOT cover them in wet towels or blankets. These could prevent their body heat from escaping and raise their temperature even higher.

STINGS AND BITES

Bee, wasp and most other insect stings or bites can be relieved by applying an ice pack or a cold compress. If a bee has left its sting in the wound, scrape it away with the edge of a knife blade, or a clean fingernail. Do not squeeze it as this might push more venom into the wound.

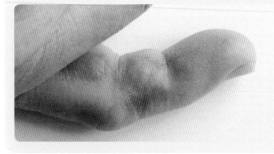

TICKS – bury their jaws in the skin when they bite, and if the body is pulled away they can leave their jaws behind and cause an infection. Grip the tick with your fingers or a pair of tweezers as close to the skin as you can and gently but firmly pull straight upwards. Try not to twist or jerk the tick as you pull, or crush its body in case you squeeze poison into your bloodstream. If the jaws do break off, try to remove them with tweezers or get medical help. Once the tick is out, clean the bite with soap and water and apply a cold pack to reduce any swelling. Then apply an antiseptic.

ANAPHYLAXIS

Anaphylaxis, or anaphylactic shock, is what happens when your body has a severe allergic reaction to something. It may be caused by eating a certain food, by a bee or wasp sting, or by a reaction to a particular material or medicine.

An allergic reaction can vary from mild itchiness, rash or swelling, to an inability to breathe and heart and circulation failure. The reaction may take place instantly or some hours later, but immediate medical treatment is vital.

Signs of anaphylaxis include:

▶ Swelling and itching, especially around the area that came into contact with the offending substance – known as an allergen. If food, for example, the swelling will be around the mouth and throat.

▶ Blotchy red skin or itchy rash spreading over the body

▶ Swollen, itchy eyes

▶ Swelling in the throat, difficulty breathing or wheezing

▶ Dizziness, anxiety and apprehension

▶ Stomach cramps, vomiting or diarrhoea

▶ Sudden drop in blood pressure leading to unconsciousness

Treatment:

1. Get medical help as quickly as possible.

2. Move the casualty away from the allergen if possible.

3. If the person is carrying an adrenalin injection, or epi-pen, they should apply it immediately. (Note: if you carry an epi-pen, make sure one of your friends or colleagues knows how to use it in case you are unable to do it yourself.)

4. If the casualty is having trouble breathing, help them sit up. If they are feeling faint, lie them flat with raised legs.

5. If they are unconscious, check their airways are clear and they are able to breathe. Then put them into the recovery position (see page 216).

CHOKING

If someone has something stuck in their throat but can breathe and cough, they may be able to cough the obstruction out. Ask if they need help. If so, apply a couple of firm blows to their back.

If they cannot speak or cough, they probably cannot breathe and will need immediate action. However, do not practise this on anyone who is not choking.

1. Strike them firmly between the shoulder blades with the heel of your hand. Do this five times, quickly checking inside their mouth after each blow to see if anything has been dislodged that can be removed. Warning: DO NOT put your fingers in their mouth or try to make the person sick.

2. If this does not work, give them up to five abdominal thrusts, checking their mouth each time as before:

   - Stand behind them and put your arms around their waist (or kneel if the casualty is a child).

   - Make a fist with one hand and place the thumb halfway between the navel and the bottom of the breastbone.

   - Hold the fist with your other hand and pull inwards and upwards sharply.

3. After five abdominal thrusts, repeat with five blows on the back, then a further five thrusts, and so on.

4. If still choking after three rounds, call 999, but continue to try to dislodge the obstruction.

5. If necessary, apply resuscitation (see page 215).

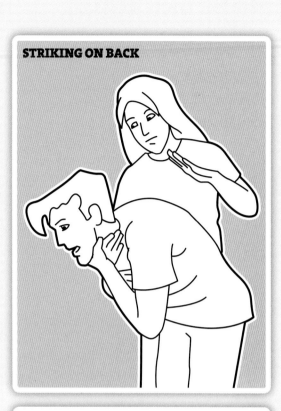

STRIKING ON BACK

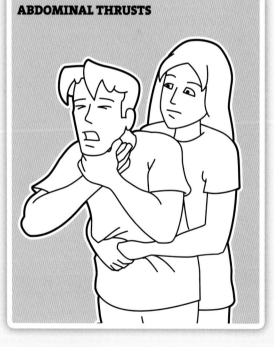

ABDOMINAL THRUSTS

BURNS AND SCALDS

Burns are caused by coming into contact with a hot object, a chemical, or electricity. Scalds are caused by hot liquid. It is important to cool the burnt area as much as possible.

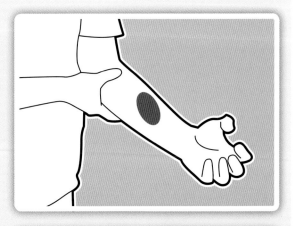

Treatment:

1. **Prevent any further burn damage by getting the casualty away from the source of the burn, for example by dousing the flames with water or wrapping a blanket around the person to put the flames out. If someone is being burned by electricity, turn off the appliance or use a non-conductive material, such as a wooden stick, to pull them away.**

WARNING

Do not put yourself at risk of getting burned.

2. **Remove any clothing or jewellery near to the burn unless it is stuck to the skin.**

3. **As soon as you can, cool down the burned area with water for at least 10 minutes. Ideally use cool or tepid running water from a tap or stream, or immerse. Do not use ice or iced water.**

4. **Keep the casualty warm with extra clothing or blankets, but do not cover the burnt area.**

5. **Once the burn has been cooled, cover the area with a large sterile dressing, a piece of cling film or a plastic bag.**

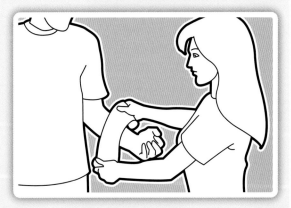

6. **If the burn is large, the skin has blistered, there are burns on the face, hands or feet, or it is an electrical or chemical burn, get medical help as soon as possible. Do not burst the blisters.**

SAFETY CHECK

Never put any kind of cream, oil or grease (such as butter) on a burn.

SEVERE BLEEDING

If someone is badly injured and bleeding severely, it is important to stop or restrict the flow of blood as quickly as possible. Too much blood loss can cause faintness, an increase in heart rate and breathing, collapse and, eventually, death. As with any injury, try to keep calm and reassure the injured person. If possible put on disposable gloves before you treat the wound.

Treatment:

1. Remove any clothing from around the wound and check to see if there is an object embedded in it.

2. If there is not an object – press down on the wound with a wad of dressing pads, swabs, or material (preferably clean), even just your hand if you have nothing else. Hold it firmly in place. Do not lift it up to check the blood flow. If the blood soaks through the pad, add another one on top. Once the bleeding has slowed or stopped, hold the padding in place with a bandage.

3. If there is an object – avoid pressing on the object itself. Instead, press firmly on either side of the object and build up padding around it. Bandage the padding to hold it in place, but try to avoid placing the bandaging so that it puts pressure on the object. Do not try to remove the object and get medical help.

4. If the wound is on an arm or leg, raise and support it above the level of the heart. Treat for shock.

5. Keep the injured person as warm and comfortable as possible and get medical help.

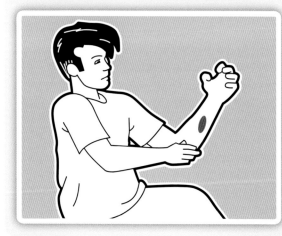

MINOR CUTS

Small cuts and scratches should be treated to prevent infection. Wash your hands thoroughly before and after treating an injury. If possible, wear disposable gloves, particularly if the casualty is bleeding.

Treatment:

1. If there is dirt in the wound, pour water on it to flush the dirt away.

2. Clean the skin around the wound.

3. Dry the area gently with a clean gauze swab.

4. Cover the wound with a sterile dressing and secure with plasters or adhesive tape. Do not use cotton wool or anything fluffy.

SPRAINS AND STRAINS

A sprain is what happens when a ligament has been overstretched or torn. Ligaments are the stretchy bands of tissue that link one bone to another at a joint. A strain is when a muscle is overstretched or torn. In terms of first aid, both injuries are treated in the same way. However, if you are unsure if the injury is a sprain or a fracture, treat it as if it is a fracture.

Signs of a sprain or strain include:

▶ Pain around the joint or muscle

▶ Bruising, tenderness and swelling

▶ Inability to put weight on a joint or use it normally

Treatment – use the RICE procedure:

1. **REST** – stop what you were doing.

2. **ICE** – put an ice pack or a cold pad on the injured area.

3. **COMFORTABLE SUPPORT** – bandage or wrap the area comfortably to provide effective support. Do not make the wrapping too tight.

4. **ELEVATE** – prop up or raise the injured part.

SAFETY CHECK

☑ Do not use a hot pack or hot water on the area.

☑ Do not massage the area.

☑ Do not put undue weight or pressure on the area.

FRACTURES

A fractured bone might be cracked or it might be completely broken. If a bone has punctured the skin or is visible through a wound, it is called an open fracture. If the skin is not punctured, it is a closed fracture.

Signs of a fracture include:

▶ **Severe pain, especially if the injured part is moved**

▶ **Swelling and bruising at the site of the injury**

▶ **The injured area may appear to be deformed in some way, or look shorter, bent or twisted**

▶ **You may see a piece of broken bone through the skin**

Treatment:

1. Try not to move the injury and send for medical help.

2. **OPEN FRACTURE**

   If it is an open fracture and the wound is bleeding, it is important to limit the loss of blood and prevent the wound from becoming infected. Cover the wound with a wad of dressing pads or clean material and press on either side of the protruding bone without pressing on the bone itself.

   ▶ Build up padding around the bone and bandage the padding to hold it in place, but try to avoid putting pressure on the bone itself. Do not give the injured person anything to eat or drink as they may need surgery. Continue as for a closed fracture.

3. **CLOSED FRACTURE**

   If it is a closed fracture, try to immobilize and support the injured part as much as possible using bandages, blankets or pieces of clothing. For example:

   ▶ Support a fractured ankle by wrapping folded T-shirts or teacloths around it and tying them in place with bandages. Do not make the bandages so tight that they cut off the person's circulation – see circulation panel opposite. Prop the leg up on a folded blanket or a backpack to reduce the swelling.

▶ Support a fractured wrist or fingers by wrapping the wrist or hand in dressing pads or soft material. Hold the dressing in place with strips of bandage. Use a triangular bandage, or a long-sleeved jumper or sweatshirt to support the lower arm across the chest so that the hand is above the heart. Do not knot the triangular bandage behind the neck as this will cause pressure on the neck. As above, do not make the bandages too tight.

CIRCULATION SAFETY CHECK

If you bandage or bind up an injury to a hand, foot, arm or leg, check that the dressings are not so tight that they prevent the person's blood from circulating around their body. Press down on a finger- or toenail and check if the colour comes back within 3 seconds. If it doesn't, or if the fingers or toes are blue, cold or numb, loosen the dressing.

MAKING A SLING FOR AN INJURED ARM

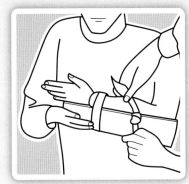

1 Support the injured arm with a piece of stiff card or wood, or a roll of paper.

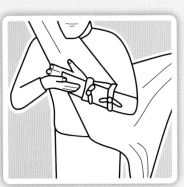

2 Gently slide the triangular bandage underneath the arm, keeping the ends free.

3 Lift the bottom corner and knot around neck. Fold the third corner over the elbow.

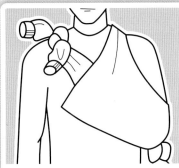

If you don't have a large bandage, use a jumper and knot the sleeves together.

With a fractured or broken ankle, wrap the foot and ankle with spare clothing, tea towels or towels. Use bandages, belts or straps to hold them in place. Keep the foot propped up off the ground.

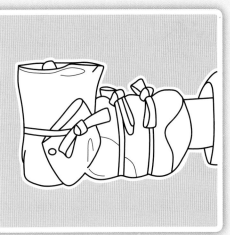

SEARCH AND RESCUE

If there is an emergency while you are travelling in a remote area, you may need to help the emergency services to find you.

BEING SEEN

If you cannot phone or send for help (see page 213) and are unable to continue your journey, the best thing is to stay where you are and wait for your home contact to realize something is wrong and alert the emergency services on your behalf.

In this situation, the first priority is to do whatever you can to make injured members of the group more comfortable and to make sure that everyone has some form of shelter, such as a bothy bag or survival blanket (see page 65), tent or bivi bag (see pages 94–95), or by building a temporary shelter (see pages 234–237).

The next priority is to make your location as visible as possible. Eventually a Search and Rescue team will try to find you so it is sensible to do what you can to mark your position with any brightly coloured, shiny or metallic clothing or materials that might be spotted from above. If there is high or open ground nearby, use this for your markers.

SIGNAL FIRES

Signal fires are an effective way of getting help. Smoke will be seen during the day, and flames at night. Prepare signal fires separately from any campfires you may build for warmth or cooking. However, if fuel is scarce or you are unable to maintain several fires, use what fire you have to keep yourself warm.

If you can build separate signal fires, try to keep them covered so that the wood is dry and ready to be lit the moment you hear or see any aircraft approaching. Keep a supply of green leaves, grass or green wood handy in case you need to make plenty of smoke. Make sure your fires are well away from trees and bushes and take care to prevent them from setting fire to nearby vegetation. Starting a forest fire will not help your situation.

For more information on building campfires, see Chapter 6, pages 120–129.

SOUND AND LIGHT

Making noise and flashing lights are also good ways to attract attention. The internationally recognized mountain rescue signal is:

- ▶ **6 quick blasts on a whistle, followed by**
- ▶ **1 minute silence, followed by**
- ▶ **6 quick blasts, and so on**

This signal works just as well for attracting attention in any other environment. If you do not have a whistle, try banging rocks or metal pots together or even shouting the signal out.

Or give the signal with flashes of light, either from a torch at night, or angle a mirror or any shiny metal surface so that it flashes in the sunlight.

The SOS message in Morse Code is another internationally recognized distress signal, and can be given as blasts of sound or flashes of light in the same way as the mountain rescue signal. The SOS signal is:

- ▶ **3 short blasts, 3 long blasts, 3 short blasts**
- ▶ **1 minute silence, then repeat**

If the signals are seen you may receive a reply, meaning 'Message Understood'.

The message understood signal is:

- ▶ **3 quick blasts, or flashes, repeated after 1 minute silence.**

Or you might see a white flare.

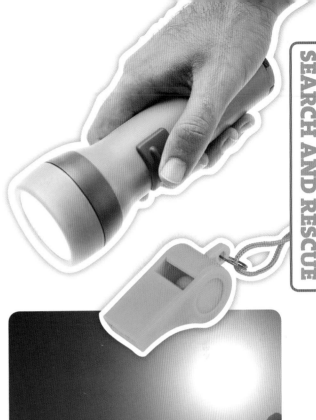

SAFETY CHECK

Do not practise sending distress signals when you are out in the open as they might be mistaken for the real thing. Calling the emergency services out when there is no emergency could cost someone else their life.

MORSE CODE

Morse code was originally designed for use with the first electric telegraph system in the 1840s. It is made up of spaced groups of short and long dots and dashes, sounds, or lights. Each group represents a letter of the alphabet. Messages can be sent by linking the groups together to make words and sentences. Morse code is still widely used and internationally recognised today, especially in an emergency situation.

It is not necessary to learn Morse code off by heart, but it is useful to carry a copy of the code with you.

The key to sending Morse code is in the timing of the dots and dashes:

▶ **A dash should be three times as long as a dot.**

▶ **The pause between each part of a letter should last as long as a single dot.**

▶ **The pause between each letter should take as long as three dots (i.e. a dash).**

▶ **The pause between each word should last as long as six dots (i.e. two dashes).**

Sending Signals:

AAAAA... Repeated as one word is a call sign meaning 'I have a message'

AAA End of sentence (More follows)

EEEEE... Repeated as one word means 'Error' (Start again from last correct word)

AR End of Message

Receiving Signals:

TTTTT... Repeated as one word means 'I am receiving you'

K I am ready (Start message)

T Word received

IMI Repeat sign (I do not understand)

R Message received

Some Useful Words:

SOS • • • — — — • • •

SEND • • • / • / — • / — • •

HELP • • • • / • / • — — • • / • — — • •

INJURY • • / — • / • — — — / • • — / • — • / — • — —

LOST • — • • / — — — / • • • / —

GROUND-TO-AIR SIGNALS

On open ground lay out markers to catch the attention of passing aircraft. Think carefully about your needs before deciding which signal to make, however, as most aircraft crew will go out of their way and take great risks in order to help someone in serious distress.

The following markers are recognized by all aircraft crew. (Alternatively, you can mark a giant SOS on the ground.)

Make the markers as large as possible. The recommended size for each symbol is 3 metres wide by 10 metres long, with about 3 metres between symbols if you need more than one.

Use rocks, or logs, or make grooves in the ground. Or better still, use your backpacks, groundsheets, clothes or anything that will stand out against the colour of the ground.

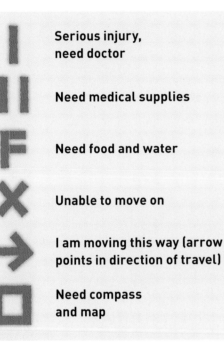

I	Serious injury, need doctor
II	Need medical supplies
F	Need food and water
X	Unable to move on
→	I am moving this way (arrow points in direction of travel)
□	Need compass and map

A	Affirmative / Yes ('Y' will also be understood for 'Yes')
N	Negative / No
K	Indicate in which direction I should travel
LL	All is well
JL	I do not understand
△	I think it is safe to land here

AIRCRAFT RESPONSE

If an aircraft pilot spots your message he or she will respond in the following ways:

1. Message received and understood

▷ In daylight – the pilot will fly the plane so that the wings tip from side to side in a rocking motion.

▷ At night – the plane will flash green lights.

2. Message received but NOT understood

▷ In daylight – the pilot will fly the plane in a right-handed circle.

▷ At night – the plane will flash red lights.

SAFETY CHECK

Once help has arrived and before you leave the site, make sure you remove any signals or markers you have made.

BODY SIGNALS

If you are spotted by an aircraft and do not have time to make ground markers, the following body signals will also be understood by an aircrew. Make the signals as clearly as you can, exaggerating the movements. Position your hands and legs carefully and notice when you should be facing the aircraft and when turned to one side. Hold a cloth in your right hand to emphasize the 'Yes' and 'No' signals.

Pick us up   **Need mechanical help**   **All is well**   **No**   **Yes**

Need medical assistance

Can proceed shortly   **Have radio**   **Land here**   **Do not attempt to land here**   **Use drop message**

IF YOU MOVE ON

If all the members of your group are able to travel and you decide that it is best to do so, leave signals behind to show that you were there but have left, incuding a large ground-to-air arrow to show the direction in which you left.

As you travel, leave other direction markers along the way so that rescuers can follow your trail. These will also help you if you lose your direction and find yourself going round in circles or need to retrace your steps.

Wherever you stop, leave written messages explaining what has happened and what you plan to do. Date the messages, put them in containers and hang them from trees or from sticks stuck in the ground. Indicate that they are there by using tracking signs as shown in the panel.

TRACKING SIGNS

You can use anything to make tracking signs – sticks, stones, rocks, tied bunches of grass, notches carved in wood, whatever you can find that won't be washed away by rain or blown away by the wind. Place them as prominently as you can so they can be easily seen and understood.

1. Direction arrows can be shown in many ways, for example:

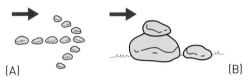

(A)   (B)

With small stones (A), or place a small stone on top of a larger one, with another small stone alongside to show the direction of travel (B).

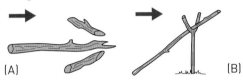

(A)   (B)

With sticks – put three sticks together to make an arrow on the ground (A), or push a forked stick into the ground and rest a pointer stick against it to show the direction of travel (B).

With long grass — tie a bunch of grass in an overhand knot and bend the top to point in the direction of travel.

2. Turn left or right

Use broken arrows (A and B), or an arrow-head carved into a stick (C) to indicate a turn to the left or right.

(A) Turn left   (B) Turn right   (C) Turn right

3. Not this way

Wherever a trail divides, put a cross of sticks or stones to show which way not to go.

4. Group has split up

Make a forked arrow with counters at the end of each arrow head to show how many people went one way and how many the other. In this example, 2 people went left and three people went right.

5. Message left here

A box with an arrow indicates where a message has been left. The number of markers inside the box says how many paces away the message is.

6. Obstacle ahead

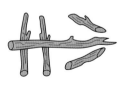

Two straight lines beneath or behind a direction arrow indicates the way ahead to cross an obstacle of some kind.

7. Water ahead

At least three wavy lines followed by a direction arrow shows that there is water ahead.

SURVIVAL

Accidents are not the only events that can create an emergency situation. The weather might suddenly worsen, for example, and you could be unable to continue your journey, or you could lose your way, or even lose all your kit. Most of the information in this book is geared towards helping you to avoid such situations, but sometimes events happen that are out of your control. For this reason, it is always best to be prepared for the worst.

DEALING WITH THE UNEXPECTED

Try though you might, it is impossible to plan and equip yourself for every eventuality. However, what you can do is learn to adapt your equipment, whatever materials you have around you and your knowledge to deal with whatever comes along.

By their nature, survival situations put us to the test. They usually involve some level of anxiety or fear, and can place us under severe physical stress and hardship. But it is apparent from those who have survived disasters that the single greatest survival skill is the right mental attitude. No matter what the situation, being confident in yourself and your ability to get through it can often make the difference between life and death.

KNOWLEDGE AND UNDERSTANDING

Confidence comes from knowledge and understanding – of your own skills and how they can be adapted to suit your environment, and of your own limits and levels of endurance. Knowing when not to push yourself, and when to rest, is as important as knowing when you need to keep going.

The following pages contain examples of ways of coping with some of the most practical issues of staying alive – finding shelter, food and water, for example. But as with most of the information in this book, this is just the beginning. In the outdoors every situation is different and there is always something new to learn and experience.

A PERSONAL SURVIVAL KIT

The aim of a survival kit is to keep it small so you can carry it with you at all times. With experience, you will discover the right kind of equipment for your needs and the size of your container, but the following list will give you a good start:

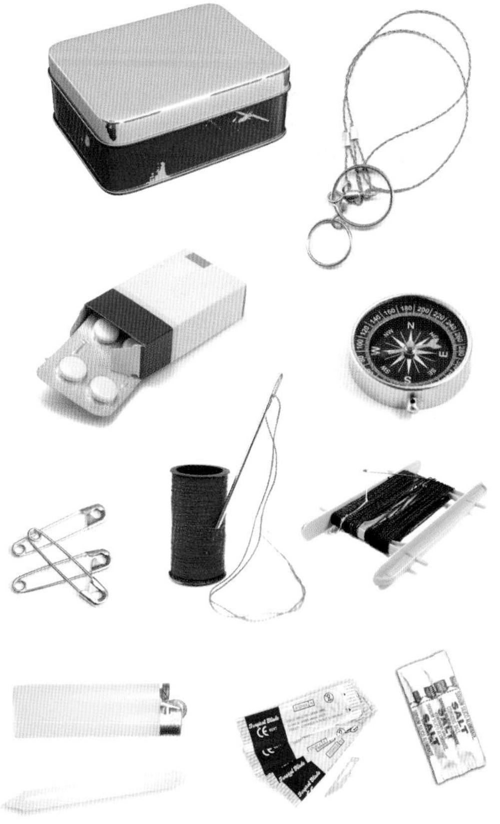

▶ **Container – the best type is an old-fashioned tobacco or sweet tin with a firmly-fitting lid. When empty, the tin can be used as a cup or pan, and the lid can be polished and used as a signalling mirror. If your box is plastic, include a signalling mirror in your kit.**

▶ **Insulation or Duct tape – use this to seal your tin, and as a piece of survival equipment.**

▶ **Firelighters – a small candle, disposable lighter, and about 15–20 strike-anywhere wooden matches wrapped in tin foil. Waterproof the matches by dipping the heads into melted candlewax. Scrape off the wax before use.**

▶ **Large needles and strong thread.**

▶ **Safety pins.**

▶ **Elastic bands.**

▶ **Thin wire.**

▶ **Scalpel blades.**

▶ **Wire saw.**

▶ **Button compass.**

▶ **Water sterilizing tablets.**

▶ **Salt.**

▶ **Glucose sweets.**

▶ **Fishing line, hooks, floats and weights. Fishing line can also be used for lashing.**

▶ **Waterproof plasters, steri-strip wound closures, antiseptic wipes.**

▶ **Strong plastic bag for carrying water or collecting it.**

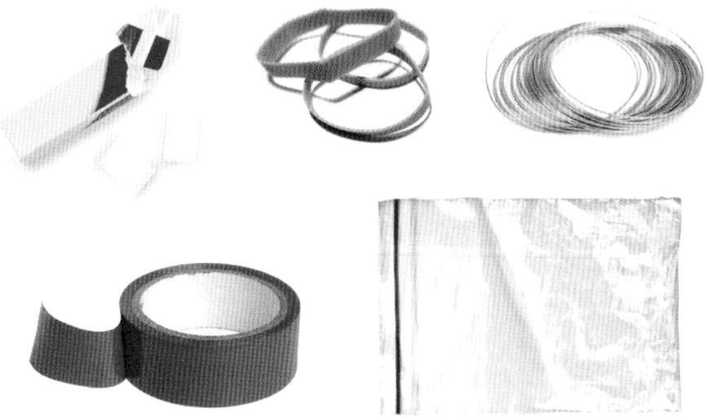

For safety and ease of packing, group small items together in zip-lock or resealable small plastic bags.

SAFETY CHECK

In addition to your survival kit, always carry a whistle, torch and pocketknife. A pen or pencil and paper are also useful.

For lists of other useful or emergency items see Chapter 3, pages 64–66.

PRIORITIZE

As with risk assessment (see pages 208–211), the first thing to do in a survival situation is take the time to decide on what your priorities should be. These will change depending on your circumstances and your surroundings.

If there are injuries, they need to be dealt with first as they will only get worse if they are left until later. The next question is whether to stay where you are or to move on. It is usually safest to set up camp where you are and wait to be rescued. However, if your immediate surroundings present a danger – from flooding, rockfalls, or exposure, for example – then it may be necessary to move on to find a safer location.

FINDING SHELTER

Protection from the elements is vitally important. Wind, rain and cold, or even extremes of heat, will quickly sap your energy and lead to hypothermia or heatstroke (see pages 218–219). A clear priority, therefore, is to make sure that you have adequate shelter.

If you have tents with you it is wise to get them up as quickly as possible. If you need to build a shelter, this will take longer and is best done in daylight so the sooner it is started the better.

Think carefully about the best place to build your shelter. Where possible, make use of hillocks, boulders, trees or bushes to provide some protection from the wind and rain, but look out for the possibility of water run-off or flooding, rockfall, insect nests or other animal invasions.

If you think you will be in one spot for some time try to make your shelter as sturdy as you can. The safer and more secure you feel, the better you will be able to deal with other difficulties. However, if you are on the move or your need for shelter is immediate, look for a quicker, short-term option that will give you some warmth and protection until you are able to find or make something better.

Building a bivouac from rope and tarpaulin, or wooden poles and branches, is described on pages 98–99. Here are a few more ideas:

For more information on setting up tents and a campsite, see Chapter 5.
For information on building campfires, see Chapter 6.

CAVES

Caves or even projecting ledges can provide instant shelter. However, make sure there are no indications of recent rockfall or soil movement above and around the entrance or inside the cave, and check for signs of bats, snakes or other wild animals. If the cave is shallow, add a lean-to made of poles and leafy branches to provide a windbreak barrier across the entrance.

Caves do not always make great long-term shelters as they tend to be cold and damp. However, if the cave is big enough you can build a campfire inside it for warmth. Do not build the fire at the entrance, however, as the smoke will be blown inside. Smoke rises, so if the fire is further back the smoke will rise to the roof of the cave and find a way out, as long as you leave an opening at the front.

SHALLOW CAVE

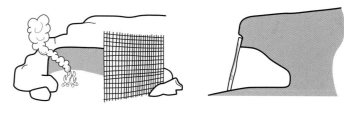

DEEPER CAVE

TOP TIPS

+ Avoid high, exposed places. If possible it is better to move downhill and out of the wind.

+ Be careful of low hollows and valley bottoms as they could be cold and damp at night.

+ Do not lie directly on the ground. If you don't have a sleeping bag, make a bed from piles of grass, leaves, branches, logs, or whatever you can find.

+ Build a reflector behind your campfire to give added warmth, see page 171.

TREES

In a wooded area you might find a fallen tree or a large broken branch which reaches to the ground. If you find a large branch that has broken away completely, lash it to the base of a fixed branch or a tree trunk to make a rough tripod structure. Weaving smaller branches and leaves into the main structure and piling earth around the base will give you additional warmth and protection.

Sometimes the entire root ball of a tree is pulled up when the tree falls, creating a great natural hollow with a 'wall' of roots on one side. Build up the sides of the hollow to make it more secure.

Be careful to site your campfire a safe distance from the tree branches.

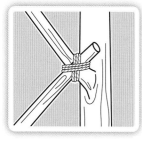

Rest the end of a broken branch in the fork of a tree and lash it in place.

HOLLOWS

Even a hollow in the ground can make a shelter, especially if there is a boulder or tree trunk to one side. Use a sturdy stick to scrape out the hollow and make it deeper. Over it, prop a lean-to made of branches or sticks covered with a tarpaulin, leaves, moss or turf. Try to slope the roof so that rainwater will run off it.

It is always worth the effort of digging a drainage ditch on either side of your hollow, especially if you are on a slope, as you could find it filling up with rainwater in the night.

If the ground is flat, try scraping out a hollow and piling earth or stones around the edges to make a low wall. Then lay a roof of branches, leaves or turf across the wall.

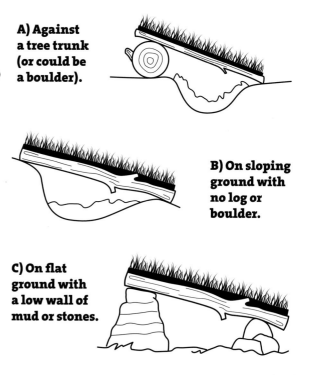

A) Against a tree trunk (or could be a boulder).

B) On sloping ground with no log or boulder.

C) On flat ground with a low wall of mud or stones.

IN AN EMERGENCY

SNOW AND ICE

SNOW HOLLOW – Deep snow can be an advantage. The simplest shelter can sometimes be found beneath the spreading branches of a tree. If the branches are low and sturdy, and the snow around the tree has built up to branch level, a natural hollow may have formed beneath the lowest branches. Dig down carefully on the leeward side of the tree and try not to dislodge the snow on the branches above.

SNOW CAVE – If the snow has drifted, tunnel into a bank to make a cave. Hollow out an area big enough to shelter in. If the snow is firm, you might manage to fit you, your equipment and a small campfire inside. If so, put the fire on the highest level at the back of the cave. Make a channel around the inside floor so that ice melt from the walls will drain into that.

Remember that hot air rises and cold air sinks, so build a sleeping platform above ground level to avoid the coldest air. Poke ventilation holes through the sides – see warning panel. Block up the entrance, but not too tightly in case the blocks freeze together overnight.

SNOW TRENCH – Alternatively, dig a trench in the snow and use a tarpaulin or a framework of sticks to form a roof. Lay conifer branches across the top and cover this with snow. Be careful to make airholes – see warning panel. Line the floor with branches, sticks or whatever you can find to keep your body off the cold ground.

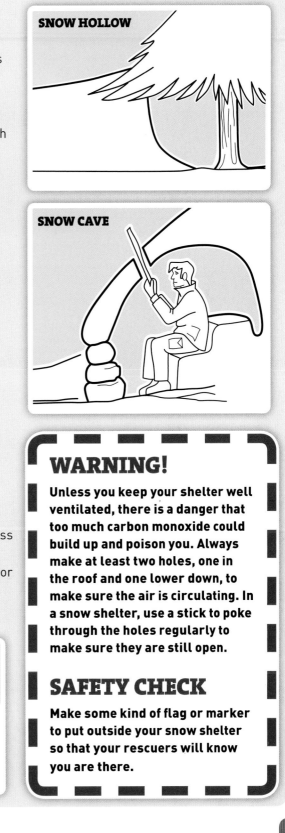

SNOW HOLLOW

SNOW CAVE

WARNING!

Unless you keep your shelter well ventilated, there is a danger that too much carbon monoxide could build up and poison you. Always make at least two holes, one in the roof and one lower down, to make sure the air is circulating. In a snow shelter, use a stick to poke through the holes regularly to make sure they are still open.

SAFETY CHECK

Make some kind of flag or marker to put outside your snow shelter so that your rescuers will know you are there.

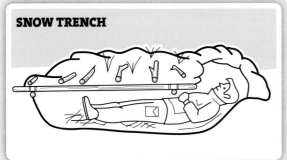

SNOW TRENCH

WATER

Finding a source of drinking water is almost as immediate a priority as finding shelter and protection from the elements. The human body loses about 2–3 litres of water each day. If we do not replace that water, we become dehydrated (see page 218) and will die in three to five days, whereas we can survive for up to three weeks without food.

FINDING WATER

The obvious place to look for water is at the bottom of a valley, ditch or gully. If there is no water on the surface but the ground looks green or gravelly, try digging down half a metre or so. In mountainous areas look in crevices for pools of rainwater. Trees and other plants are always a sign that there is water of some sort and, as all animals need water, it is worth following any well-trodden animal trails.

SAFETY CHECK

Always be careful of water collected in the wild, especially from stagnant pools and puddles or where the mud looks slimy or green. If you find a stream, make sure there are no dead animals in it for at least half a kilometre upstream of where you take your water. The best solution is to filter all ground water through a sock or other material, preferably filled with sand or moss, then boil it for about 5 minutes – see also page 140.

TOP TIPS

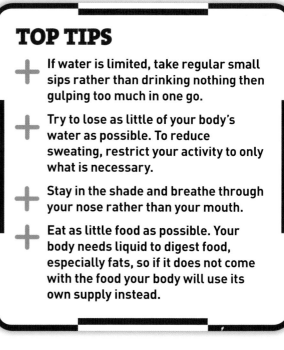

+ If water is limited, take regular small sips rather than drinking nothing then gulping too much in one go.

+ Try to lose as little of your body's water as possible. To reduce sweating, restrict your activity to only what is necessary.

+ Stay in the shade and breathe through your nose rather than your mouth.

+ Eat as little food as possible. Your body needs liquid to digest food, especially fats, so if it does not come with the food your body will use its own supply instead.

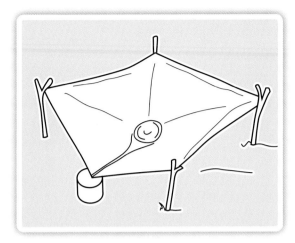

RAINWATER

Always collect rainwater even if you have another source nearby. Even allowing for air pollution, rainwater is always pure enough to be drinkable. Put out whatever containers you can find. If you have any plastic or waterproof bags or sheets, large pieces of metal or foil, or even tree bark, use them to make a rain collector.

Spread out the material as widely as you can and peg out the corners or tie them to sticks stuck in the ground so that the collector is lifted off the ground at a slight angle. Put a clean stone or some other object in the centre to create a pool and place a container at the lowest point to catch the run off. Make sure to replace the container at regular intervals so it does not overflow, and keep your containers covered once they are full.

DEW

If there is no rain there may at least be dew. If you are surrounded by vegetation, drag a clean cloth over grass and other plants to soak up the dew. Then wring it out into a container. You will need to do this early in the morning, before the dew evaporates in the sun.

CONDENSATION

Plants suck up water from the soil and release it from their leaves. If you have plastic bags, tie them around a branch of leaves growing on a tree or bush in the sunlight. Secure the neck to prevent the moisture escaping from the bag, but try not to squash the leaves against the sides of the bag. Moisture from the leaves will condense on the sides of the plastic and collect at the bottom of the bag.

Alternatively, gather fresh foliage and put it inside a bag, on top of a layer of stones so the water collects at the bottom of the bag. Prop up the top of the bag to keep it clear of the foliage. Angle the bag or scoop out a small depression below one side of it so that the water will trickle down and collect in one spot. Change the vegetation when the water stops condensing.

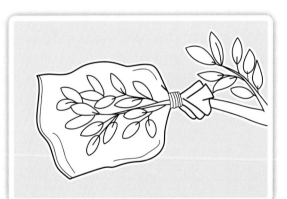

FOOD

We need food to give us the energy to stay alive, and we need a variety of food – we cannot survive by eating just one type of food day after day (see page 18). In the wild, this is a plus point as it means that our bodies can digest almost any type of food (as long as it is not poisonous), but it can also make the job of hunting and gathering food more complicated.

Wherever you are in the world there is likely to be something you can eat. The difficulty may be in recognizing it. There are a great many books, websites and courses available that can teach you how to recognize, gather and hunt for wild food. The following information is a very simple guide to a few survival basics.

IS IT EDIBLE?

Many thousands of wild plants are edible in some form or another, whether it is their leaves, stems, roots, fruit, nuts, seeds or grains. However, a few can make us very ill or can be deadly. Sometimes one part of a plant is edible while another part is not, or is only edible when cooked.

To know which plants are safe and good to eat requires either learning them off by heart, or carrying out a slow and careful process of testing – see opposite. As a golden rule, **IF IN DOUBT, DO NOT EAT IT.**

For more information on wild fungi, see Chapter 2, page 35.

Dandelion is a widespread edible plant. The young leaves can be eaten raw and the older ones cooked. Dandelion roots can also be boiled or roasted.

FOOD TESTING

Always test a potential new food source before eating it. Take each stage slowly and one step at a time. Only one person should do the testing. If you react badly, drink lots of water (hot if possible) and do not eat anything else until you have recovered. If necessary, make yourself vomit.

1. Smell – crush or break open the plant and smell it. If it smells bad, or smells of bitter almonds or peaches, do not eat it – see Warning panel opposite.

2. Feel – rub a little of the juice on the inside of your arm. Wait about 20 minutes to see if a rash, itching or swelling appears.

3. Taste – hold a small amount against your lips for 5 seconds then take it away. Wait a further 20 minutes and if there is no burning, stinging, numbness or other irritation do the same thing:
   – against the corner of your mouth
   – then the tip of your tongue
   – then under your tongue
   – then chew it

4. Swallow – swallow a small piece and wait for five hours. Do not eat or drink anything else during this time. If you have no unpleasant reaction, such as stomach pain, nausea, belly pain or diarrhoea, sore throat or numbness, the plant is probably safe to eat – but in small amounts to begin with.

WARNING

▶ Do not eat any plant that has a milky sap unless you know it is safe to eat (such as dandelion).

▶ Do not eat red plants unless you know they are safe. The highly poisonous hemlock plant, for example, has red or purple streaks or splotches on its stem although the feathery leaves and white flowers can be mistaken for parsley or wild carrot.

▶ Do not eat anything that smells or tastes of bitter almonds or peaches. Both these flavours indicate the presence of poisonous hydrocyanic (or prussic) acid.

▶ Do not eat something you think you recognize unless you are certain it is the right one. A number of poisonous plants look very like edible ones. Poisonous plants such as cowbane, hemlock or fool's parsley, for example, can be mistaken for edible cow parsley.

Nettle is a common nutritious plant. Young shoots can be steamed or boiled to make tea, or eaten like spinach. Older leaves should be boiled and sieved to remove the fibres and added to soups or stews.

FISH

It is perfectly possible to get all of the nutrients your body needs from plants, as long as you eat a wide variety and include some nuts, grains, or pulses. However, if you are close to a river, lake, or the sea and can construct a net or hooks and a line, fish are an excellent food source (as are seaweeds and some shellfish – see pages 44–45).

Most fish are edible, although some taste better than others. A number of freshwater and saltwater fish have sharp teeth or spines and some have poisonous spines and should be handled with care. A few fish also secrete a poisonous mucus over their skin so if a fish is unfamiliar to you always remove the skin and bones before eating it. A few species of tropical fish have poisonous flesh.

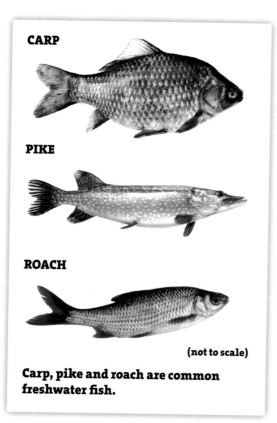

CARP

PIKE

ROACH

(not to scale)

Carp, pike and roach are common freshwater fish.

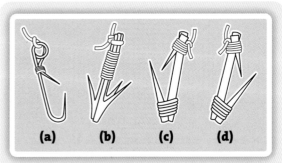

You can make a fishing hook from a bent pin (a), plant thorns (b), a sharp sliver of wood (c), or bone (d).

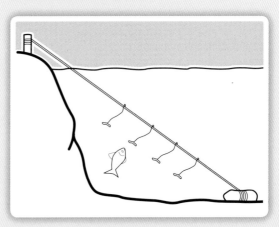

A practical way to catch fish is to set up one or more night lines, each with several baited hooks spaced along it. Tie one end of the line to a tree or stick firmly set in the bank. Attach the hooks with shorter lengths of line and bait them with worms, maggots or insects. Tie the end of the line to a weight and lower it carefully into the water so that the hooks are spread out.

WARNING

If you find a dead fish do not eat it, no matter how fresh it looks. Unless dried or smoked, the flesh of a dead fish deteriorates very rapidly and is dangerous to eat.

For more information on fishing, see Chapter 8, pages 206–207.

MEAT

Hunting animals for meat requires knowledge and experience, and unless you have this you will spend far more energy than you can afford or are likely to gain from catching your food in this way. If you get hungry enough, some insects and other invertebrates are a much more practical source of food.

Grasshoppers, ants, worms, slugs, snails, caterpillars and grubs are a good source of protein, fat and carbohydrate and are eaten widely in some parts of the world. It is best to remove the wings and legs of larger insects and to squeeze the innards out of hairy caterpillars rather than eat the skin.

Invertebrates can be boiled or roasted. If you really cannot bear the thought of eating them, try mashing them to a pulp and carefully roasting or drying the pulp into a powder. The powder can be mixed with other foods to disguise it while still giving you the nutritional value it contains.

WARNING

Avoid brightly coloured snails, caterpillars or other insects as they are likely to be poisonous. Spiders are also best avoided.

TOP TIPS

+ Start by eating only the plants you recognize, such as nettles, dandelions or wild garlic.

+ If you find a good source of plant food, do not pick the entire plant or over-collect it. Leave enough of the plant to grow again.

+ Test and introduce one new food at a time.

+ Don't eat too much of a new food at once – give your body a chance to get used to it.

+ Don't assume that anything another animal eats can be eaten by you.

+ Do not eat anything that looks old or unhealthy, or has a bad smell.

For information on cooking without utensils, see Chapter 5, pages 148-151.

MORE INFORMATION AND FURTHER READING

SURFING WEBSITES

▶ Not all information found on the internet is true, accurate, or up to date. Check that the website giving the information is a reliable source. A professional website will always have an 'About us' or 'Who we are' section on their site and will list a contact address or phone number.

▶ If you bump into a site that contains upsetting or scary images or information, use the 'Back' button or turn the computer off.

INTERNET SAFETY

The internet is a fantastic way to get information or advice on just about every subject under the sun. But as with most things, it also has its dangers. Make sure you are 'street smart' and aware of the dangers before you set off to explore.
If you are under 18, never give out your personal details without the permission of a parent or carer.

▶ It is tempting to download free movies, music or other material from a website but remember that most of this material is protected by someone's copyright so downloading it illegally for free is much the same thing as shoplifting, and it is a crime.

▶ Downloading material from unlicensed or illegal websites also opens up the possibility of downloading a virus that could damage your computer.

REPORT IT!

If you receive bullying or inappropriate messages, images or other material over the internet, you should tell an adult you trust, and you or they should report it to one of the following organizations:

▶ The Child Exploitation and Online Protection (CEOP) centre: **www.ceop.gov.uk**

▶ The Internet Watch Foundation (IWF): **www.iwf.org.uk**

Further information on using the internet safely can be found at:

▶ **www.thinkuknow.co.uk** an information website run by CEOP, for children, teenagers and adults.

▶ **www.direct.gov.uk** information for parents on internet safety and laws.

▶ **http://kids.direct.gov.uk** an interactive information website for children containing information on internet safety.

▶ **www.kidscape.org.uk** an advice and information website for children and adults on cyber bullying and online safety.

USEFUL ADDRESSES

Here is a round-up of useful websites that amplify or extend the information given in this book. All of these addresses were correct at the time of publication but please remember that website addresses often change.

ACCOMMODATION

www.yha.org.uk nationwide budget accommodation with the Youth Hostel Association.

ADVENTURES AND CHALLENGES

www.dofe.org the Duke of Edinburgh's Award (DofE) programme for young people aged 14–25 involves achieving awards by taking part in a range of activities, including volunteering, fitness, skills and undertaking an expedition.

www.jointheadventure.com Use this Scout website to find out about volunteering opportunities for young adults – add to your CV, travel, and take part in great activities.

www.scout.org.uk The Scout Association offers challenge, adventure and over 200 activities to young people (girls and boys) aged 6-25 as well as a wide range of flexible volunteering opportunities for adults. See also pages 248–249.

CONSERVATION AND WILDLIFE

www.cpre.org.uk Campaign to Protect Rural England.

www.direct.gov.uk/en/Environmentandgreener living/index.htm information on the environment and greener living.

www.energysavingtrust.org.uk ways to save energy and live a greener life.

www.infoscotland.com/gogreener working towards a more sustainable future in Scotland.

www.keepbritaintidy.org.uk working towards a cleaner, greener England; includes Eco-Schools projects.

www.lnt.org Leave No Trace: advice and information on how to enjoy the outside while making a minimal impact on the environment.

www.rspb.org.uk the leading society for the protection of birdlife; website includes information and guidelines on watching birds safely and responsibly.

www.rspca.org.uk registered charity to prevent cruelty to animals, and alleviate their suffering.

www.wildlifetrusts.org voluntary organization dedicated to conserving the full range of the UK's habitats and species; a total of 47 local wildlife trusts across the whole of the UK, the Isle of Man and Alderney.

www.woodlandtrust.org.uk the UK's leading woodland conservation charity.

www.wwf.org.uk WorldWide Fund for Nature; leading conservation body which works to safeguard the natural world.

EMERGENCIES

Accidents and leisure safety

www.rospa.com Royal Society for the Prevention of Accidents; information, advice and training on all aspects of avoiding accidents in all areas of life – at work, in the home, on the roads, in schools, at leisure and on (or near) water.

First aid kits and training

To purchase kits online and learn life-saving skills:

www.firstaid.org.uk St Andrew's First Aid (St Andrew's Ambulance Association); in Scotland.

www.recfirstaid.net Rescue Emergency Care.

www.redcross.org.uk British Red Cross.

www.sja.org.uk St John Ambulance.

Life-saving skills

www.lifesavers.org.uk the Royal Lifesaving Society UK; for lifesaving courses and learning what to do in an emergency.

Ticks, Lyme disease & Weil's disease

www.ramblers.org.uk Ramblers Association; click on 'Walking information'/'Practical information'/'Health and safety'.

www.lymediseaseaction.org.uk practical information on Lyme disease.

www.rospa.com to download a factsheet on Weil's disease (leptospirosis) click on 'Leisure safety'/'Leisure safety information' /'Information sheets'.

GENERAL HEALTH AND ADVICE

www.bbc.co.uk/health - includes First Aid information.

www.direct.gov.uk for Government information on carrying knives, click on 'Crime Prevention'.

www.eatwell.gov.uk for information about food and nutrition.

www.nhs.uk/livewell the National Health website for advice and services.

www.ruthinking.co.uk information about adolescence and relationships.

www.thesite.org information and advice for young adults.

www.thinkuknow.co.uk information on safely using modern technology, such as the internet, mobile phones etc.

SPORTS AND INTERESTS

www.adventure.visitscotland.com includes information on adventure and outdoor sports in Scotland.

www.efds.co.uk English Federation of Disability Sport; working to promote sports involvement for disabled people in England.

www.sportengland.org for general information on community sports in England.

Archery

www.gnas.org for information about archery in Great Britain and Northern Ireland.

Caving and potholing

www.trycaving.co.uk for information on caving clubs in the UK.

Climbing, mountaineering and abseiling

www.abcclimbingwalls.co.uk Association of British Climbing Walls.

www.mcofs.org.uk the Mountaineering Council of Scotland, the MCofS, represents mountaineers, climbing and hill walking enthusiasts in Scotland.

www.mountaineering.ie for walkers and climbers in Ireland.

www.nicas.co.uk the National Indoor Climbing Achievement Scheme (NICAS) to promote and develop achievement in climbing artificial surfaces.

www.pyb.co.uk the National Mountain Centre, based in Wales.

www.thebmc.co.uk the British Mountaineering Council.

www.ukclimbing.com climbing holidays in the UK.

Cycling

www.ctc.org.uk the UK's National Cyclists' Organization; includes information on clubs, training courses and off-road mountain biking.

www.sustrans.org.uk an organization working to improve and open up more cycling routes; includes information on routes around the country, and the National Cycle Network.

Fishing

www.anglingtrust.net for information on fishing, clubs and competitions.

www.paauk.com the Professional Anglers Association.

Fossil hunting

www.discoveringfossils.co.uk how to do it and where to do it.

Geocaching

For information about this high-tech treasure-hunting sport using GPS navigation devices:

www.gagb.org.uk

www.geocaching.com

Horseriding

www.bhs.org.uk the British Horse Society; for approved horseriding centres.

www.pcuk.org youth organization for youngsters interested in ponies and riding.

www.rda.org.uk volunteer groups dedicated to improving the lives of people with disabilities, through the provision of opportunities for riding or carriage driving.

www.ride-uk.org.uk for the National Bridleroute network for riders throughout the country; including trail guides and riding holidays for horse and pony owners.

Pioneering

www.pioneeringmadeeasy.co.uk information and instructions for pioneering projects, including the look-out tower given in this book.

MORE INFORMATION AND FURTHER READING

Running and athletics

www.uka.org.uk the national governing body for athletics in the UK; Olympic and Paralympic sport from grassroots to top competitions.

Space

www.bbc.co.uk/science/space information on all aspects of space and astronomy.

www.bnsc.gov.uk British National Space Centre's Learning Zone.

www.schoolsobservatory.org.uk website run by the National Schools Observatory; lets you look at the stars!

Water sports

www.ara-rowing.org Amateur Rowing Association, for information on rowing clubs and courses.

www.asto.org.uk the Association of Sail Training Organizations

www.bcu.org.uk British Canoe Union – governing body for paddle sports in the UK, with information and links to clubs in your part of the country.

www.britishwaterski.org.uk site run by the National Governing Body for water skiing in Great Britain.

www.dragonboat.org.uk the British Dragon Boat Racing Association.

www.dsp.uk.com and **www.adventuresoffshore.co.uk** for sailing experiences and courses.

www.rya.org.uk Royal Yachting Association; includes information on clubs and training centres for sailing, windsurfing and powerboating (including jet skis).

www.sailing.org the International Sailing Federation official website.

www.ukwindsurfing.com United Kingdom Windsurfing Association (competitive windsurfing).

WALKING, RAMBLING AND THE COUNTRYSIDE CODE

www.breathingplaces.org/public BBC website on finding outdoor areas to visit throughout the UK; including guided walks.

www.britishorienteering.org.uk orienteering events and courses.

www.ccw.gov.uk (in Welsh or English) Countryside Council (Wales).

www.countrysideaccess.gov.uk Countryside Agency (England).

www.countrysiderecreation.com Countryside Access and Activities Network (Northern Ireland).

www.forestholidays.co.uk for holidays on Forestry Commission land.

www.forestry.gov.uk a guide to Britain's forests and woods.

www.geomag.bgs.ac.uk British Geological website; contains online calculators that will work out the Magnetic Declination or Grid Magnetic Angle for you.

www.go4awalk.com stacked with information, advice and details of walks in the UK.

www.goodbeachguide.co.uk for information on Britain's beaches.

www.moorlandassociation.org for details of the moorland code and information about Britain's moorlands.

www.nationaltrail.co.uk for information about long-distance walking and cycling routes in England and Wales.

www.naturalengland.org.uk good links to a variety of countryside organizations.

www.nnr-scotland.org.uk for information on nature reserves in Scotland (includes information on guided walks).

www.ordnancesurvey.co.uk for detailed maps of the UK.

www.outdooraccess-scotland.com Outdoor Access (Scotland).

www.ramblers.org.uk the Ramblers Association (Britain), for lots of information about outdoor walking, including guided walks, routes, etc.

www.snh.org.uk Scottish Natural Heritage (Scotland). For information on long-distance trails in Scotland.

www.ypte.org.uk/residential-courses.php the Young People's Trust for the Environment and Nature Conservation; offer residential Environmental Discovery courses.

SCOUTING – JOIN THE ADVENTURE OF A LIFETIME

The Scout Association offers challenge and adventure to 400,000 young people in the UK, helping girls and boys reach their potential by working in teams, taking responsibility and learning by doing.

This is delivered through a youth programme that is open to everyone aged 6-25, regardless of background, religion or race. It is made possible by our dedicated adult volunteers.

Our young people ...

▶ get to make friends and try new things

▶ earn badges and awards including the Duke of Edinburgh's Awards

▶ try over 200 different adventurous activities

▶ get to camp, travel overseas and meet Scouts across the world

▶ learn Scouting skills and pass them on

▶ lead small teams, learn leadership skills and do other things that look great on a CV

Our volunteers ...

▶ are each part of a team of 100,000 adults helping us to deliver Scouting across the UK

▶ give over 364 million hours to volunteer within their communities

▶ offer opportunities for 400,000 young people in the UK alone

▶ are contributing to an international movement that has 28 million Members in 218 countries around the world

▶ take part in training for their role and their own personal development (for example, in any five-year period Scouting trains in excess of 70,000 adults in basic life-saving skills)

▶ contribute to the largest membership organisation in the world working for peace

Our challenge ...

Even with 100,000 adult volunteers, we still have over 30,000 young people on joining lists across the country, waiting to take part in Scouting. And that is where you come in. We are looking for enthusiastic adult volunteers who can help us offer adventure and opportunities for more young people within their local communities . . . and to join the adventure themselves!

So why should I volunteer?

Without our adult volunteers we could not deliver the youth programme we currently offer and would not be able to meet our aims of increasing the opportunities available for young people. In fact, Scouting simply could not exist without the skills and enthusiasm of thousands of adult helpers.

Whether you have several hours a week or a year, or you are looking for a one-off volunteering project, there are opportunities for you to contribute to what we do and have fun! We have opportunities local to you, ranging from leader to treasurer, website designer to volunteer manager and we offer opportunities based on the time you can give and your skills and interests.

What is in it for me?

We hope you will have fun and enjoy the opportunity to meet other people. We will also offer you a wide range of personal development opportunities including externally recognized training and qualifications. We offer a training scheme that allows you to participate and develop in areas such as leadership, management, working with young people and practical skills. Again, this is based around your time commitments, your existing skills and your own personal development.

The contribution our volunteers make to their communities is recognized outside The Scout Association. Our partnerships with the Institute of Leadership and Management, the Open College Network and the Institute of Training and Occupational Learning are all recognition of the quality and standard our volunteers maintain.

So what next?

▶ Take a look at **www.scouts.org.uk** for more information about Scouting across the country and what it can offer to young people and adults.

▶ To find out how you can be part of it and how flexible volunteering opportunities fit around you, visit **www.scouts.org.uk/join** or call 0845 300 1818.

▶ Take a look at **www.do-it.org**, the volunteering website that gives you more information about volunteering and specific Scouting opportunities within your area.

Did you know?

▶ More young people do adventurous activities as Scouts than with any other organization.

▶ The number of adult volunteers in Scouting is larger than the workforces of the BBC (27,000), and McDonald's (67,000) combined.

▶ Scouting's Chief Scout, Bear Grylls, was the youngest person to climb Everest.

▶ No other organization offers such a range of challenging or exciting activities as Scouting.

▶ The youngest person to walk to the South Pole was a Scout (Andrew Cooney).

▶ Each year Scouts undertaking the Queen's Scout Award walk the equivalent distance of once round the world.

▶ Each year Scouts spend over 2 million nights away from home.

▶ 11 of the 12 people to walk on the moon were Scouts.

▶ You are never more than 10 miles from a Scout meeting place.

▶ Scouting is the largest membership organization in the world.

▶ Scouting is the only organization to operate in all but six of the countries of the world.

▶ There have been enough people involved in Scouting in the UK since 1907 (10 million) to fill London's Wembley stadium 111 times over. That's approximately 1/6 of the population of the UK.

▶ Each year 10,000 Scouts from the UK travel to every continent in the world to work on community projects.

▶ In the last 15 years UK Scouting has raised over £500,000 to support development projects and other charities around the world such as The Queen's Jubilee Fund, RNID, Sherpa 88, Water Aid, Unite.

QUICK TIPS

We would especially like to thank the many Scout leaders – and Scouts themselves – who, based on their experience in the field, provided tips for this book, including the following:

David Anderson, Steve Baker, Chas Cochand, Keith Evans, Andy Dalrymple, Nigel Davey, Rosemary Davies, Graham Duckworth, Ben Foster, Shirley Gilbertson, Alan Hill, Glynn Hill, Tom Hillbeck, Alison Light, Neil Lines, Sharon Martin, Colin Mills, Matthew Newell, Gordon Niven, Alan Norton, Trevor Padget, Michelle Palmer, Simon R. Patrick, Robin Shaw, Brian Sheen, Ness Smith, Chris Strong, Graham Strowes, Jayne Vauthan, David Voy, Daniel Warmington, David Waugh, Brian Webb, Sarah Webb, Mike Wenham, Doug Wilson, Dave Woods, Allison Worth, Cliff, Denise, John, Michael

Many of their tips are already within the book – but here are some more of our favourites to leave you with lots of ideas!

KIT PACKING

Pack your kit in separate plastic bags so that it is easy to see what you have got and prevents you from losing stuff.

DAY AT A TIME

Roll all the clothing for one day together, then you do not have to tip out your kit bag each day to find your clothes.

WET WIPES

When out on a hike, use wet wipes to clean your hands before eating.

RUBBISH ON THE MOVE

When hiking/camping up in the hills, take an empty wide-necked plastic bottle with you. It weighs almost nothing, and you can use it as a sealable rubbish bin.

WORMS IN YOUR THERMOS

A thermos mug can be used as a container e.g.: for holding worms for fishing. They can't climb out!

NO RUSTY BLADES

Wipe a white candle over the blades of a saw or edge of an axe to prevent rust forming.

TENT REPAIRS

When you pitch your tent, put a roll of duct tape around your tent pole and it will always be handy for any repairs.

NO SPIDERS!

A dixie lid (cooking pot lid) full of conkers at the door of the tent keeps the spiders out.

NIGHT LIGHTS

Hang up glow sticks inside your tent.

CAMPING TIPS

1. Take a cheap camping mat and cut one third off. Make a simple cover by sewing part of an old hike tent groundsheet into a bag to go over it. The resulting mat has a multitude of uses from sitting on damp ground, to sitting on while canoeing.

2. Sleep out without a tent. Resolve to try and spend at least one night at camp under the stars. Unforgettable!

COLD IN YOUR SLEEPING BAG?

To make a good hot water-bottle, fill a metal drinking bottle with very hot water and slide it into a thick sock (so it doesn't burn you).

WATER SENSE

When you use a platypus/camelback hydration system or any other type of hydration system i.e. with a hose and a bite piece, use a 35mm film canister to cover the bite piece when you are not drinking, so that the mouth piece doesn't drag in the mud when you take your backpack off.

STICKY HANDS

When gathering firewood from conifers, hands can become coated in resin which is sticky and difficult to wash off. Use cooking oil to remove the resin from your hands.

HUNTING FOR WOOD

When looking for firewood in a pine forest, look up not down. The wood on the floor will be damp but there will be dead wood which has fallen into the lower branches. These will have been 'air dried' so make great tinder and should catch very easily.

FIRE TIPS

1. The bark of the silver birch tree will provide you with fire-lighting wood that will light even when it's wet.

2. Polish the base of a soft drinks can so that it is like a mirror. Point it to a bright sun and hold a piece of dark-coloured tinder in the focal point (about 5cm away from the base). After a few seconds you should see smoke. And if you really want to impress, how about making fire from water! This takes a lot of practice and patience but does work. Put a sheet of clingfilm in a mug. Half fill the mug and gently lift the clingfilm and wrap around the water, making a 'water crystal ball'. Under bright sunlight, hold the ball over your dark-coloured tinder, moving it up and down until you produce a bright dot that will light the tinder.

3. When you are building a fire, use a large piece of log to lean your sticks against. It acts as a reflector for the heat.

CAMPFIRE 'BLOW POKER'

Take a short length of metal tubing (about 6 inches) and push a length of plastic tubing on the end. Point the metal part into the fire where you want air, then blow. It gives a very effective jet of air just where you need it.

A FRUITY HOT DRINK

Add hot water to orange or blackcurrant squash for an instant fruit tea!

TIDE SAFETY MARKER

Don't risk getting cut off by tides. When exploring around the beach, rock pools or coves, always put in a marker 1 metre above the wet water mark. Check it constantly. If the water moves towards the stick . . . the tide is coming in!

JAMMY CAMPFIRE DOUGHNUTS

Spread jam over one slice of bread (no butter) and cut into quarters. Dip each quarter into a batter mix and fry in a cooking pan with oil until the sandwich turns golden brown. Turn over and do the other side, drain and dip in sugar. Take care when they come out of the pan – the jam will be very hot!

RAPID RICE

One the best tricks we use at camp is boil-in-the-bag rice. No mess. No cleaning burnt pans. And each portion does two people.

CAMPFIRE FOOD

Round lids from big tins of Christmas biscuits are really effective pizza ovens on an open fire. Use the lid as the base, pierce a couple of holes in the tin and leave on the embers for 5-10 minutes before using. Coat hooks through the holes are effective for lifting out of the fire.

CHOCOLATE PORRIDGE

To make a great breakfast when hill walking, boil up a pan of water and make a mug of hot chocolate drink. Then pour the drink over a bowl full of instant cereal like 'Readybrek'.

INDEX

ACKNOWLEDGEMENTS

The Scout Association and publishers would like to thank the following:

- the many Scout leaders and Scouts whose expertise over the years has contributed to the knowledge gained and included in this book

- the Red Cross, for checking (through The Scout Association) the first aid information given on pages 214–225

- Nicola Ashby, Greg Stewart, Paul Wilkinson, Jess Kelly, Barnaby Poulton and Chris James at The Scout Association

- Mandie Howard, Mike Morris and Rosemary Reames

The information given and websites listed on pages 244–247 are accurate at the time of going to press, but the publishers will be happy to rectify any errors or omissions on future reprints.

Copyright material

Picture credits